CARDUS ON THE ASHES

Also published by Souvenir Press

CARDUS ON CRICKET
CARDUS IN THE COVERS
PLAY RESUMED WITH CARDUS
A FOURTH INNINGS WITH CARDUS
THE ROSES MATCHES 1919–1939
A CARDUS FOR ALL SEASONS
AUSTRALIAN SUMMER

Full reports and scores of the Test matches
discussed in the present book will be found
in the titles above.

CARDUS ON THE ASHES

Neville Cardus

Edited by
Margaret Hughes

SOUVENIR PRESS

Photoset in Great Britain by
Rowland Phototypesetting Ltd,
Bury St Edmunds, Suffolk
Printed in Great Britain by
Mackays of Chatham plc, Chatham, Kent

CONTENTS

INTRODUCTION

INVASION (May 1930)

IN 1862 occurred a romantic event in the history of these islands. A cricket team set sail from England to Australia in a paddle-steamer—a simple-hearted and bewhiskered company bound for the other side of the world on a day in late summer. There was no noise made about their going; they went quietly, and nobody ever heard of them again until Christmas. The sense of adventure is quickened at the thought of this voyage of discovery, over great seas in a vessel which to us of today must have seemed a precarious cockle-shell. No quest of empire builder was more romantically English—the earth encompassed, all for cricket, in days when no ship could confidently boast mastery over the seas. Today our cricketers journey to Australia in a sort of floating domesticity; from hour to hour we hear of them, and we send on each tour an army of them. How many men took part in the Odyssey of 1862? Exactly twelve! Their names today are mute and inglorious: H. H. Stephenson, W. Caffyn, G. Griffith, W. Mortlock, W. Mudie, T. Sewall, C. Lawrence, G. Bennet, T. Hearne, G. Wells, Iddison, and E. Stephenson. Poor anonymous pioneers; your names might as well have been Noakes and Stoakes and Stiles and Thompson! Our age knows you not, nor can we quite see the glamour that touched your enterprise to a land legendary enough in your time. Today it is not much more dangerous to travel to Australia by aeroplane than it is to travel by motor car from Manchester to London. The world is charted in all its parts; few voyages of discovery are left for man to make now. But in 1862 what did the foreigners think of us as a people that we spanned the earth for the cause not only of Empire, but of cricket? The foreigner still thinks the English serve sport too zealously; he would rather we listened day by day to tenors baying of love to the moon. Well, cricket is the national art of our land; by cricket the average Englishman is rendered sensitive not only to the power of combat, to the fascination of a struggle for a prize, but also to beauty and courage spent in the game's performance.

As we recollect in tranquillity the typical acts and scenes in the history of Test matches between England and Australia, we can get the sense of a national play set now in one land and now in another—with the dividing seas the orchestra! The characters and their settings and deeds are now outside time; once again Memory, the artist, has been at work. Spofforth spinning Grace and his men to ruin in the first home defeat of England at the Oval in 1882, the crowd dying a thousand deaths while twelve successive maidens are bowled. A. G. Steel at Lord's in 1884, his bat a hammer in a forge, the field ablaze with his innings of 148 against Spofforth, Boyle, Giffen, and Palmer. Australia scoring 551 at the Oval the same summer, 211 by Murdoch, despite an England XI composed of all the talents. Grace asking Lyttelton in this match to take off his stumper's pads and bowl; Lyttelton getting four wickets for 19, and the Old Man saying: 'Get back to your pads, young man. Your lobs are worse than I expected!' Bonnor's thunderous innings of 128 at Sydney in 1885, an innings to be seen for ever in a light of legendary awe. Arthur Shrewsbury a pillar classically calm, a support for All-England at Lords in 1886. Turner and Ferris mowing down English wickets day by day in the summer of 1888. England winning by ten runs at Sydney in 1894, after Australia had batted first and scored 586; the noise of rain in the night, surely it was heard by Stoddart, England's captain, when he was dying. Albert Ward and J. T. Brown in triumphant action at Melbourne in 1895, Porthos and D'Artagnan! Ranjitsinhji in the Old Trafford Test match of 1896, conjuring 154 out of Australian bowlers, glancing to leg Ernest Jones's fast bumpers off his left ear. Tom Richardson breaking his lion's heart in the same mighty battle, bowling for hours and hours, dead to pain, dead to the joy of his own unbounded health and activity, a man with only one idea: 'We must win.' Richardson tired of vain things at the end, when

for all his heroic endeavour, a missed catch lost England the
game . . . The frieze is endless; victors and vanquished
intermingle, equal in their deathlessness. Eternal sunshine
falls on them; MacLaren the last of the Romans; Trumper, a
Saladin cleaving the silken cushion with his scimitar; Woolley
at bay at Lord's, hounded like a lovely stag by Gregory and
Macdonald; Macartney the Figaro of cricketers—Rossini's
Figaro, impudent, dry-humoured, cynical and audacious to
all bowlers; M. A. Noble, deep in thought as he walks the
field plotting England's downfall; Darling at Old Trafford,
playing an innings for death or glory under a sky of rags;
poor Fred Tate the gods' sport in the same tragic game—
England lost by three runs and Tate's was the last wicket to
go! Hobbs, majestic at both ends of the world . . . There is
no last act to this national play; no limit to the span of the arch
of climax. It is a saga in which no twilight falls upon the gods.

Fifty years ago a match between England and Australia was
ancient history before the earth's other side knew of the
result. Today a decision in Melbourne is news all over the
Empire a few minutes after the drawing of the stumps. In the
vivid light of Sydney some happy man makes a winning hit; by
the time he has removed his pads and smoked his cigarette,
men and women in the gloom of a winter's day in London are
turning to the stop-press news, half afraid of the worst. When
Gilligan's team fought for the rubber during the winter of
1924–1925, the result of the Test match was chosen in preference to any other event in the world's daily dish of happen-
ings, as the text for the newspaper posters. On the morning of
23rd January 1925, when most of us watched the dawn break
as we waited for telegrams from Adelaide to let us know
whether the two remaining English wickets had been able to
score 22 and win the match—on this dreadful morning the
special editions came out even while breakfast was being
eaten—if eaten at all—in lighted chilly rooms. I happened to
be in a city street at the critical moment; I bought a paper but
put it in my pocket without looking at the news. I walked half
a mile knowing that in my possession were tidings of joy or
sorrow; it was a thrilling thought that I was carrying about
with me rare combustible stuff. At last, I ventured to look at
the stop-press column; my approach to it was gradual. No

sooner had I seen that England had lost by 11 runs than a perfect stranger dashed up to me, snatched the paper from my hands—leaving bits of it in my fingers—and hurled himself into the pages of it. He read the result, said: 'Oh, my God!' and vanished into the fog. This event may be taken as typical of the nation's attitude to Test matches these last few years. Great crowds have flocked outside newspaper offices; a general election night has not been more feverish. In 1921 the Prime Minister of England arrived at Lord's for a Test match—and was obliged to take his place in a queue a mile long. Well might the foreigner regard our cricket with amazement. In August 1914 *Punch* printed a cartoon showing two Prussians contemptuously discussing England's chances in the War: 'Still kicking the cricket ball aboudt,' said one of them. Flannelled fools!

In quick time did Australia take to the game; not very many years after Stephenson's tour in 1869, Australia was able to challenge our best in England. Cricket has thriven for a long time in the West Indies and South Africa and in India, but so far only the Australians have ever been able to defeat an England XI in this country.* Even on a wet English wicket, the odds are unusually level in a Test match between England and Australia. It is not hard to account for Australia's genius at cricket; the climate there, and the beautiful pitches, are all in favour of close technical study and practice. Then there is the fact of an environment that makes for supple limbs, a quick eye, and good health in general. Yet, with all these considerations taken into account we must needs continue to stand in mingled perplexity and admiration at the thought that Australia, with a population that could be put into London, has year after year been able to produce cricketers good enough to challenge all comers, from England or elsewhere.

The Australians have brought characteristics of their own to cricket, temperamental and technical. In a land of flawless turf, too much dependence on a mechanical spin would have landed bowlers nowhere; Australians have generally had to use their heads to get batsmen into difficulties. Spofforth was the first cricketer really to subtilise bowling by variety of curve

* Written in 1930.

and pace through the air. It is a mistake to think of him as a
fast bowler pure and simple. He could exploit entirely different balls in one and the same over, and hide them all under a
mask of similitude. Albert Trott was once found, when he was
learning to play, attacking a wicket which was concealed from
him behind a wide box. 'What's the idea?' somebody asked
him. 'That there box,' he replied, 'is George Giffen's bat. I'm
trying to get round it.' Poor Albert Trott, a genius amongst
bowlers if ever there lived one. He did the 'hat trick' twice in
one innings during his benefit match, and did not realise, until
the engagement was all over in two days, that he had, while in
the throes of inspiration, bowled himself into the bankruptcy
court. Temperamentally the Australians have always been
tough; they tightened up the psychology of cricket at a time
when easy-going English worthies like A. N. Hornby and
C. I. Thornton were taking it all as a great joke, an eternal
holiday for eternal schoolboys. Australian cricket has never
come under the influences of village cricket or the public
schools; consequently it has gained in high seriousness and
arrogance what it has lost in geniality and affable manners.
There has never been a comic character amongst Australian
players, not one Tom Emmett or Johnny Briggs. They are
men of war most times. Even when the Australian batsman is
brilliant to watch, he is at the same time a dour fellow. Your
Spooner drives past cover-point with a courtliness that causes
you to forget he is at bottom an antagonist, the bowler his
enemy. You feel that a Spooner is batting not for the contest's
prize but simply for beauty's sake. The Australians have
shown us many handsome batsmen, but one and all, they have
worn their plumes with a difference. They have hit the ball
hard and beautifully—but also have they always hit the ball
vindictively. Lust for spoils, not some power above mortal
combat, has been the motive force. Even Victor Trumper was
a *conquistador*. And there was little humour or graciousness
about the incomparable Macartney. His every innings was a
scherzo—in a battle symphony; there was a touch of the
macabre in the way he led bowlers along a dancing track to
their ruin. His brilliance was not sunny; out of his bat's end
shot the lightning that works havoc. The Australian sharpens
cricket continuously with temper. 'The best way to get an

Australian batsman to play an innings,' said Aubrey Faulkner to me once, 'is to tell him that the bowling of the other side is terribly difficult.' In 1912, when the Triangular Tournament was fought in this country, the Australians were playing England at Lord's. One of the South Africans being without a game himself, was watching the contest from the Australians' dressing-room at Lord's. S. F. Barnes, bowling magnificently, quickly got one or two wickets. Macartney was putting on his pads when our South African said to him, as he looked through the window into the field of play: 'My goodness, Charlie, Barnes is doing the very devil's tricks with the ball today. You'd better be careful—cut out all your fancy work this time.' Macartney was heard to mutter under his breath. He tightened his last buckle, took up his bat, stuck out his chin. When he walked down the pavilion steps to go in next he was livid with rage. The Australian is not in the habit of turning the other cheek.

I suppose Spofforth was what Emerson would have called a 'Representative Man' of Australian cricket. He had the lean-ness suspected by Caesar; look at the portraits of him in Mr Beldham's book on 'Great Bowlers', and you will feel that in this man some spirit of destruction was contained which broke forth in sinister, Spring-heel Jack leapings. When Spofforth stepped on to an English field such an east wind of antagonism blew as the worthy and eminent Victorians had never before known: a killing, chilling wind fit to freeze our grass and dry up nature in our soil. He bowled men out voraciously; it is hard to think he ever had his relaxations, even when the other side's poorest batsmen were in. He has himself left on record a proof of how grimly he took the game to heart, how jealous he was of his sovereignty: 'We were playing against eighteen in the north,' he once told Mr Bettesworth, 'and the son of an influential man in the town had made the top score in the first innings. In the evening the father came to our hotel and said that his son could play the "demon bowler" all day. I told the old gentleman, in fun (!) that it was only because I was so good-natured that I had let his son get any runs at all, and that I really thought I should have to bowl him out in the first over for a duck's egg in the next innings. A friend of mine at once made a bet that I would do so, and it was immediately taken. I didn't like this at all, because the boy was really a good bat. However, I felt bound to go through with it now, especially as the father laughed at me for making such a rash statement. The next day, when the son came in, I made a fuss about arranging my field, and put them all very close in. Then I bowled him a slow, but it didn't work. Next time I sent down one as fast as I could. He played it. Nothing came of the third ball either, and things were getting serious. But with the last ball—four balls in an over—the leg stump was taken right out of the ground and sent over Blackham's head. I think the father was convinced that I was a man of my word.' Comment upon this 'reminiscence' would spoil it. Spofforth's appetite for wickets grew with each day's eating. He seems to have had a Mephisthophelean personality; he stalked over the field like a spirit of denial. An old player described him to me once in these terms: 'He was always fixin' you with his eye. Once I went out to bat at the Oval in a Test match. I had to pass him on my way to the wicket; he was getting ready to bowl. As I walked down the pitch to the crease I happened to turn round and look at him over my shoulder. His eyes were on me all the time, and he would never let me get away from 'em!' It is often claimed he was the greatest bowler the game has ever known. Well, his best ball was an off-break. At the present time there is an effective counter to the off-break. The ball, after all, comes in to the bat; the modern player puts his right foot across the wicket and, as the off-break turns, he 'backs up', protects his wicket with his pads, and places the ball to the on-side, with the spin. Today the off-break is not a deadly means of bowling down a first-class batsman's wicket; it must be supported by at least three fieldsmen arranged close to the batsman on the leg-side. Spofforth used to place a man at mid-on near to the batsman: a device which anticipated the leg-trap of modern cricket history. But the point I am trying to make about Spofforth's best trick—the off-break—is that it comes in to the bat's face. It is not as deadly as the ball which breaks from the leg-stump to the off—and goes away from the bat. On this technical ground alone I submit that Barnes was Spofforth's superior. I leave out of account the fact that on the beautiful Australian pitches of our period Barnes has achieved bowling performances which are equal to anything done by Spofforth on the rough English wickets of his period. But Spofforth was more than a deadly bowler for a day; he was a seminal force in the development of cricket. As we have seen, he brought bowling under the control of mind; he pointed out, perhaps for the first time, that a ball could be deadly not only of itself but by reason of its place in a context. Moreover, his spirit lived after him; it went into Australian cricket for good and all. For from Spofforth came Giffen and Trumble and Noble and Macdonald, all of them alike in their Machiavellianism.

The present age knows Spofforth only as a legend. But they have seen Macdonald, who, not less than the 'Demon' bowler, sums up in his own skill and psychology the Australian cricketer today and for ever. He has Spofforth's pace, though not his many masks and contrivances. When Macdonald bowls slow he is not really on the kill. Macdonald also lacks Spofforth's unappeasable appetite; there are moments when he will not spend his energy on the small fry of batsmen. But how true to the traditional 'cornstalk' Macdonald holds himself. The sunshine of his land has gone into his body, making warm music of motion play throughout his suppleness. That sunshine, though, has not entered his mind. He is indeed the true Australian by reason of a want of juice in his temperament; the sun of Australia dries up the humours that breed urbanity in a man (there has never been an Australian humorist who was not satirical). Macdonald bowls fast and destructively, not out of the gusto of a Walter Brearley. When Brearley was upsetting wickets he reminded us of the hearty gale that turns head over heels the old woman and her apple stall. Macdonald's speed is seen by the imagination as a cold spear, flashing to destroy. Look at him as he runs to bowl: immediately his power is to be felt by all. We never have need to argue the fact of greatness; it knocks you over at first sight. Macdonald is under no obligation to be in form to convince us of his genius; personality transcends the utilitarian values. Judge the artisan by results, not the genius. Macdonald is possessed by an incalculable spirit; he does not always seem himself to understand the comings and goings of the forces within him. One day sees him masterful; it is then that his right arm is a wheel of war and pestilence. On another day his demon sleeps; now he is an ineffectual Lucifer of fast bowlers, 'dispossessed, chucked down'. Little use for Macdonald's captain to try to goad him out of his moments of majestic indifference. He rises in such periods beyond the Australian type; he is not responsive to the call for a rally, an 'effort'. As well might a demand be made on Mount Etna when Mount Etna is sleeping.

At his best Macdonald will be remembered as one of the great fast bowlers of all time. When in 1921 he attacked for Australia with Gregory, we saw a sight as thrilling in its contrasted beauty as any ever witnessed on a cricket field —Gregory thundering over the earth, shaking it, and leaping up at the wicket by a great act of strength; Macdonald at the other end running along a curve silently, his arm sinuous, his wrist poising the ball before letting it go—the cobra's poise. Gregory bowled until he was dead tired; like Tom Richardson, he was one of nature's toilers under the sun, though he lacked Richardson's action, and wasted much of his gusto on the air. Macdonald's attack is always under the influence of a man mixed in his elements. Against a bad batting side Macdonald is as likely as not to bowl with a contemptuous slackening of his fires. I have seen him toss up slow off-breaks to frail batsmen, toss them up sardonically by the hour. Then I have seen him sweep these weaklings out of sight by sudden strokes of speed, as though he had impatiently said: 'Out of my way, scum!' In his prime, he was at his greatest against a great batsman. I have known him confront Hobbs at the Oval like one who for a long time has awaited this moment. He has taken the ball as though by right—before his captain has given it to him. He has seemed to cry out: 'This man is mine!'

Australia had her fast bowlers before Macdonald was given to her. But, like Gregory, they belonged to what George Lohmann called 'the brute force' school. Remember Cotter and Ernest Jones. ('Yes, I'd say he *was* a fast bowler all right!') Macdonald's pace, like that of all the game's really genuine fast bowlers, was the product of a rhythmical body action, and flexible wrists and fingers. His greatness resided wholly in his fast bowling—graceful and lissome fast bowling. The man has never been seen to make an awkward or angular movement; even when he tossed the ball up the pitch to the bowler at the other end, the curve of the flight through the air seemed somehow more beautiful than when other men threw. When he was on the kill, in the 1921 Test matches, his superb mingling of the rhythm of life with the dissonances of temper and conquest, rendered him the Australian cricketer seen *sub specie aeternitatis*. There never was a cricketer of loftier disdain. At Trent Bridge I saw him at the end of a sweltering day. Notts had scored nearly 400 and it was six o'clock. Macdonald's captain—he was playing for Lancashire now— asked him for one final onslaught before close of play. Macdonald had bowled for hours, but he bowled again. He sent down an over of brutal bumpers. An honest yeoman named Flint hit three of these bumpers for fours; the last ball of the over he hooked to the square-leg ropes for six. Macdonald, even before Flint's mighty stroke was finished, turned on his heel indifferently and slouched to his position in the field at mid-off. He did not even look where Flint's hit had gone. And somehow it was Flint that seemed the futile man. An onlooker in the crowd said: 'There's the Australian for you, all over.' Macdonald spat on the grass—the 'Digger' from head to foot. Macdonald, Trumble, Noble, Darling, Griffin, Clem Hill, Iredale—all of them grim men of war, all of them sprung from the loins of Spofforth. Trumper, a genius, transcended the type. But even he did not make us completely forget it. Over his play was cast a robe of purple; underneath were the cannons of battle. He hit the ball with a vehement antagonism which was never to be felt in any stroke by Spooner, Palairet, or Woolley. When Trumper went out of his crease to a half-volley he did so like a lithe and beautiful animal on the kill. Look at the photographs of him, doubting young Thomases of the sceptical present, and see how far he would venture beyond the crease's rim at the sight of a well-tossed ball; his bat is held up behind him punitively, he is leaping to the ball, his every muscle responding to the demands of the will to power and victory. In 1902, at Old Trafford, MacLaren lost the toss for England on a soft dead turf. Even Rhodes could not turn the ball. England's problem was to keep the Australian batsmen quiet until after the lunch interval; by then the pitch would be dry and helpful to

England's attack. MacLaren's strategy was to hold down at all costs the score of Trumper, so to place the field as to block his strokes. After the interval, wickets would fall rapidly enough; for two hours all eyes and hands had to concentrate on Trumper, the man with countless hits. 'Never mind about getting him out,' said MacLaren, 'if his score is not big at lunch we'll have the lot of them back in the pavilion for next to nothing by half-past three.' Men were placed on the boundary to save the fours. MacLaren put a lifetime of experience in his setting of the field. And at the lunch interval, after two hours of play, Trumper was 103 not out and the Australians' total was 173 for one. Many years afterwards, MacLaren was taken to task in my company for his inability to 'keep Trumper quiet' on this occasion. 'Did you know how to set a field in those days, Archie?' asked the critic. 'Why didn't you exploit the inner and outer ring?' 'Inner and outer ring?' queried MacLaren pityingly. 'My God! Inner and outer ring!' I had my men on the rails; I had 'em fairly close up for any mishits! Inner and outer ring! You can only put nine men to field, no matter how you arrange them. Victor hit two balls on to the adjoining practice ground before the match was ten minutes started. Now I couldn't place my long-on in the practice ground . . . could I?'

This match, and the match which succeeded it a week or two later at the Oval, possessed the fury of demons. At Manchester, Australia scored 299; Trumper got out after lunch on the first day and then, as MacLaren had anticipated, Australia collapsed. (How superb the opportunism of Trumper on the easy pitch of the first morning!) England went in to tackle Trumble on a 'glue-pot'; before close of play, five of our best batsmen were out for 70. Next day F. S. Jackson and Braund had the lee-way to make up; on a baking ground they had to toil like mules. These two batsmen held the fifth English wicket while 141 runs were scored. England at their first innings' end, were only 37 behind. Australia then had to face Lockwood on an impossible pitch. Trumper, Duff, and Hill were 'settled' (as Mr Micawber would say) for 10 runs. Under a threatening sky, out of which sunlight touched the scene fitfully, Darling shook his bat at the English attack. He hit at everything—and set to Fred Tate the chance of an easy catch. Tate missed it—perhaps the most fateful missed catch in the history of Test cricket between England and Australia. England on the third day were left with 124 to get for victory in a match which, if they lost, would give Australia the rubber. At lunch England were 36 for none, MacLaren and Palairet undefeated. An hour later England were 70 for two; only 54 needed now, and who to get them? Why, the flower of English batsmanship: MacLaren, Ranjitsinhji, F. S. Jackson, Braund, Abel, not to mention Lilley, Lockwood, and Rhodes. MacLaren threw his wicket away trying to hit a boundary, for he saw clouds of rain coming up the sky. This was the age in which batsmen actually directed their cricket according to the state of the weather and the game. Trumble bowled off-breaks over the wicket. Ranjitsinhji was like a man palsied; he quickly died the death. Three men were put on the boundary for Lilley, and Trumble tossed him a tempting ball. Lilley accepted the challenge (what is the name of the modern batsman who, with a Test match at stake, would have tried as Lilley did to hit a four in the face of three outfields?). Lilley made his stroke beautifully, but Clem Hill, lust giving him speed incredible, caught the ball; he ran twenty yards after holding it. 'A sinful catch,' said a parson in the crowd, which it was. England wanted eight runs to win when Tate, England's last hope, came to the wicket. He was scourged abominably, poor Fred, an honest craftsman made for pastoral humours at Horsham, not for thunder amongst gods on Olympus. Tate arrived at the wicket knowing that with two good hits he could achieve an immortality worth having, knowing, too, that by a single mistake he would go down the ages as one of the tragic comedians of cricket—a source of the pitiless laughter which must always flow whenever circumstances take hold of a small man and demand that he shall strike the heroic attitude. Before Tate could get his lungs used to the tight air on this bodeful Saturday afternoon of 26th July 1902, a cloudburst put an end to the action—for forty minutes. But Tate was not free to hope that merciful rain was going to rescue him from responsibility. All through the heavy showers the sun shone. Tate, as he saw the clearing skies, must have been like a man on a rack waiting for torturers ironically taking their time.

I was a small boy in 1902. If I live to a hundred I shall never forget the scene when the Australians came on to the field again, after the rain stopped. They went without a word into their positions. Clem Hill's face was white, not from fear, but from determination. Rhodes was Tate's helpmate at the death. To tell of the bitter end I can do no better than draw on first impressions.

At six minutes to five the game went forward again. Saunders bowled at Tate—a fast one. Tate saw something hit the ground and he made a reflex action at it. Click! Tate looked round wildly. What had happened? A voice came to him over the wet grass, sounding like a distant sea in his ears. The crowd was cheering; he had snicked a boundary. Another snick like that and the game is England's, and Tate assured of an honourable posterity. The ball was returned from the ring, and Darling rearranged his field, slightly but portentously, while Saunders bent down to a sawdust heap. Tate got himself down on his bat once more; a wheel went round in his head. 'Bat straight . . . don't move it . . . bat straight . . . block hole . . . can't hit wicket . . . don't move . . . block hole . . . bat straight . . .' Saunders' fourth ball was not only good enough for Tate's frail bat; it would have bowled most cricketers. It was fast through the air and—it was a shooter. It broke Tate's wicket, and no doubt Tate's heart and the heart of the crowd. England lost by three runs, and a week afterwards Tate met the Australians again in Brighton on a Saturday afternoon, when the sea was in and the air full of warm sunshine. He was graciously permitted to play an innings of 22 not out against them—a capital innings at that.

Of Jessop's match-winning innings on the Oval Test match of August 1902, cricket has never been more marvellously touched by genius. In an hour and a quarter Jessop added 104, on a drying wicket, in the face of a conquering Australian eleven. Jessop was not a C. I. Thornton; his hits were not so much stupendous as rapid. He possessed not only the hitter's full-lengthed body-drives, but also the authentic batsman's short-lengthed strokes, the cut and the hook. No slogger could have survived the deadly science of Australia's bowling on 13th August 1902. The innings was a case of technique controlled by imagination. Skill is not of much avail if it is left to work by the rote which skill can so easily set into motion. The mind, the act of vision, must be there to keep skill a servant, to prevent it from becoming master. With all his swiftness of eye and foot, his supple energy, his responsive technique, Jessop could not have won England one of the most famous of all cricket victories, had not he thought that it could all be done, and willed the deed faithfully.

I do not digress overmuch from the theme of Australian cricket by discussing two games which were won mainly by opportunist batsmanship. In recent years the notion has got abroad that Australian batsmanship is invariably dour, and that for a proper exploitation of it the Test match without a time-limit is required. During the Australian season of 1928–1929 the Australians no doubt did, knowing that they lacked match-winning bowlers, score runs at a slow pace. For that matter, so did the Englishmen, who could boast Larwood and Tate. Both sides while batting acted according to the dismal philosophy of 'safety first—and last.' Few attempts were made to hit hard anything but the loosest ball. Matches dragged on day after day; a week was not enough time for the forcing of a decision. The scoring topped aggregates not dreamed of in the heyday of Trumper, Noble, Hill, Stoddart, Tyldesley, and R. E. Foster. Skill and the sportsman's love of a hazard were denied; cricket resolved itself into a dreary trial of physical endurance. But I deny that these methods were characteristically Australian. The worst example of safety-first batsmanship perpetuated out of season for its own sake was shown by the Englishmen at Brisbane on 4th December 1928. England batted first and scored 521. Australia collapsed for 122; not only that, but they lost through accident and illness the services of two of their greatest all-round men, Gregory and Kellaway. Enjoying an advantage of 399 against a crippled team, England batted again, and in five minutes short of six hours made 342 for eight wickets. The pitch was easy of pace. One Englishman stayed in three hours and a half for 72, after reaching the wicket when his side were 424 ahead, with seven wickets in hand. Another Englishman began his innings when his side were 516 ahead, with six wickets in hand. He so far forgot the meaning of cricket as to bat, in these circumstances, three hours for 65 not out. Never did it happen before the War that a Test match batsman played three hours for sixty or seventy runs on an easy pitch when his team was 400 or 500 in front.

It is somehow hard to comprehend the ideals of Test match cricket in these terms. But I do know that Test matches in Australia before 1914 were fought under the 'no time limit' rule, and that players did not then hug runs covetously for no reason at all reconcilable with sport. I decline to believe that a great cricketer can ever submit to joyless parsimonious measures unless driven to them by force of circumstances. When in 1921 the Australians found themselves sure masters of a weak English eleven in this country they did not spare the bowling. Right and left they hit, defiantly, handsomely. In 1921 the Australians scored throughout the season at the rate of 80 or 90 runs an hour; the brilliance of their cricket turned every field of play into a cloth of gold.

I can recall not a single instance in the game's records where the Australians have not, while winning a match, played triumphantly. Australian batting has always been stern and Fabian in the presence of a stronger foe. All the great Australian cricketers have, as I say, been men with an eye for opportunity. A Noble, a Collins, has stone-walled for hours waiting for the tide to turn Australia's way. In 1905, the Australian XI, finding themselves a weak bowling side, sought to make a draw of all the Test matches. To that end, a clever bowler like Armstrong was willing to render his arts negative by bowling wide on the leg-side, the aim being not to get English wickets but to kill time in a three-day match. You will find ample evidence in the history of Test matches that, at the right moment, the Australians can be terribly canny, and ready to withdraw into a protective shell for hours at a stretch. But no Australian XI of my acquaintance has shown quarter to English bowling when the bowling has been manifestly weak, or when the Englishmen have been thrust beyond all doubt into a hopeless corner. It has yet to be recorded that any Australian batsman born to hit weak bowling fiercely has turned himself day in and day out into a stone-waller, against nature, and all for the cause of war by attrition. The eye for the main chance has directed Australian cricket policy always; Trumper and Macartney are the only cricketers who in the encounters between England and Australia have scored individual hundreds before luncheon on the first day of the match. Yet driven into a corner there is no end to the patience of an Australian batsman. At Manchester in 1921 Collins was the personification of obstinacy for five hours; he scored in that time forty runs, each fruitful stroke made as though under protest. Runs were of no value to Australia that day; only the clock had to be frustrated. The Australian view of cricket is apparently competitive first and last. Often enough an Australian team, once the rubber has been settled, has found nothing in the game worth their while to do. They have relaxed even their skill. At the Oval in 1921 on the closing day of the fifth Test match—the Australians had won the rubber in the third—Armstrong condescendingly allowed inexpert bowlers to help English batsmen to score runs at ease. Armstrong himself retired to the deep-field, and once, while his men were changing positions between overs, he picked up a newspaper which had blown to him from the crowd—and he looked affably into its pages. Armstrong had a sublime unconcern for those useless but charming amenities which in its country are indulged in because they *are* useless and charming. Once his great Eleven of 1921 had grasped the rubber's prize, it seemed that Armstrong lost all interest in cricket. He was the Australian every inch when, on the first day of the Test match at the Oval in 1921, he would not agree to continue play, after an interruption by rain, until the crowd gathered in front of the pavilion and threatened a riot. The summer had been torrents of sunshine week after week; then, the weather broke on the Saturday of 13th August, while England were batting prosperously. The rain lasted for no more than an hour, and with the ground thirsty as dust, the wicket was soon quite fit for play again. But Armstrong did not come forth with Tennyson to inspect the pitch. The crowd walked over the field, and saw for themselves that the earth was dry and hard once more. At last Armstrong agreed to look at the wicket. Amidst catcalls he ambled, pipe in mouth, to the 'middle', in company with Tennyson. Arrived there he went through an act of no small irony. He bent down to the ground, which was now innocent of moisture, and pretended to press his thumb into the turf. He lifted himself up and jerked his hand downwards as though getting rid of disgusting quantities of mud from his finger-ends. And also he wiped his hands on one another, every gesture elaborate, so that the crowd could see them. Play was 'then resumed', as the newspapers put it.

Absence of cant from Australian cricket can be very refreshing in a land where at times we no doubt incline towards sentimentality in cricket. The Australians are not in the habit of excusing themselves after defeat. When, at Brisbane, in December 1928, Australia were beaten by 675 runs—the most pronounced success by runs in the history of Test matches—Australia, as we have seen, lost half-way through the engagement the services of Gregory and Kellaway. But these accidents were stoically taken as all in the day's work by the Australians. It was different when, in 1924–1925, England lost the rubber in Australia. The injury to Tate's toe-nail was bewailed throughout the Empire. In 1905 Darling's team lost the rubber, and England in every Test match won the toss. The Australian captain did not as a consequence suggest that tossing for innings should be abolished. But in 1924–1925, when Gilligan lost the toss four times in five matches—and the rubber easily—the newspapers in this country wept tears, and announced the tidings of 'Gilligan's bad luck' until most Englishmen must have felt ashamed. Fortunately our cricketers are not as bad as our Press would have us imagine. But the game has been none the better, especially the Test matches between England and Australia, since the 'popular' prints discovered that after all there is 'copy' in cricket. It is a game which because of its fine shades of technique, its uncommon aesthetic appeal, cannot be used for the purposes of 'stunt' news. In the absence of some adventitious interest, grossly worked up—'patriotism', 'bad luck', and other spell-binders—cricket will not sell the papers. During the summer of 1926, the Test matches in this country were put into a world of abnormal sensation by Fleet Street. Sometimes the Australians and English cricketers alike were forgotten in the hunt for the 'amazing' incident. I recollect a newspaper poster which was published before lunch on the Monday of the second Test match at Lord's:

WHO DID IT
LORD'S LEAKING HOSE
Bardsley's Fine Innings

If modern Test matches are not as interesting as they were of old it may be because the Press has so drenched players in limelight that they have grown immobile through self-consciousness. The game, left to itself, it not naturally given to a crisis every hour. Cricket can from time to time achieve climaxes of intolerable drama. But because it is the most artistic of games, these climaxes come at the *end* of an act; they invariably happen after long preparation. Australia gets five English wickets down for 48, and Jessop arrives—*deus ex machina*. In great cricket the storm follows a calm; sensation is honestly brewed in the cauldron of intent sport, hour by hour. The Australians may possibly have erred now and again by confusing willow with the steel of the battle-axe. A mistake on the side of dignity, at any rate. So far, it is not Australian cricketers or the Australian Press that is to blame for the creation of an atmosphere in which a Test match between England and Australia can easily suffer a drastic cheapening.

The Australian view of cricket, dour and realistic, has not been an original contribution. If Australia had never been discovered, Lancashire and Yorkshire would just the same have played each other on Bank Holidays. Nor have Australian batsmen taught anything which Englishmen would not have found out for themselves. It is in the subtlety of their bowling that we must look for the Australians' unique contribution. Environment had a lot to do with it, of course. The problem of a flawless pitch at Sydney has invariably sharpened the wits of the players condemned to bowl on it. In England a man's natural spin can be left to work more or less automatically; rain and sunshine will lend a potent enough assistance. Day by day the Australian bowler needs to toil by the sweat of the brow; 'Bowling is a black man's job in this country', Hugh Trumble once complained. Yet, on turf cruelly hard and smooth, Australians have learned arts of spin as clever as any known to cricketers nurtured in this green and pleasant land. As I write the complaint goes round that the modern cricket pitch, elaborately rolled, renders a man's spin null and void. Well, the pitches in Australia have always been made for batsmen; cast-iron to the feet, glossy to the eyes. And on these 'perfect' wickets, George Giffen learned to turn the ball; so, too, did Hugh Trumble, Palmer, Ferris, Howell, Noble, Armstrong, and—in our own period—Mailey. Only the other day, so to speak, the best of our modern batsmen, armed with broad pads, were being spun to destruction on Australian grounds by Mailey. In the Australian season of 1920–1921, when Mailey won a rubber, little was heard about the 'impossibility' of spin bowling on modern wickets. It is not in Australia, the place of the batsman's ideal wicket, but in England, where rain is always with us, that the bowler is helped to get on with his work by alterations in the size of the stumps and the shape of the ball. The Australians' bowling has so largely been governed by a dry climate that, so far, they have possessed only one slow left-hander of the kind common enough on our pliable turf. Ferris alone of Australia's roll of great bowlers can be put into the category of Briggs, Peel, Blythe, and Rhodes. The typical Australian bowler is medium paced. On pitches made not for a day, but for all time, fast bowling is horse's work. In the same circumstances, slow spin, unless in the 'googly' manner, is easy prey for good batsmen. Australian bowling, therefore, has in the main mingled spin and pace in proportion; enough speed to attune with the fast, hard earth, and enough break to make the difference between a true and a sliced stroke. To these two ancient tricks the Australians have brought changeful flight —according to the teachings of Spofforth. With fast bowling pure and simple, Australia has had little to do.* Ernest Jones, Macdonald, Gregory, and Cotter are four names only against the long succession of fast bowlers, from the round-arm slinging school to Larwood. (I take Lord Harris's word for it that Spofforth is not to be included in the fast bowlers 'pure and simple'. I doubt if Macdonald, even, can really be so described.) 'The whole art of bowling,' we have been told by B. J. T. Bosanquet, 'is to make the batsman think that the ball is going to be of one kind when it is really of quite a different nature.' Spofforth, Giffen, Noble, Trumble—they

* Not so since World War II.

were all artificers who began to study their batsmen the moment they met them in the pavilion in good time before a match began. Giffen would set himself at twelve o'clock to get Arthur Shrewsbury out at 4.15 precisly, by means of a far-seeing plan of varied balls, the crucial one to be delivered after a tireless succession of others which had never once suggested that the 'trick-card' was in Giffen's hand at all. Shrewsbury, however, exercised Grace's policy of play each ball on its mertis, and, as a consequence, Giffen frequently wore his mask in vain. For a mask is only of use to conceal something that somebody is expecting to see. Shrewsbury, while batting, 'expected' nothing; he waited for a ball to come along and then saw the object as in itself it really was. An eminent Victorian!

I have often wondered whether the great Australian medium-paced bowlers of old would be as successful today as they were when tackling batsmen of a chivalrous epoch in the history of English cricket. During the tour of Stoddart's team to Australia in 1894–1895, the English captain fell a victim to a piece of strategy of Giffen. I will here describe this strategy for the delectation of the modern professional batsman. Giffen (it was a Test match) tossed a ball up to Stoddart, a half-volley to the off-side. Stoddart's left leg flashed over the wicket and the bat banged a four through the covers. Giffen then shortened his length a shade, and dropped the ball a tiny bit wider. Again did Stoddart's bat flash, but this time the ball was slightly beyond the reach of his blade's middle. A catch to the off-side field followed.

'Strategy?' asks the modern batsman. 'Child's play, I call it! Catch me having a bang at a ball wide to the off. Catch me, in fact, banging at a half-volley within hitting range!' A Giffen might well angle in vain nowadays. The medium-paced bowlers of Australia's classical period sought to circumvent their country's beautiful pitches by playing upon a batsman's impatience, or by challenging his vanity. In modern Test cricket it would often seem that batsmen are not harassed by either of these mortal failings. There's little point in a bowler sending out decoys to an enemy who prefers to fight underground and gain the victory by the imperceptible sapper's methods.

Playing as they have done with an eye on the main chance,

the Australian game has been technically assimilative rather than inventive. Spofforth, even, acquired his first dodges from Englishmen and then adapted them to the special conditions of cricket as he found it here and in his own country. In the English winter of 1863–1864, George Parr's XI visited Australia, and with them was Tarrant. 'When I saw Tarrant,' Spofforth told Mr Bettesworth, 'he was the fastest bowler I'd ever seen. I tried to copy him. My one aim was to bowl as fast as possible.' But ten years later, W. G. Grace took a team to Australia, and it was then that Spofforth found out from old English masters the right way of his greatness. 'When Southerton and Shaw came over their bowling was a revelation to me, and I didn't see why I shouldn't copy and combine the styles of all three. I soon found that variation of pace was the most important thing of all.' The Australian opportunism again. They do not plunge into the unknown experimentally; they borrow the tools of other men's fashioning. B. J. T. Bosanquet invented the 'googly', and in 1904 won a Test match in Australia by means of the off-break bowled with a leg-break action. But not until long after South African cricketers had, in 1907, proved to the whole world that the 'googly' was a good trick—not until well after that date did an Australian bowler have anything to do with a ball which asks for a good deal of faith in its exponents. But once an Australian, name of Mailey, did cultivate the 'googly', he mastered it and, by combining it with insidious flight, made it almost his own.

R. E. Foster wrote a prophetic comment upon 'googly' bowling. 'I think it will cause a deterioration in batting. It must be realised that this type of bowling is practically in its infancy, and if persevered with—as it surely will be—must improve and become very difficult to deal with. Now a batsman when he goes in may receive a ball which either breaks from the off, perhaps from leg, or, again, may come straight through very quickly. If he survives half a dozen overs he ought to be getting set, but such bowling never allows a batsman to get really set, because he can never make or go for his accustomed shots. The ball just short of a half-volley, which he is accustomed to drive between cover and extra cover, now bothers him, and prevents him from doing so, owing to his inability to discover which way and how much the ball is going to break. And as this bowling improves, the difficulty will become increased, till those beautiful drives we are wont to expect from great batsmen will become a thing of the past.'

The school of the 'googly' is on the wane; possibly the ball demanded studies which are more exacting than can be accommodated to the life of a professional cricketer, who naturally enough buys his skill in the cheapest market. The 'googly' can be mastered only by long labour and much philosophy. As I write, there is only one authentic 'googly' bowler playing—his name Freeman.

Cricket has conquered the English-speaking world, maybe. But to this day it takes an Australian side to make a Test match with England. Australia still holds the inalienable right to contemplate the majesty of an all-England XI, and to cry out to other ambitious cricketers from across the seas: 'Hands off; this is mine own enemy!'

1902

BY THREE RUNS

THE GREATEST TEST MATCH AT OLD TRAFFORD

THE most thrilling finish of all the Test matches ever fought at Old Trafford happened on the Saturday afternoon of July 26th, 1902. It was the decisive game of the rubber, and Australia won it by three runs, snatching the spoils from the lion's mouth. The match at the end seemed to get right out of the control of the men that were making it; it seemed to take on a being of its own, a volition of its own, and the mightiest cricketers in the land looked as though they were in the grip of a power of which they could feel the presence but whose ends they could not understand. As events rushed them to crisis even MacLaren, Ranjitsinhji, Trumper, Noble and Darling—most regal of cricketers— could only utter: 'Here we do but as we may; no further dare.' The game, in Kipling's term, was more than the player of the game.

The match was designed, surely, by the gods for their sport. Even the victors were abominably scourged. On the second day, when the issue was anybody's, Darling played an innings which, as things turned out, must be said to have won Australia's laurels as much as anything else. Australia in their second innings had lost 3 wickets—those of Trumper, Duff and Hill—for 10 runs and now possessed an advantage worth no more than 47. Under a sky of rags, the fitful and sinister sunlight coming through, Darling let all his superb might go at the English attack. His hitting had not the joyfulness of mastership in it; its note was desperation. He plainly felt the coils of circumstance about him; he plainly was aware of the demon of conflict that had the game in grip. And the defiant action of his bat was like a fist shaken at the unfriendly

heavens. It was in this innings of Darling's that the gods
played their first cruel trick. For with Darling's score only 17
he was impelled to sky a ball to the deep field—a high but easy
catch. And who was the wight that the ironic powers had
decreed should shoulder the responsibility of taking that
crucial catch? His name was Tate—Tate of Sussex, a kindly
fellow who never did harm to a soul. The humour of the gods
really began when this cricketer was asked to play for England
instead of George Hirst. Tate was a capital bowler, but as
soon as he was seen in the company of the great the question
went out: 'What is he doing in this galley?' Tate had not the
stern fibre of character that can survive in an air of high
tragedy; his bent was for pastoral comedy down at Horsham.
Tate missed the catch, and never looked like holding it. As he
stood under the ball, which hung for a while in the air—an
eternity to Tate—and then dropped like a stone, his face
turned white. Darling survived to make 37 out of a total of 86.
Had Tate held the catch Australia could hardly have got a
score of more than 50, for Lockwood and Rhodes, that Friday
afternoon, bowled magnificently. Yet when Tate laid himself
down to rest in the evening, can he not be imagined as saying
to himself: 'Well, it's nearly all over now, and as far as Tate of
Sussex is concerned, the worst must have happened. I never
asked to play for England—they thrust greatness on me
—and I'll be well out of it this time tomorrow, back to
Brighton, and who'll remember my missed catch after a
week? What's a muff in the field in a cricketer's career?
—everybody makes them.' If Tate did console his spirit in this
way the poor man did not know he was born. The gods had
not finished with him; the next day he was to be put on the
rack and have coals of fire heaped on his head.

On the Saturday England were left with 124 to get for
victory. A tiny score—with the cream of batsmanship at
hand. But there had been five hours of rain in the night, and
Trumble and Saunders were bowling for Australia. Still,
England seemed nicely placed at lunch; the total 36 for none
and MacLaren and Palairet undefeated. The crowd took its
sustenance light-heartedly; everybody lived at ease in a fool's
paradise as rosily lighted as Tate's. Here, again, was the
humorous touch of the gods: men that are taken suddenly out

of contentment are the more likely to writhe in Gehenna. After lunch the sun got to work on the wicket, and straightway Palairet was bowled by an intolerable break from Saunders. Tyldesley came in, and, with MacLaren, the game was forced. The play of these two batsmen gave the crowd the first hint that all was not yet settled in England's favour, for it was the play of cricketers driven to desperate remedies. The runs, they seemed to say, can only be got if we hurry; there's the sun as well as Trumble and Saunders to frustrate. Tyldesley jumped to the bowling; he hit 16 runs in quick time before he was caught in the slips. England 68 for 2—56 wanted now, And, said the crowd, not yet sniffing the evil in the wind, *only* 56, with Ranji, Abel, Jackson, Braund and Lilley to come, to say nothing of Rhodes and Lockwood. Why, the game is England's! Four runs after Tyldesley's downfall MacLaren was caught by Duff in the long field. An indiscreet stroke, yet whose was the right to blame the man for making it? It had come off time after time during his priceless innings of 35, and England could not afford to throw a single possible run away. MacLaren had played like a gambler at a table—not looking as though he were making runs, but rather as one who had ample boundaries at his bat's end to bank on every throw of the dice.

Abel and Ranji were in when at last the multitude unmistakingly saw the evil day face to face. For what sort of a Ranji was this? Palsy was on him. You could have sworn that he shook at the knees. It looked like Ranji; his shirt rippled in the wind even as it did on that day at Old Trafford six years earlier than this, the day on which he conjured 154 runs out of the Australians. Yes, it looked like Ranji—the same slight body, the same inscrutable, bland face. Alas! the spirit had gone—here was a deserted shrine. Thousands of eyes turned away from Ranji and looked to Abel for succour. Ah, this is better—the pertness of little Abel lightened the soul. He made gallant runs—a boundary over Hill's head. 'Cheeky' work this—batsmanship with *gaminerie*. 'Bravo-Bobby!' shouted the Old Trafford crowd. At 92 Ranji was out, leg-before-wicket to Trumble. Well, the sophist crowd told itself, that was bound to happen; he never looked good for any at all. But 5 runs more and Trumble bowled Abel.

England 97 for 5—27 needed. 'It's quite all right,' said a parson on the half-crown stand; 'there's really no cause for anxiety. To doubt the ability of Jackson, Braund, Lilley, Lockwood and Rhodes to get a paltry 27 runs would be scandalous. Besides, I do believe that fellow Tate is a batsman—he has an average of 16 for Sussex.' The century went up with cheers to herald it—the crowd made as much of joyful noise as it could, presumably in the hope that cheering would put a better face on the scoring-board. Jackson, who made a century in the first innings, scored seven in his best 'Parliamentary' manner—neat, politic runs. Then he was caught by Gregory, and now the cat was indeed out of the bag; sophistry passed away from the heaped-up ranks. 'Who'd 'a' thowt it?' said a man on the sixpenny side. Who, indeed? At that very moment of agony at Old Trafford, people far away in the city read in the latest editions, 'England 92 for 3', and agreed that it wasn't worth the journey to Old Trafford, that it had been a good match, that the Australians were fine sportsmen, and jolly good losers.

Sixteen runs—four good boundaries or four bad ones— would bring the game into England's keeping when Lilley reached the wicket.

He was frankly and unashamedly in some slight panic. He hit out impetuously, as who should say: 'For the Lord's sake let it be settled and done with quickly.' Braund was overthrown at 109, and Lockwood made not a run. Lilley lashed his bat about like a man distraught. Rhodes is his companion now, and stands on guard ever so cool. Eight runs will do it, and 'There goes four to them!' affirms the red-hot crowd as Lilley accomplishes a grand drive into the deep. 'Well hit, sir!' shouts our parson. 'Nothing like taking your courage in both hands against these Australian fellows. Well hit, sir!' Glem Hill is seen running along the boundary's edge as though the fiend were after him. Trying to save the four, is he?—even from as certain a boundary hit as this! Extraordinary men, Australians; never give anything away. Hill, in fact, saved the boundary in the most decisive manner in the world by holding the ball one-handed before it pitched. The impetus of his run carried him twenty yards beyond the place where he made the catch—a catch which put incredulity into the face of every man and woman at Old Trafford that day. 'A sinful catch,' said the parson. Tate, the last man in, watched Rhodes ward off three balls from Trumble, and then rain stopped play. Yes, rain stopped play for forty minutes—and England eight runs short of triumph with the last men in. But though it was heavy rain there was always a bright sky not far away— another piece of subtle torture by the gods, for nobody could think that the weather was going to put an end to the afternoon. It would clear up all right in time; the agony had to be gone through. The crowd sat around the empty field, waiting, but hardly daring to hope. The tension was severe. Yet surely there were calm minds here and there. Why, under a covered stand sat two old gentlemen who were obviously *quite* indifferent to the issue. One was actually reading to the other the leading article from one of the morning papers. Moreover, he was reading it in a controlled and deliberately articulated voice. 'Sir M. Hicks-Beach argued yesterday,' he read, 'that even if Ireland was overtaxed in 1894, its grievance was less today, because taxation had not increased quite so rapidly in Ireland as in the United Kingdom.' And the other old gentleman, so far was he from troubling his head needlessly over a mere cricket match, promptly took up the points in the argument, and he too spoke in a perfectly controlled and deliberately articulated voice. 'Two wrongs,' he commented, 'do not make a right.' Excited about England and Australia? Not a bit of it, sir! We trust we are old and sensible enough to put a correct valuation on a game of cricket.

In the pavilion Tate was dying a thousand deaths. All depended on him—Rhodes was safe enough. In his head, maybe, notions went round and round like a wheel. 'You've only to keep your bat straight,' he might well have said to himself time after time. 'Don't even move it from the block-hole. I've heard tell if you keep your bat quite still it's a thousand to one against any ball hitting the wicket' . . . At six minutes to five the Australians went into action again. Saunders bowled at Tate—a fast one. Tate saw something hit the ground and he made a reflex action at it. Click! Tate looked wildly around him. What had happened? A noise came to him over the wet grass, sounding like a distant sea.

The crowd was cheering; he had snicked a boundary. Another snick like that and the game is England's and Tate safe for posterity! The ball was returned from the ring, and Darling slightly but impressively rearranged his field, the while Saunders bent down to a sawdust heap. Bloodless, calculating Australians they were. Tate got himself down on his bat once more, and the wheel in his poor head went round faster and faster. '. . . Bat straight . . . don't move . . . can't hit wicket . . . block-hole . . . don't move . . . Bat straight . . . can't hit wicket . . .' And the gods fooled him to the top of his bent—to the last. Saunder's fourth ball was not only good enough for Tate's frail bat; it was good enough for the best bat in England. It was fast through the air and—it was a shooter. It broke Tate's wicket, and, no doubt, broke Tate's heart and the heart of the crowd.

In twenty minutes Old Trafford was deserted save for one or two groundsmen who tended to the battlefield. The figures on the score-board had revolved, obliterating all records of the match from the face of it, which now looked vacantly over the grass. The gods had finished their sport—finished even with Tate. Yet not quite. A week later, on the Saturday afternoon following this, Tate met the Australians again in his beloved Sussex, and he was graciously permitted to play an innings of 22 not out against them—and a capital innings at that.

SPOFFORTH

'THE DEMON BOWLER'

WHAT manner of man was Spofforth? How did he bowl? Was he fast, fast medium, or did he mix them? Did the man himself, his personal aspect, get on the nerves of batsmen? These are questions typical of the curiosity in our age about 'The Demon Bowler'. The great cricketer can establish no permanent affirmations of his prowess; Spofforth was the strongest living force in the game some four decades ago, and today his might is with the might of Bahram; he is no more than a name pronounced by greybeards in the ears of their children.

There are, of course, young sceptics about in these times. 'Spofforth?' they ask. 'See, now, was he post- or pre-Fuller Pilch? The Demon Bowler? Well, well, perhaps he was—in the early 'eighties' view of the demoniac. But, we ask you, how could the early 'eighties know what velocity really is capable of? The conception of velocity changes from age to age; it is not a fixed idea. The early 'eighties looks a sleepy age to us who have seen the speeding-up since the twentieth century came in. The aeroplane does give one a positive idea of velocity. But the early 'eighties! Come, come, what could they know of speed then? The 'eighties went about in four-wheelers—and, bless us, active men and women were from time to time knocked down in the streets by four-wheelers, though how they managed it is rather baffling. Obviously their view of pace was different from this age's, which boasts an endorsed licence. Would your Spofforth have seemed streaked lightning today? We pause for a reply.'

But the old men, who saw the glory of Spofforth, need not argue on this point; they are, indeed, at liberty to admit that Spofforth was not strictly a fast bowler in his best years. The belief that he came into George Lohmann's classification of 'brute-strength' bowlers they can put down to callow innocence. Spofforth bowled fast in 1878, on his first visit to England, and that his speed was alarming has been testified by C. W. Alcock—for one—who, as he lived long enough to know Richardson and Lockwood, must be accepted as a witness with a modern notion of velocity. When Spofforth came to England again in 1882, though, and accomplished his mightiest deeds, he was no longer a fast bowler pure and simpler. It is doubtful whether he ever was one, for the Hon. E. Lyttelton has spoken of the Spofforth of 1878 as a bowler with a 'marvellous change of length and speed'. And the characteristic of his work in his heyday has been settled once and for all by Lord Harris in these sentences: 'It is quite a mistake to suppose Spofforth won his great reputation in England as a fast bowler. True, he was very fast before he came to England in 1878, and on occasion I have seen him bowl very fast here, but, so he told me, he soon found that on our softer wickets he could do so much that, instead of bowling fast with an occasional "judgment" ball, as he called it, he changed to bowling the medium-paced ball as a rule, with an occasional fast one, and so became one of the best bowlers ever seen; in my opinion the best I have ever played.' Here, in fact, we get at the real value of Spofforth's contribution to cricket—and a great cricketer's work is not wholly to be judged by wickets taken or runs scored, but by his expansion of the technique that came to his hand in his day.

The claim has been put forward by admirers of Spofforth that he was the first bowler to study variation of pace. No slight to Spofforth's genius will happen if this claim is shown to be extravagant. Great men do not begin epochs, but rather are a fine flowering of them. It is only the 'freak artists' who cannot be seen as links in a chain of development. Spofforth's indebtedness to English bowlers—pioneers of our game in Australia—has not been insisted on half enough, yet Spofforth himself has gladly and generously admitted it. In our winter of 1863–4 Parr's XI visited Australia, and with them was Tarrant. 'When I saw Tarrant,' Spofforth once told Mr W. A. Bettesworth, 'he was the fastest bowler I ever saw. I tried to copy him. My one aim was to bowl as fast as possible, without any other idea at all.' But ten years after this, W. G. Grace's team went to Australia, and then it was that Spofforth was put on the track of his greatness. 'When Southerton and Alfred Shaw came over to Australia their bowling was a revelation, and I didn't see any reason why I shouldn't copy them, and Tarrant as well, and try to combine all three. I soon found that variation in pace was the most important thing of all.' Thus the master pays his debt, does justice to the great pioneers—those that had to be quit of a world with their work to be done. 'W. G.' and Spofforth were inveterate foes on the cricket field. An intriguing thought (as they say in the drawing-rooms) that in these two old masters we have a case of cause and effect! We have seen how Spofforth was prompted to cultivate variations by Shaw and Southerton in 1874. Well, some half-dozen years earlier, bowling was either fast or slow; the cricketer was a rare bird who could get the

two paces under one control. And Grace scattered fast bowling all over the field just as easily as he scattered slow bowling.
It was Grace that drove bowlers into low cunning. Can we say,
then, that Grace was the cause of Shaw and Southerton, who
were, in a way, the cause of Spofforth? Of course Spofforth
expanded the art of variation immensely by bringing his own
keen brain to the study of it. Not even George Lohmann or
George Giffen had a subtler changefulness. He saw no use in
'leg traps' or 'off theories'; he was always making a direct
attack on the batsman's defence. He was master of break-
back, yorker, top spin, and 'hanging' spin. He would 'deliver'
from various points of the bowling crease, and so obtain
different lines of flight into the batsman. Also he would bowl
now from the edge of the crease and now straight over the
wicket—and obtain much the same line of flight! Even the
onlooker in the pavilion was frequently at a loss whether his
run to the wicket suggested a fast or a slow ball; batsmen were
afflicted with dubiety even after the ball had left the bowler's
grip. There is a story of a young Cambridge cricketer who,
certain that the slow one was coming along, played forward
gracefully. A second later Blackham, the wicket-keeper, was
addressing him most politely: 'Your bat, sir?'

But we can no more account for the prowess of Spofforth
wholly in terms of technique than we can account for any
man's genius in terms of technique. Lancashire once had a
bowler in the XI who possibly knew every trick of the trade
that ever was, but because he was short of 'personality' he
could not get a footing even on the upper slopes of greatness.
There is no doubting that Spofforth did 'get on batsmen's
nerves'. He had a dark, Mephistophelian aspect; tall, sinuous
—the 'spirit of denial' to highly strung cricketers. An old
player once spoke somewhat in these terms to the writer, of
his first taste of Spofforth: 'It was at the Oval. I were in right
form and not afeared of him when I goes in to bat. He'd just
taken a wicket, but I walks into t' middle jaunty like, flicking
my bat, makin' rare fancy cuts through t' slips as I went over t'
grass. Well, at the Oval you have to pass t' bowler on the way
to t' crease, and as I got near Mr Spofforth he sort of fixed me.
His look went through me like a red-hot poker. But I walks on
past him along t' wicket to t' batting end. And half-way down

somethin' made me turn round and look back at him over my shoulder. And there he was, still fixin' me with his eye.' One can even today get a good idea of Spofforth's demoniac air from the portraits in Mr Beldam's *Famous Bowlers*. They were taken long after his days in the sun were over, yet there lurks in the pictures of the man a sense of sinister power. The bowling action is Spring-heel-Jackish; the form of him lithe in an inimical way; his face set in hard, predatory lines. He was the Australian of Australians, a stark man who let in with him the coldest blast of antagonism that ever blew over a June field. Armstrong had Falstaffian humours compared with Spofforth. We shall not look upon his like again, no doubt. At which sentiment all honest batsmen will say, in Mr Pecksniff's language: 'What a soothing reflection is that!'

VICTOR TRUMPER

WHEN Victor Trumper died on June 28th, 1915 at the age of thirty-seven and seven months, nearly all Sydney lined the pavements to mourn. It was like a Royal funeral, and rightly so. For Victor was the Prince of Batsmen. Measured by statistics his achievements have been left far behind. In Test cricket against England and South Africa he played eighty-nine innings, eight times not out, highest score an undefeated 214, for a total of 3,164 runs, average 39.04. His record as a batsman v. England was seventy-four innings, five not outs, highest score 185 undefeated, for 2,264 runs, average 32.81—an average excelled not only by Bradman, Clem Hill, Ponsford, Sutcliffe, Hammond, Woolley, Hutton, Leyland, and Compton, but by A. P. F. Chapman, Peter May, Cowdrey and Cyril Washbrook. But Trumper opened Australia's innings many times in Tests limited to three days, moreover on pitches not elaborately prepared. The first game between England and Australia I saw as a boy began with Albert Cotter, Australia's terrifically fast bowler, sending three balls in the morning's opening over—flying far above J. J. Kelly's (the wicket-keeper) head.

Trumper commanded the qualities which in my opinion are the sign of the truly great batsman—effortless mastery, ability to cope with the finest attack on the most vicious pitches and a method and style beautiful to see. He had, so A. C. MacLaren once told me, six different strokes for the same kind of ball. MacLaren, in fact, paid to Victor the highest compliment ever paid by any master-cricketer to another. 'They called me the embodiment of the Grand Manner . . . but compared to Victor I was as a pretty good cab-horse to a Derby winner.' Trumper, said C. B. Fry, 'played a defensive stroke *as a last resort.*' In 1902, summer in England was wet, with flashes of burning sun. In those days wickets soon became 'sticky' as they dried. And in 1902 spin bowlers thrived in plenty: Haigh, Rhodes, Blythe, Wass (fast from leg stump to off, in fact a fast Charles Parker!), Walter Mead, J. T. Hearne, S. F. Barnes, to name just a few. In 1902, Victor scored eleven centuries in a season's total of 2,570 runs, average 48.49. His rate of scoring was round about 40 an hour. His strokes, gallant, audacious yet always stylish, took the watcher's breath away. Bowlers, put to the brilliant sword, four boundaries an over, were obliged to join in the crowd's applause. Do I overpraise?—very well let me quote from the restrained prose of the MCCs 'Cricket Scores and Biographies'. 'For Trumper, the English season of 1902 was triumphal progress, and those who were fortunate to witness his amazing brilliance will never be able to forget the unrivalled skill and resource he displayed. On "sticky" wickets he hit with freedom whilst everybody else were puddling about the crease, unable to make headway and content if they could keep up their wickets . . .' He scored a Test match century before lunch, in this his 'wonderful year', at Old Trafford. MacLaren lost the toss and the slow wet turf would certainly become a batsman's death pitch somewhere near half-past three. So MacLaren's strategy was, of course, to keep Trumper quiet at all costs, for two hours. But Trumper drove on rapid feet. And when the bowlers were compelled to pitch a shade short Trumper cut them late, astonishing even MacLaren and Braund, two of the greatest slip fieldsmen of all time. On that morning at Old Trafford, July 24th (a three-day match remember) the ground was too soft to allow Lockwood, (a fast bowler in a thousand) to bowl until Australia's total had soared to 129 for none in an hour and a quarter. After lunch Lockwood came on and took 6 for 48. England lost by 3 runs; so it will be apparent to the most sceptical intelligence that Trumper won the match, and the rubber, before the first day's lunch, despite MacLaren's design, supported by Rhodes, F. S. Jackson, Fred Tate and Braund, to 'keep him quiet'.

In the upstairs tea-room at Kennington Oval hangs a photo of Trumper jumping to drive, yards out of his crease, lightly balanced. Some years ago I was admiring this photo for the hundredth time when an England player, then in his pomp, asked me, as he also looked at the photo, 'was Trumper really any good?' 'Why do you ask?' I said, and this English International replied, 'Well—just look where he is—easy to stump if he misses.' I could not resist telling him that he, at any rate, seldom exposed himself to any such hazard, 'You've never been that far out of your crease in your life.' This International must remain, for the purpose and good manners of this article, as anonymous as his batting.

Trumper, of course, was not all gallant attack, flags flying, his sword a chivalrous lance, though essentially he was a chivalrous batsman at any time, good days or ill. More than half-a-century ago, a Leicestershire professional named A. E. Knight wrote a cricket book. He was an educated man, but he called in the assistance, as literary adviser, of E. V. Lucas. Knight was a member of P. F. Warner's England team of 1903–04, and he saw, though he did not take part in, the first game of the rubber when Trumper scored 185 not out, trying in vain to save Australia, 292 behind on the first innings, from defeat. Knight wrote this way of Trumper that day. 'A slender figure, wan and drawn of face, but spiritualised with the delicacy of ill-health, glides to the wicket . . . He took guard quickly, more quickly took a glance round the field. "Dreams of summer dawn in night of rain" presented no fresher vision than this boy's play to that black sea which hid the blistered grass of the Sydney hill. Not in his fascinating collection of strokes, nor in their frank and open execution merely, lay the charm. It was a man playing away a power which was himself rather than in him. With luxuriant masterfulness, yet with unlaboured easy naturalness, he diverted the ball in every conceivable direction which his genius willed . . .' Would that cricketers today could write of the game this way or find such a 'ghost!'

'Luxuriant masterfulness' and 'charm'—here are the absolutely right words for any description or pen-picture of Trumper. Though he might drive, hook and cut with a mingled power of shoulder and a rapidity of wrist, he never seemed to belabour, to 'murder' bowlers. He was not, as Bradman was, a 'killer'. His strokes might plunder; they never insulted the bowler, never stunned him into indignity. Always was Trumper playing on safety's verge, taking the chance which is the breath of life to any great player. His batsmanship was as courteous as it was punitive and cavalier. When I was not much more than a child I adored Victor Trumper. Indeed I found myself in a predicament. Patriotic as most small boys, I of course wanted England to beat Australia every time. But also I wanted Victor to bat well in every innings. I got out of the dilemma by the most artful prayer ever delivered to Omnipotence. 'Please God,' prayed this small boy that was once myself, 'Please God, make Victor Trumper score a century tomorrow—out of an Australian total of 120 all out.'

During his first trip to England in 1899, when just twenty-one, Trumper scored 135 not out v. England in his first Lord's Test match. And in this same season of his English baptism he scored 300 v. Sussex at Hove in 6 hours 20 minutes. In the Test v. England at Sheffield in 1902 he scored on a bad wicket 62 out of 80 in fifty-five minutes. For New South Wales on a terrifying wicket at Sydney in 1905 he scored 101 out of 139 in fifty-seven minutes. He scored 108 before lunch v. Gloucestershire in 1905. He was sadly on the way to a fatal sickness when he came to England in 1909 for the last time; but a flash of the old lovely dauntless Victor came out in the Oval Test against an England attack composed of Barnes, D. W. Carr, Rhodes and Woolley. And against the great England team which won the rubber in Australia in 1911–12, he reached 113 in three hours and three-quarters against Barnes, J. W. H. T. Douglas, Frank Foster (a fearsome new-ball trio!), J. W.

Hearne and Woolley. For Victor to bat as long as nearly four hours for a century!—the disease that killed him was already at work.

'The shadow stayed not, but the splendour stays . . .' Trumper had no conscious style; but he was, as C. B. Fry put it, *all* style. The majesty of MacLaren, the young gracefulness of Spooner, the lion leap of Jessop, the sword-thrust of J. T. Tyldesley—I must of course keep my comparisons to his period—these rare excellencies were balanced proportionately in Victor, so perfectly named. M. A. Noble, great Australian captain of cricket, told me of a match between New South Wales and South Australia at Sydney. Ernest Jones was then one of the world's fastest bowlers, but for a while he was suspected of an occasional throw. When Noble went in to bat, number four, a young New South Wales player, having his baptism more or less, was batting at the other end, not out twenty or so. Noble immediately received a ball from Jones which, on a flawless wicket, pitched on the off stump and missed the leg stump by an inch, travelling some ninety miles an hour. At the overs end Noble went mid-wicket to talk to the young batsman who was, so to say, on trial: 'Look, son,' said Noble, 'you've been in longer than I . . . don't you think that "Jonah" is chucking a few?' And the young man replied, 'Yes sir, I think he is. But don't say anything about it or they might take him off!' His name was Victor Trumper.

ARTHUR MAILEY

IT is generally agreed nowadays that the most harmful obsession ever to afflict cricket is the tyranny of the seam, the persistent mania for swing bowling, more or less dependent for success on a new ball. No great skill is needed to manipulate the seam. At any rate, it is a kind of bowling not difficult to exploit with effect by any strong armed young man after a year or two of practice. But the worst thing to be said of seam bowling is that it is boring to watch, mechanical and, at bottom, unimaginative and inartistic.

How different is leg-spin, how fascinating it is to watch a skillful bowler of leg-spin! In all my long years as a watcher and student of the game I can recall few pleasures finer than have blessed me as I watched, years ago, Arthur Mailey spinning the ball leisurely from the back of his hand against some of the greatest batsmen England has known. In the rubber of 1920/21, in Australia, Mailey made his Test match début and in five Test matches, all played to a finish, he took 36 wickets, average 26.27. Among his victims were Hobbs (three times), Hendren (twice), Woolley, J. W. Hearne, Makepeace, Russell, Rhodes and Douglas.

In a brief six or seven year career of International cricket the reward for his constantly amusing the skilful art was 99 wickets, average 33.91 runs each. Terribly expensive, no doubt, according to the skinflint economy of our seamster Scrooges of 1963. It is doubtful, in fact, if Mailey would get a place at all in modern first-class matches in this country. The fact that he played cricket for fun would, in itself, keep his claims and talents under severe and suspicious scrutiny.

Arthur Mailey was, and I hope still is, a man of humour and fantasy. All cricketers who knew him in his active period—if so perspiring a word as active can be applied to him at all—loved him, love him yet; and they send to him far away to Sydney, warm wishes as he recovers from his recent illness. He first came to England in 1921, one of Armstrong's invincible XI, which contained the terrible fast attack of Gregory and Macdonald, who on wickets not yet repaired after the 1914/18 war, and in a hot summer everyday, were a perpetual danger to limb and thorax. Of this rough-riding Australian XI Cecil Parkin said; 'They've brought two killers with 'em, also a funeral director and a gravestone maker.' (H. Carter was in private life connected with 'funeral parlours', and T. J. E. Andrews with gravestones.) I could never fit Arthur into this company of unsmiling Ironsides. He was so casual, so apparently lazy. He never seemed to exert himself when he bowled in a few easy strides, and an almost negligent swing-over of the arm. But the left side of his body pointed classically down the wicket. It was a beautiful action, with a strong leverage of the wrist. He bowled any amount of full tosses. 'If ever I bowl a maiden,' he once said to me, 'it's the batsman's fault, not mine.' No bowler who loves the arts of leg-spin and 'googly' likes to send down a maiden. Some Australian wit—I think it was Ray Robinson—maintained that Mailey bowled leg-spin like a millionaire and Grimmett like a miser. Few leg-spinners have put onto a cricket ball a spin as tremendous as Mailey's. One morning in the nets at Perth, Western Australia, he bowled at me. A half-volley floated slowly towards me, hit the hard earth, then whipped away with an enormous acceleration of speed. I drove blindly at it, and the ball gyrated still faster over the back-net into the Australian bush. It was never recovered. 'That was a devil of a ball, Arthur,' I said. 'Yes,' he replied, 'it's the ball you criticise Patsy Hendren for not driving past cover for four.' Mailey bowled his gigantic leg-break at me on one other occasion. At midnight in London, on a lovely June night, along the pavement in Piccadilly. But it wasn't a cricket ball he bowled at me this time. It was an apple. And after pitching on the pavement it spun over Piccadilly to the rails of the Green Park—or thereabouts.

He was born in a slum, one of the Sydney 'larrikins'. It is a mystery where he got his fantastic and civilised mind from in the Sydney of those days. For he was (and is) a man of very rare sensitiveness and sophistication. He was a cartoonist on the Sydney newspapers, with a broad, unambiguous and deft pen. He has written one of the most engaging books in the literature of cricket: 'Ten for 66 and All That', named to commemorate one of his most distinguished and laughable bowling performances—all the Gloucestershire wickets in one innings at Cheltenham in 1921. He turned up one morning in his dinner-jacket to play at Kennington Oval.

In the January of 1925, Hobbs and Rhodes achieved the great first-wicket stand of 283, batting the Saturday through. Then, on Monday, Mailey clean bowled Hobbs—with a full toss! 'I never bowled a ball which gave me more pleasure. It made the pavilion cat laugh,' said Arthur. He bought his wickets. On the flawless Australian pitches of his day, a slow bowler simply *had* to speculate. England's own marvellous title 'Tich' Freeman was not a dangerous spinner in Australia.

He who in England took 304 wickets at 18.05 each in 1928, and 298 at 15.26 in 1933, could trouble Australian batsmen in 1924/5 only to the extent of 8 for 459 in Test matches, the reason being that he lacked Mailey's strong wrist leverage. Mailey, of course, bowled the 'googly'; but not only spin but curving flight was one of his most dangerously alluring tricks. He bowled, in short, with intelligence, imagination—and humour. He even revelled in the massive total of 1,107, scored by Victoria against New South Wales in the Australian summer of 1926/7. His analysis worked out at 4 wickets for (approximately) 340 runs. 'This analysis,' explained Arthur, 'scarcely did me justice. Three catches were dropped off me—all by a man in the pavilion wearing a bowler hat.'

Such charm of character has made cricket the great game it has been, a greatness far above competitive and statistical estimation. I have travelled much with Arthur, over the seas between England and Australia. On one voyage our cabins were next to one another. And at our table sat a pretty and witty girl from Sydney. Arthur and I simultaneously 'fell for her'. But at Colombo, a middle-aged judge came on board. The young girl left us at our table after dinner to dance with him, promising to return to us 'soon'. She was still dancing with the judge towards midnight. So I said to Arthur: 'Come, let's go to bed. Teach her a lesson. When she comes back here, we'll be gone.' 'Right,' said Arthur, 'teach her a lesson. That's the way to handle 'em.' We retired in dudgeon to our cabins, but I waited in mine, listening to Arthur as I heard him—so I thought—prepare for bed. At last I heard his electric switch turn out the light. After a few moments of silence, I crept out of my cabin. I hadn't undressed at all. Then I went up to the deck alongside the dancing floor, peeping through the window, looking for the pretty Sydney girl. Stealthily I crept along. Stealthily I turned a corner—and collided with Arthur. He was still in his dinner-jacket. He had been waiting in his cabin until, as he imagined, *I* had gone to bed. This was one of the laughs of a lifetime.

Such cricketers as Arthur Mailey, as I say, have given to the game its unique character as well as skill of a very select order. He played cricket as a way, or at least one way, of his life. And he has lived a rich and varied life, with a relish he has conveyed through a spinning ball to thousands of lovers of the fine points of the game. Best of all, he has, by being Mailey the cricketer and Arthur the happy Australian, made friends in two hemispheres, amongst whom I count myself—one who owes him much for many hours of pleasure that has enhanced the appreciation and understanding both of life and friendship.

1925

THE TEST MATCHES

A T the moment of writing the fifth Test match is not finished. England has been skittled out on a Sydney wicket for 167 and 88 for five—a convulsion and collapse which takes much of the gilt from the gingerbread made in the earlier matches by our XI, thanks to ginger supplied by Hobbs, Sutcliffe, and Tate. The tour, after all, does not establish that English cricket has improved over-much since the great Attila ride of Armstrong in 1921. Gilligan's team, with the services of the best bowler in the world, has lost the rubber easily to an Australian XI which at the winter's beginning had to make good the loss of Armstrong, Macartney, and Macdonald—not to mention a decline in the skill of Gregory and Bardsley.

The English team as a whole failed to live up to the reputation in batsmanship it spread about the country last summer when confronted by the bowlers of South Africa. Hearne, Hendren, Woolley, and Sandham have not put a fresh polish to their names. 'Sutcliffe and Hobbs out—all out', the Australian newspapers were declaring as far back as a month ago; and the other day an Australian bowler, who has since the war dealt hard blows to English cricket here, gave me his word that Australia fears no English batsman of the moment save Hobbs and Sutcliffe—'and does not fear Sutcliffe after Hobbs is out'. The wavering of Woolley, Hearne, and Hendren, their consistent inability since 1921 to re-produce against Australia their county form, is hard to explain; you cannot get to the root of the trouble in terms of technique. The skill of these three batsmen is surely beyond suspicion—though personally I have always questioned Hearne's footwork against a spinning ball. Many judges of cricket would place Hearne, Hendren, Woolley, and Sandham technically in a class rather above Sutcliffe's. Are we, then, to account for their failures against Australia by a reference to 'nerves'? Every cricketer will smile at the idea of a scarified Woolley, or of a Hearne subject to any kind of emotional reaction. My own contribution to the problem is this: Hearne, Hendren, and Woolley have found it difficult to reproduce their true quality *in the crucial moments* of the winter's Tests because of their dubious experiences with Australian bowling since 1921. It is only too likely that they have not been free to give undivided minds to the job of cutting and driving Mailey and Gregory; the possibility is that reputation has all the time been staring them in the face. A test-match batsman needs to feel pleased with himself from the outset of an innings; he will discover it hard enough even then to score heavily and comfortably. A cricketer cannot hope to master Gregory and Mailey in Australia and at the same time deliver himself from the influence of an 'inferiority complex'. For Test-match purposes nothing succeeds like success; that is the Australian philosophy, as may be proved by the alacrity with which the Australian Selection Committee got rid of Bardsley and Macartney.

Yet despite the holes in the armour, Gilligan's team fought magnificently in the decisive games, and came as close to recovering the Ashes as any team in the past that has lost them. An accident to Tate in the third Test is certain to be regarded by many of the historians as the factor that at bottom settled the issue. But others, with more reason, will argue that the English team would have won the rubber if our Selection Committee had chosen one more bowler of pace and physique as a helpmate to Tate. Generations yet unborn will some day ask—and in vain—why in 1924–25 we sent to Australia a team that included five slow bowlers and not one trustworthy bowler of speed, save Tate. Before the side sailed from England last September, most judges of the game here (one refers to players as well as to newspaper critics) doubted the wisdom of trusting to middle-aged Douglas on Australian grounds, and to Howell, who had already, in 1921, revealed himself a doubtful force on the wickets of Sydney and Melbourne, and who, moreover, was known to be a poor bat and field. It is, of course, easy to win cricket matches backwards; none the less, criticism is at liberty to ask whether with, say, Geary in the English XI we should have had to suffer the two decisive Australian last-wicket stands in the first Test, and the equally decisive ninth Australian wicket stand in the second Test. In these two games it was the Australian 'tail' that piled on just those runs which in the long run broke England's back; the Australian 'tail', it seems, was able to accomplish what it did accomplish because Tate had utterly spent himself in a noble and successful onslaught against Australia's best batsmen. There was no other English bowler at hand possessing the pace which, as a rule, will give the happy dispatch to such as Hartkopf and Mailey—both of them batsmen, one would say, of the kind that fall easy game to Parkin, who is celebrated even in London for his prowess among 'the rabbits'. But Parkin, and Macaulay, too, for that matter, were not taken to Australia; both are admitted on all hands to be fine bowlers, but, seemingly, both are very naughty boys. The tour will probably be known to posterity as that on which Sutcliffe achieved in a few months a fame not exceeded by Ranjitsinhji himself in a long and miraculous career. Sutcliffe, unlike Hearne and Hendren, found the air of Test cricket bracing—or rather, sustaining. He was as much at ease in mind during the agonies of the deciding match of the rubber as the average good cricketer is in week-by-week county matches. The country may or may not possess one or two other young cricketers of the Sutcliffe stamp: the pity is that next summer the illuminating light of representative cricket will not be spread frequently, few matches outside of the county programme having been arranged. County routine does not always give a born Test-match player a keen enough spur; we nearly lost Sutcliffe—we certainly did 'waste' him in 1920–21—through taking his stature in county games to be his true stature. Many cricketers somehow can loom big in none other but big engagements. There is another reason for deploring the scarcity of representative matches in next summer's programme. In the absence of the searching event, not only is the tough temperament unable to show and assert itself, but the flaccid temperament gets a chance of hiding itself. We may be sure that one or two of this winter's broken reeds will stand upright yet again in the balmy air of county cricket next season.

J. HOBBS: AN APPRECIATION

THAT the first century of the season should usually come from Hobbs is, as Mr Square in *Tom Jones* would have said, in accordance with the eternal fitness of things. For Hobbs is indisputably our leading batsman; moreover, he is an out-and-out product of the modern game. Were a Martian to come upon us, wanting an introduction to the science of batting as we know it today, he need go no farther than the Oval some morning when Hobbs is at his best. And, truth to tell, Hobbs is always at his best, even if he fails to put up a big score. This is no paradox. There are cricketers who can give a glimpse of their mettle even in the very process of getting clean bowled, just as a tyro may hit a ball to the boundary time after time, yet only to convince us of his total lack of art. Whoever saw MacLaren act in any way unbecoming to a great cricketer? I always think of him today as I saw him once playing forward to Blythe beautifully, a majestic rhythm governing the slightest movement. He was clean bowled on the occasion I have in mind, for none, but nobody other than a giant of the game could have made a duck so immaculately. He played cricket as some proud Roman might have played it.

Hobbs, without possessing MacLaren's magnificence, can similarly convince us even on his unfruitful days. Rarely does he lose his wicket through incorrect or, rather, inartistic play. He does, of course, deviate from the conventions; that is because, like the artist he is, Hobbs cannot go on from day to day just scoring runs in the way that comes easiest to him.* No artist is happy moving along the lines where resistance is least, and Hobbs is for ever seeking to widen the scope of his

---

* This was written of the Hobbs of 1919.

craft—experimenting, creating obstacles for the sheer joy of overcoming them. So does a Chopin choose to write a study for black notes only, a Chardin paint a white tablecloth against a white background! Any green boy fresh from his coach at a public school may hit a ball on the off stump past cover; Hobbs often prefers to get it round to the on with a daring hook shot. Of course it is risky, and now and again he pays the penalty.

At the beginning of a certain bygone summer an amount of gloom set in at the Oval because Hobbs failed several innings in succession. Was his day over? asked the Jeremiahs. And then, just before the Lancashire match in London, Hobbs decided he had been playing a little too confidently, trying his on shots before getting the pace of the wicket. In this match he promised himself he would take no undue risks. As a result he got a century. And he would get a century every time he batted if he chose to 'sit on the splice' and wait for the inevitable loose ones. Fortunately for the glory of modern cricket, Hobbs sees in the game more of art than of science. Like Peter Pan, he is ever out for 'an awfully big adventure'.

I have said that Hobbs in himself would provide an ample idea of the scope of modern batting technique. And I should say that the great batsman of today differs from the great batsman of yesterday in his fuller command over back play as an offensive factor, and in his ability to combine it easefully with forward play. Men like Hobbs have worked out a method of back play such as few cricketers of the 'eighties dreamt of, though there have, of course, always been geniuses who 'builded wiser than they knew'—wiser, that is, than the law taught them. Such a one was Arthur Shrewsbury, whose back play was faultless, no matter how bad the wicket. But how far cricketers of yesterday were, in the lump, from realising the full scope of back play we may understand from this sentence in Grace's book on cricket:

'Whatever you do, do not get in front of the wicket when you play the ball . . . My experience has shown me that by keeping your right foot firmly in its place and drawing back the left until the heels are almost touching, one can resort to what is called the glide stroke and place the ball to leg.'

The G.O.M. was, of course, laying down a canon taught by

experience of the bowling of his day.* But other times other manners. Bowling is not as accurate now as it was in the Shaw and Attenwell epoch, but it turns more than it did in those times and is distinctly shorter. Two conclusions emerge if we consider these changes. The 'classical' forward stroke was, from its very muscular action, slightly speculative; that is to say, one did not actually see the ball at the moment the bat met it. The stroke assumed that the ball on pitching would follow more or less along the line of flight. In that case the stationary right leg as a *point d'appui* for the lunge forward was a sound enough rule. If the ball turned out rather shorter than you had at first calculated, you could, as the G.O.M. instructs, play back at it simply by drawing in the left leg.

But latterly we have had scores of good bowlers (I am speaking of bowling on the average during the last dozen years) whose deliveries you could not just trust to follow along the line after pitching. Some of them—Vogler, Faulkner, Bosanquet, Hordern—did not even break the way their finger and wrist action indicated; they were 'googly' men—bowlers of 'wrong 'uns'. To cope with these, the more or less speculative lunge forward was suicidal. Better to run out, if it was a case of forward play at all. Most of these men, however, bowled rather short of a length, so that if your right foot was grounded stiff just behind the popping crease, you met the ball as it was turning and, what was more dangerous still, taking an upward trajectory. In 1912 the South Africans went to pieces in the Triangular Tests mainly because of immobile play on the right foot. This defect, as Mr E. H. D. Sewell once shrewdly pointed out, was probably due to the fact that in South Africa cricket is played on matting, and that a batsman tends to ground his right foot behind the edge of the matting and keep it there. Whatever the cause, fast-footedness was the South Africans' ruin against Barnes.

Batsmen like Hobbs (but today there are few!) meet the 'new' bowling mainly by using the feet as batsmen never used them before. They go back right on the wicket, when they cannot jump to the pitch, thus giving the ball time to work off

* Grace himself did not always obey his own rulings; see the portraits of Mr Beldam's book on *Great Batsmen*.

its spin and devil and so become more playable. They simply have to move the right leg across the wicket (to the horror of the old 'uns!) so that it may be used as a pivot on which to swing the body for the hook stroke to a break-back—the pads quite legitimately protecting the stumps. Hobbs has this stroke to perfection.

Old cricketers may argue with some force that modern batting—even that of Hobbs—is not as delightful to watch as batting was when it was three-parts forward play. The grace of forward play comes from the longer swing that can be got if you move your left leg fairly well out. But a flowing rhythmical movement is not the only way in which great batting may titillate the aesthetic emotions. If Hobbs, for instance, finds the wicket or the bowling rather against a free forward game, then he makes the main factor in his back play take the form of wrist-work. And who will deny the fascination of wrist-work? Why, the most stylish bat of the last twenty years, and that is R. H. Spooner, appealed to us less by his forward play than by wrist action used in conjunction with back play.

With Hobbs, when he is on a bad turf, back play is made positively dramatic. He times his strokes so beautifully that you catch your breath as you see the ball on the very wicket. Then he gives you that wonderfully quick swing round, the right leg as pivot, and you have the finest on-side shot of recent years! The drive through the covers is sweet, but Hobbs on the on-side is majestic. Besides, given a fast wicket, Hobbs can play the conventional forward game with the best of them. How superbly adaptable is his style we can understand from his success in this country, in South Africa, in Australia, against all conceivable sorts of bowling. The modern batsmen may have the good fortune to play on better wickets than those which fell to cricketers of yesterday, but, to be just to them, let us realise that they have bowling infinitely more diversified to tackle.*

Hobbs has mastered great bowlers in the 'classical' manner, and Rhodes, Blythe, Noble, J. T. Hearne will compare with any of the bowlers of the 'eighties and 'nineties; he has also

---

* Again, let me make it plain that I refer to bowling during the Barnes–Vogler–Foster period.

mastered the greatest of the modernists—Hordern, Schwarz, Faulkner, Barnes, Hirst, F. R. Foster, 'googly' men, leg-break-cum-off-break, swerve or what you will. He learnt all the well-tried tricks of the trade from Tom Hayward, and he has added a few of his very own.

M. A. NOBLE

THE general law which divides human mentality into two contrasted types—making of us Liberals and Conservatives in politics, classicists and romancists in the arts and literature, Platonists and Aristoteleans in philosophy —would seem to operate even in our sports and pastimes. In cricket, at any rate, we have our Frys and our Ranjis, our Trumpers and our Nobles. M. A. Noble was in the classic school through and through, and that much can be said without contradicting the view that also he was definitely a player of today. For it is possible to be classic without being pedantic. Noble's style scrupulously observed all the principles which long experience has sanctioned, but with him these principles had, so to speak, developed naturally, and the ease with which he was able to adapt them, especially in his batting, to every change in the technique of the game, was a striking justification of their undiminishing utility.

As a bowler he was far enough advanced to cultivate the swerve, but even here he never forgot the time-honoured axiom about good length being the basis of good bowling. Too many of our 'swervers' can only bring off their effects by over-pitching, and indeed the very conditions which are required to induce the swerve, render it difficult not to overpitch. Before a ball will curl, obviously it must be in the air for a longish time, and take an uncommonly spacious curve in its flight. The trouble, therefore, is to swerve without presenting the batsman with the full toss or half-volley which can so easily be hit to the boundary. Noble solved the problem like the thoughtful student he was. He got the necessary addition to his curve in the air at his end of the pitch—not at the batsman's. This he managed by going down rather low on his right knee in the act of delivery, and by releasing the ball from the hand farther back in the swing over than is usual. The ball thus was impelled from a conveniently low altitude, and as a consequence, the upward trajectory was a little higher than the average bowler's, and so the ball gained the extra air in which to lose its spin—and this must happen before the swerve will take effect—all of which operations happened well away from the batsman's reach. His swerve was done so subtly that the batsman hardly saw it at all, for it was less a curve in from the right or the left than a vertical swerve. There was perhaps a slight swing from leg, but the chief danger came from the ball that dropped suddenly down just when it appeared certain to be a delightful half-volley. There was, however, nothing sensational in Noble's swerve; even a purist like Alfred Shaw might have cultivated it had he played the game today. As has been said, Noble always tried to keep his length classically correct. He also had the conventional off-break of the fast medium bowler. But, first and last, it was his generalship that gave the quality to his bowling which made it difficult on all wickets. He was a master of deceptive flight, as, indeed, most great Australian bowlers invariably are. They need to be, too, playing as they do in a country where the hard, fast grounds so often make break almost impossible.

Noble's batting was in all its details quite classical; here no notably modern characteristic entered at all. His play did not fire the imagination of the crowd, like Trumper's; rather, it compelled admiration. There was thoughtfulness in his very stance at the wicket, and every action pointed to a deliberate and studiously cultivated method.

The art of a Trumper is like the art in a bird's flight, an art that knows not how wonderful it is. With Noble there was always a sense of effort; we did not feel, as we did with Trumper, that batting was for him a superb dissipation, a spontaneous spreading of fine feathers. He gave us the impression, always, that there was some difficult obstacle in the attack, to be overcome only by hard work and untiring determination. His was the skill that comes not exactly 'to the manner born', but through diligently scorning delights and living laborious days. He played back to an extent uncommon among Australians. But it was back play of an extremely graceful and polished kind. He did not dab at the ball, bringing the bat from just behind the right leg with a cramped wrist action, as some batsmen do. His bat, even in his very late defensive strokes, came down from above with a full swing; it was as free and as rhythmic as in a forward shot. He combined caution with enterprise in a way that is typical of the average Australian cricketer. In his brilliant moments his off-drive was worth a day's walk to see.

P. F. Warner has described Noble as the wisest of all Australian captains, and though this is high praise, remembering Giffen and Darling, it must come very near the truth. On the field he was the picture of concentration. His temperament inclined him naturally towards the more scientific aspects of the game, and he usually wore the expression of a mathematician tussling with a stiff proposition. He played the game for all he was worth—as though, indeed, a kingdom depended on it. It will be best to remember him as a long-limbed and tense-featured giant standing abstractedly between the overs at point (where, by the way, he was one of the finest fielders of them all) knitting his brows and letting the whole world go by, save the particular scene of the moment—the warm sun and the grass, the silently moving men in white, and the dire necessity of another wicket before lunch.

A. P. F. CHAPMAN

A. P. F. ('PERCY') CHAPMAN was in his youth and early manhood every schoolboy's summer night's dream of the ideal cricketer. He was tallish, with fair crinkly hair, good build, but not yet at all adipose. He was actually slender, supple, swift and strong. His pink chubby face beamed good-nature. There was a hint of an aureole about his head as he fielded or batted in the sun. The gods gave him everything, gifts for the game, health, good material fortune, then they ironically took away these benefactions towards his life's end. But while it lasted his day was glorious and by no means short, for it covered nearly twenty years, during which he scored some 16,000 runs, at an average of 31. His severest and most elderly critics argued that he had an 'edge' to his bat, and that he flashed it riskily at the ball on the offside, even if it was swinging away. Of course he did!—this was the happy cavalier way he played, whether for Cambridge University, the Gentlemen v. the Players, for Kent, or, if it came to that (which it did), for England. He was a left-hander, and any left-handed batsman playing for Kent in Woolley's period would have been well advised to try batting right-handed, so as to avoid an 'odorous' comparison. The plain—no, the beautiful—truth is that Chapman could get runs at one end of the wicket, with Woolley in possession at the other, and remain well within the picture's frame, a picture of perfect summer at Maidstone, at the time a day of timeless sunshine, now far away and part of dead history and embalmed statistics. At Maidstone on Saturday June 18th 1927, the sun shone gloriously. Lancashire were going neck-and-neck for the County Championship; and at once Kent were brutally pressed to the wall. On a 'flying' wicket, drying after yesterday's rain, E. A. Macdonald bowled at a hair-raising pace, endangering thorax, breastbone and cranium. He was one of the greatest, fastest and most beautiful bowlers ever seen. And once seen never forgotten. This beautiful day at Maidstone the easy, effortless silent onslaught of Mac-donald on Kent mocked the landscape's peaceful bountiful setting. Five Kent wickets were swept aside, as trees before a hurricane—Hardinge, Ashdown, A. J. Evans, Woolley and Ames, who hit bravely for 36 out of 70. Hardinge was run-out, and Woolley succumbed to Sibbles. But Macdonald was the first cause of the Kent subsidence.

After lunch, two young amateurs guarded the wicket. Fat 'Dick' Tyldesley said to Peter Eckersley, his captain, 'Hey, skipper, Ah'll go on at t'other end—'ere's a couple of them cooloured caps coomin' in.' Then Tyldesley received the surprise of his life. One of these young amateurs was Percy

Chapman, the other G. B. Legge. Each scored a century, adding 284 in two hours and a half. But it was Chapman who turned Kent's day; it was Chapman who counter attacked against the horribly menacingly advancing Macdonald. Will it nowadays be believed that Chapman, on this sadly departed afternoon at Maidstone, coming to the crease when the world's fastest bowler was 'on the kill' and his side's innings foundering all hands—will it be believed that in these circumstances Chapman, in three hours, cut, drove and hooked 260—repeat two hundred and sixty? He stood on tiptoe to Macdonald and hooked him so that the ball sometimes soared away like a helicopter for six. He lay back and cut him. He put his right foot down the wicket and, laughing as he did so, drove Tyldesley's potential leg-spin into the next field amongst the ruminant cows. In this incredible innings, Chapman hit five sixes and thirty-two fours. Macdonald's bowling analysis ended at 25 overs, 3 maidens, one hundred and eighteen runs, three wickets. He applauded when Chapman pulled him for a huge six, which promised to pass beyond recall. 'It was infectious,' said Macdonald, after Kent's and Chapman's innings was over; 'infectious. I felt that I was taking part in Percy's cricket.' A tribute in a million!

Chapman scored a century for Cambridge in the University match of 1922, 102 not out, and he had so far in this season been out of luck. A week later he scored 160 for the Gentlemen against the Players, also at Lord's. I doubt if he ever afterwards equalled this gay but secure masterpiece of batsmanship. With A. W. Carr at the other end, the turf at Lord's was blistered and the windows of Tavern and Long Room threatened. These two amateurs—Carr the filibuster, the pirate, and Chapman the knight at arms (but not pale!), plundered one hundred and fifty runs in an hour and three-quarters, from a superb attack, the cream of our professional bowling, an attack consisting of Parkin, Kennedy, Macaulay, Woolley and J. W. Hearne. (That year Parkin took 189 wickets, average 17.46; Kennedy 205, average 16.80; and Macaulay 133, average 14.67.) Such driving as Carr's that afternoon has not been equalled since, even by Dexter, Chapman, less pugilistic than Carr, appealed more than the grimly-visaged Notts' captain to carefree raptures. Chapman wasn't exactly a stylist; I should perhaps best describe him as a 'dashing' batsman. Sometimes he played at a ball with his feet too far from the pitch of it. But always was he good to look at. Often he lost poise as he swung his bat trying a hit to the on. Seldom were his offside strokes not brilliant. They might now and again astonish the slips, and cause bowlers to throw up their hands to heaven, but they didn't offend good taste. The charm of his batting was that his finest hits were as impulsive as his 'chancy' ones. He didn't achieve a great stroke by taking more thought than he did when blundering into a mistimed one. Good or bad, superb or out-of-touch, his cricket was a quick unpremeditated expression of the springy youth in him. He came by his best strokes, powerful and radiant, exactly as he came by his indiscreet strokes—simply by a natural blend of intuition and born cricket sense. At his best he was aggressively nonchalant.

He captained England with an enjoyment which might have provoked frowns from Sir Leonard and Peter May. Yet he was far more than the *Amateur in excelsis*. He knew the game. And he had the knack of bringing the best out of players of all sorts of temperament. He made them feel at home. He removed the chains of routine. And, of course, he was fortunate to have at his call and in his ranks players as great and experienced as Hobbs, Sutcliffe, D. R. Jardine, Hammond, Hendren and Duckworth. He led the great company which won the rubber in Australia in 1928–29. He had, in 1926, been made captain of England in the fifth Test at Kennington Oval, when and where England recovered the 'Ashes' after having lost three consecutive rubbers. The England team in Australia for 1928–1929 won the first four tests, losing only the fifth, in which Chapman was unable to play. Here are the names of this great company: Chapman, Jardine, Hobbs, Sutcliffe, Hammond, Hendren, J. C. White, Larwood, Tate, Geary, Duckworth—with Ernest Tyldesley, Leyland, Philip Mead and Freeman not good enough to find a certain place! Hammond in this rubber, scored 905 in nine Test match innings, once not out.

In the next rubber, following that of 1928–29, fought in England, Chapman had to surrender to Woodfull. This was Bradman's first English rubber; and he staggered us all with

974 runs in seven Test innings, averaging 139.14. Chapman was dropped from the captaincy for the deciding Test of the series—also at Kennington Oval. Time brings in revenges. But this dropping of Chapman was scarcely just. England were on even terms with Australia before this Oval match began. He had led England to victory against Australia six times, losing once only. And in this same rubber of his deposition he scored a century at Lord's. In this extraordinary match England, batting first, totalled 425, a safe enough foundation, surely, in a four-day match. Australia responded with 729 for six—declared, Bradman 254. Hopelessly downhill, England then lost five wickets for 147. Chapman came in at this deplorable hour for England. Before scoring he spooned up a ball on the offside, the easiest catch in the world. But Ponsford and Vic Richardson looked at each other and the ball fell harmlessly to the earth. Laughing like the Cheshire cat, Chapman proceeded to drive, cleave and cast the Australian attack far and wide. He scored 121 in two hours and a half, with four sixes.

Australia were left to get seventy-two to win, a merely formal job for Ponsford and Woodfull in the afternoon's mellowing warmth. Splendid bowling by Tate and Robins caused the crowd to stir, actually to hope. Robins bowled-Ponsford. Then Chapman, with one of the most wonderful catches of his life—and he was a fieldsman marked out of ten thousand—dismissed Bradman for a single. Bradman lay back to cut Tate, a great stroke from the meat of the bat, sending out a crack of vehement triumph. Eyes flashed to the boundary, where third man instinctively jerked himself to action. Chapman, in the gulley, was standing in his favourite position as the ball was bowled by Tate, his legs apart, arms folded. When Bradman made the stroke, Chapman bent down, picked the ball up half-an-inch from the grass, threw up a catch beyond belief, and assumed his usual stance in the 'gulley'—legs apart, arms folded. The roar of the crowd expressed amazement and joy. As Bradman was departing for the Pavilion, maybe the most astounded man of all, I was watching the game in front of the Tavern, standing there with Sir James Barrie. 'Why is he going away?' asked Barrie, as Bradman left the crease. 'But surely,' I said, 'surely, Sir

James, you saw that marvellous catch by Chapman?' 'Oh, yes,' replied Barrie, 'I saw it all right. But what evidence have we that the ball which Chapman threw up in the air is the same ball that left Bradman's bat?'

This same Chapman, embodiment of cricket in youth and early manhood, fell into tragically premature age. For years he remained rosy, ageless. Time and life trapped him, this same Percy Chapman, who, while he lived and loved his days in the sun, might well have imagined they would have no end at all. He was a pride of Kent cricket and an adornment to the England XI in a golden age. He will be thought of for years to come with affection and admiration—and sadness.

1926

THE AUSTRALIANS

No doubt I shall court folly if I make a few judgments about the form of the Australians on the strength of what I have seen of them at the nets. But it would ill become me NOT to take a risk or two in my work—because I am always complaining that cricketers do not risk half enough nowadays when they are at the wicket. I shall therefore attempt a few 'anticipations' about the Australians' prospects and ability in this country this summer. And if my judgments should prove absurd as time goes on, I trust my readers will give my daring as much applause as they give to the batsman who courageously 'has a go' and gets bowled middle stump in the attempt.

To the critic with some eye for inborn style and culture, it was plain enough in the nets at Lord's the other afternoon that Macartney, Gregory, Taylor, and Bardsley are the four unmistakable masters in the Australian team. And on the evidence of the discerning eye Ryder, Hendry, Everett, Ponsford, Richardson, Collins, and Andrews are good but by no means unprecedentedly great cricketers. Much has been written lately of Arthur Richardson's off-break. True, he bowls it well enough. But surely no modern English batsman is going to be outwitted by an off-break. If the two-eyed stance, with its exploitation of the pads, 'the second line of defence', cannot 'back up' and so frustrate the off-break —then what use is the two-eyed stance at all? Richardson apparently bowls off-breaks in the old-fashioned manner; that is to say, he pitches the ball off the wicket with the intention of hitting the stumps. To an off-break directed in this style a batsman may use his pads almost indiscriminately. The best off-spin bowler since the war has been Parkin. But

Parkin discovered long ago that off-breaks pitched outside the stumps in the Richardson fashion are useless against county batsmen who understand the art of pad-play. Parkin was compelled to pitch his break-back *on* the wicket and depend upon assistance from fieldsmen arranged in the shape of a leg-trap. Even then it was only Parkin's extraordinary nip from the ground, the acute angle of the rise of his off-break, that made his leg-trap successful. I doubt whether Richardson is master of half of the command which Parkin at his best held over the off-break a few years ago. My view, therefore, is that on sticky or fast wickets Richardson ought not to worry accomplished batsmen over much.

The eye for style also sees little of out-of-way quality in the attack of Hendry and Ryder. Apparently both of them are good utility bowlers, more or less dependent on the new ball for their 'devil'. I suspect, too, that Everett's bowling is pretty straight once the seam has been flattened. The Australian attack, indeed, seems likely to hang upon Gregory, Mailey, and Grimmett. If all three strike their finest form England will be lucky not to be beaten in the rubber. I must, of course, give a few reasons calculated to support this drastic statement.

The Australian batting will be good enough on all wickets —this was established beyond argument at the Lord's practices. With Gregory at anything like his fastest as a bowler, few of our batsmen, save Hobbs, Sutcliffe, and Carr, will be able to 'stop him' while he is fresh. For, to say the truth, English cricket is today almost as unfamiliar with authentic fast bowling as it was in 1921. Macdonald did not often take it into his head to bowl his fastest in county cricket last summer; whenever he did there was hardly a county cricketer in the game who was not easy prey for him. Gregory, of course, never was as fine a bowler as Macdonald. It is probably true, too, that over a longish period he cannot sustain his fastest pace. But there is little evidence that Gregory will not bowl this season for short spells with a speed and vitality likely enough to make *our* fastest bowler appear just fast-medium. There are, I am aware, good judges of the game who think that in the big matches now upon us Gregory will be a failure because he was not successful in Australia last winter. This opinion does not take into account the extra 'life' and 'kick'

Gregory is almost certain to get out of English wickets. And even if Gregory should prove more or less ineffective, the Australians may still be dangerous enough with Grimmett and Mailey in deadly form. For the solemn truth is that, apart from Hobbs and Woolley, English cricket is badly off at the moment for batsmen who are clever against slow spin bowling. Australia's attack, I admit, will scarcely be deadly if Gregory and one of the googly bowlers should lose their skill in the same season. When the 'googly' bowler is good he is very, very good; when he is bad he is merely ridiculous!

THE FIRST TEST

WITHIN the next day or two we may be led by news from Lord's to understand that the lamented first Test at Trent Bridge was not, after all, a weary waste of waters. That short spell of fifty minutes' batting by England surely taught a lesson. Did not the ease and confidence of the cricket of Hobbs and Sutcliffe demonstrate most palpably that the atmosphere of this summer's Test matches is going to be vastly different from that of the 1921 games here? In the season of Armstrong's supremacy the first half-hour of every crucial match saw England struggling in an oppressive inimical air. Gregory was a devouring flame, and the English batsmen made of very perishable stuff.

How changed the aspect of everything, in the brief cricket which was our portion at Nottingham! Gregory worked nobly to recapture his old thunder, but in vain. The wicket, no doubt, was easy—yet I thought there were signs in his laboured action that here was a Gregory who had bated, dwindled—'fallen away vilely since the last action'. And at the other end of the pitch no Macdonald flashed lightning at English batsmen—only Macartney, who has had to relearn his bowling. Macartney is clever with his left-handed spin stuff, but who, a year or two ago, could have foreseen an

Australian XI so doubtful in attack that Macartney would be put to the necessity of taking to bowling again? Macartney is still the world's most original batsman, a brilliant maker of snapdragon runs. But Macartney, in this year of grace, one of Australia's first two Test match bowlers, on a comfortable Trent Bridge wicket—what a fall must indeed have happened in Australian confidence and power from that notable and convinced masterfulness of Armstrong's men!

Opinion amongst cricketers throughout the country has crystallised to this view—the present Australian team is weak in attack. Will not our Selection Committee pick the England XI on this knowledge? So far, it would seem, they have worked with eyes entirely on Australia's batting strength. Apparently, they have argued that since the Australians are likely to bat down almost to the last man, so, too, must England. Surely this is to look at England's problem this year from the wrong end. If Australia is weakish in bowling, we do not need to concentrate so much on the batting of our XI that our bowling becomes rather scant. If Australia's strong arm is batsmanship (and it is), then we ought to make *our* attack our strongest arm. Collins holds the rubber; therefore England must take the offensive. And in this country it is bowling and fielding that win matches. We shall play Collins's game if England goes into action with less than our strongest available attack. It is to his batsmen that the Australian captain is looking this year to save a difficult situation caused by a shortage in Australian bowlers of high-class at the present time. England will not win the rubber unless her attack is good enough to break through the enemy's one and only flank that matters.

Our Selection Committee, no doubt, cannot forget that it was the English 'tail' which largely was responsible for the disasters in Australia in 1924–1925. My view is that on English wickets, and against this latest Australian team, the problem is not at all the same problem Gilligan had to tackle on perfect Australian wickets: In England a total of 500 is not wanted for the purposes of match-winning cricket within three days. On the flawless turf of Sydney, with time of no consequence, batting and fielding achieve the victory. At home, even on a good English wicket, a score of 300 will always be ample as a foundation for Test match conquests—if your attack is re-sourceful enough. Here, then, is the point of my argument: An England XI with six 'specialist' batsmen, supported by useful work from the others, ought to get runs enough *against Collins's doubtful bowling*—runs enough, that is, to give our very best bowlers the cue for victory. If we neglect our attack (I will persist in this view whatever the result at Lord's) by playing too many batsmen who cannot bowl really well, Australia's batsmen will have a good chance of retrieving any difficult situation into which their side's dubious bowling may land them.

This week-end Root, Tate, Kilner, with Hearne and Woolley to wheel a few up from time to time, might contrive to make a match-winning attack. But it is not the best English attack conceivable; a better could be found, I think, without leaving our batting at all short. Working from this point of view in strategy I name the following eleven cricketers as the most likely of all to win England the rubber this summer: Hobbs, Sutcliffe, Hendren, Woolley, Carr, Stevens, Kilner, Tate, Larwood, Root, and Strudwick—with Rhodes to play instead of Larwood on a wet wicket.

THE OVAL—VICTORY AT LAST

THE old writers used to call on the Muses for guidance whenever they had a difficult work on hand. If the Muse of History will deign to recognise the uses of the humble cricket reporter, I petition her now to give me aid. Heaven knows it is wanted, for as I write against time, this vital Test match is raging away at the Oval; England is winning; every ball bowled is being hurled across the wicket with bitter English determination; while a crowd gets madder and madder. If one's eyes are taken away from the action for a second something is bound to happen and a roar of triumph or frustration will set one's heart thumping apprehensively, for fear of having missed a superb piece of cricket.

Under the nose of this press box men and women are sitting spellbound now flushed joyously, now silent in expectation. And we poor galley slaves must somehow get down on to paper our facts, our impressions. Never before have I known a field as tense as this. The air is throbbing as history is beaten out in the hot forge of the game.

Years and years have we been waiting for this hour of revenge, and after long eating of the bread of humiliation here come Victory with her wine at last. No wonder the packed multitude lifted up its voice this afternoon as one by one they watched the smashing of the shackles of Australia which have held English cricket these many summers.

When Macartney fell to a slip catch the clamour of the crowd was not merely jubilant; in it could be heard the note of savagery. 'Die and be damned,' said the Oval, and then magnanimously cheered every Australian counter stroke. The enemy were caught in a trap of their own making. The 'timeless' Test match was invented by them, not us. Here, as Corporal Nym would say, is where the humour of today's fight comes in.

The English innings closed at twenty-past three. Rain held back the morning's play till a quarter-past twelve, and again at twenty-past one heavy showers fell and prevented a resumption till a quarter-past three. Twenty minutes afterwards Australia's heavy task started. They required to make 415 for victory and the Ashes. The rain made fast bowling rise awkwardly, and also it helped the spin bowler. But the turf could hardly have been more difficult than it was yesterday between noon and lunch time. It was faster and a little rougher, and perhaps for that reason a good ball gained in deadliness.

Collins sent Ponsford in with Woodfull to open his innings —a doubtful move, I thought, though plainly made with the intention of sparing Bardsley from Larwood's first devastating energies. Woodfull and Ponsford were terribly in earnest. Australia were not going to be beaten, we thought, in a hurry. As Larwood ran to the wicket and opened England's fire the silence on the ground was painful. He galloped along the earth like a young horse. His right arm shot forth its violent speed.

Ponsford was nearly caught at slip straightaway; as the stroke went at blinding pace from his bat the crowd's heart jumped into its mouth, and a man somewhere said 'Oh my God.' He spoke for thousands. In Larwood's second over we had tasted blood. Woodfull flashed a speculative bat at the lightning ball and Geary accomplished a lovely catch. The good tree Woodfull was thus felled to earth at one blow. The roar of the crowd must have been heard half a mile away by women in Kennington making tea. Woodfull could safely have left alone the rising ball that got him out, and as he walked back to the pavilion his face was twitching with mortification.

Macartney came in next. At last we saw him the most solemn of men. Where were his quips now, his whims and oddities, that were wont to set Armstrong's table in a roar. He took his guard as cannily as any Makepeace. But once he got to work he was his own quick-silver self. His bat made brave play here and there. He drove Tate through the covers with a stroke that had the bloom of a peach. He hit Larwood fiercely to leg. The little man was ready to play a jewel of an innings to shine through the encircling gloom for Australia.

He hit, as I say, Larwood for four to leg. The next ball, like that which was Woodfull's undoing, rose high outside the off stump, but it was a little wider; Macartney tried to cut it in his own coxcomb fashion. He too sent a catch to Geary, who again had safe, capacious hands. Macartney took off his gloves as he walked away from the wicket, for the last time in a Test match. The sound made by his bat as it sent the catch to Geary might have been the noise of Australia's cracking foundations, and with the old enemy's score still 31 Ponsford edged a beautiful spinning away ball to the slips, where Larwood tumbled forward, all eager, excited boyishness, and hugged his prize. Hats were thrown into the air from the black ranks of the crowd. Acclamation and lust for conquest and vengeance have never on any cricket field deafened ears as they were deafened now.

Collins was the living image of the will-to-survive when he reached the wicket. But even he could not hang on. Rhodes ensnared him in the slips at 35, and four wickets had toppled in the Australian camp at half-past four.

The match was won and lost at this very moment. Even the hardened old fighter Bardsley must have realised that it was only a matter of time now for England's victory. He played dourly, nonetheless, for eighty minutes. Then Rhodes tempted him to hit, and he skied a ball against the spin, high to Woolley moving from the slips behind the wicket to the leg side. But before he got out Bardsley and Andrews scored 28 for the fifth wicket, which was taken when Andrews let his bat fly at a by no means short-pitched ball from Larwood, only to see Tate hold a catch at forward leg from what might be called a good bad stroke. It was good because it was an authentic hit, and bad because no cricketer in a difficult period ought ever to 'let fly', as cricketers say, at a fast ball's pitch.

Bardsley was sixth out at 83; Gregory was a victim to recklessness at the same total; Richardson, with desperation making a sullen light behind his spectacles, drove a spiteful boundary to the one from Rhodes, who immediately afterwards bowled him with a ball that 'made pace' from the ground. Richardson's bat came down, too late, with a thud that might have been his heart making a beat of palpitation.

Let the rest of the Australian innings be silence. The ninth wicket was worth 27—forlorn play but plucky by Oldfield and Grimmett. Oldfield was not to be disturbed even by a dire period out of his customary air of cool cocksureness. At four minutes past six Mailey's leg stump was knocked flat to the earth, and at long last English cricket was free to throw out its chest.

The crowd ran over the Oval and massed itself in front of the pavilion and demanded a sight of its heroes. English and Australian cricketers alike were given a resonant 'All hail!' to the tune of the 'Bow Bells'. The happy thousands sang 'We want Herbert' (meaning Sutcliffe). 'We want Collins', 'We want Chapman', 'We want Jack Hobbs', 'We want Rhodes'. Everybody stayed there for half an hour at least—men and women, boys and girls—all well aware that they were living through a moment which in the after years they will boast about to their children, telling them as they do so that giants walked the cricket fields in their days.

Frankly, the Australians batting was disappointing to those of us who, while we prayed for an English win, also wanted to see a stern fight. The Australian innings did not keep in tune with the titanic girth and temper of the match as it was played from Saturday till Tuesday.

No conceivable team could have scored 415 on this afternoon's wicket, but we have one or two county elevens that might have tackled the English bowling with a more consistent show of common sense than Australia did. Woodfull, Andrews, Macartney, Bardsley, Gregory, and Richardson may be said to have lost their wickets by indiscreet, impatient hits. The tactics of this 'suicide club' were astonishing in a team which has learned its Test cricket in a land where the clock is never an enemy. May it be whispered that Collins and his men have proved themselves today not entirely lacking in human hearts and human nerves. The batting appeared suspiciously like that of 'rattled' cricketers. Macartney burnt his own wings, and nobody will scold him for that; he has always been a lovely wayward butterfly. But why Woodfull should have flicked at the off-side ball, and why Bardsley, Andrews, and Gregory should have made the rash strokes they did make can surely be accounted for only on the assumption that they for the moment forgot the Australian habit of Fabian doggedness in the face of odds.

The English bowling, apart from Larwood's first few overs, was not exactly of the battering-ram order. Rhodes spun the ball in his old way of curving guile masked by simplicity. Nonetheless he invited the batsmen to be accessories after the act of their own destruction. Geary and Tate were everyday 'up and down' bowlers. I imagine that had Australia been beginning a match against this attack they would have got a good score. Once Woodfull and Macartney were out there seemed a readiness on the part of most of the others to make the worst of a bad job. The difficulties of the wicket and the bowling alike were exaggerated. Larwood, with careful nursing, might develop into the best fast bowler of recent years, though he is not tall enough ever to rank with the great fast bowlers of Test cricket.

The sight of Rhodes getting Australians confused into knots at his time of life was beautiful—and a little sardonic. He takes his farewell from Test matches, even as Hobbs does, with immense honour. Had he played in the earlier Tests, especially at Leeds, we might have recovered the 'Ashes' before today.

Australian critics maintain that their eleven of this tour is not truly representative of the best of their country's cricket at the moment. Be that as it may, it is certain that England has won the rubber with a side a little below the best available here. Woolley is no longer dependable, either as batsman, bowler, or fieldsman; Hendren never has been a Test match batsman; Stevens, Geary, and (on current form) Tate are not amongst our eleven cleverest cricketers. But for Hobbs and Sutcliffe the English second innings would have broken down in a moment of crisis—even as it broke down last evening against tired bowling on an improving turf.

The gods gave Australia a rare chance on the unpleasant wicket before lunch on Tuesday. They did not jump to it, and so the gods had no further use for the Australians. When the gods would destroy, the old saying has it, they first make mad. There were certainly some signs of blind folly in the Australians' batting this afternoon—and at the very stage where the situation called for the authentic shrewdness and patience of Australia.

LESSONS FROM THE 1926 TESTS

THE Test matches may fairly be said to have exposed the limitations of the seam-swerve bowler. Yet it is only the other day, so to speak, that he was full in the fashion. Some fourteen months ago, I wrote an article in which I pointed out that most modern swerve bowlers were dependent on the new ball, and that immediately after its gloss and shine had passed away, there were few swerve bowlers who could exploit any deadlier trick than an up-and-down medium-paced length, a little too short for a good hit.

This view of the 'fashionable' bowling was not common at the time I argued it out in print. Truth to tell, I had not myself then quite gathered together *all* the evidence. And I could not get away from the fact that our greatest bowler was Tate—essentially a seam-swerver. Day after day, I watched cricket in all parts of the country—and watched it from a place situated behind the bowler's arm. And slowly I was forced to the conclusion that our average bowler dwindled sadly in deadliness as the ball got 'older' and its seam got flatter. Tate's persistent success, I decided, was the consequence not so much of his late 'swing' as of some physical vitality generated from his strong shoulders.

The Test match at Leeds would probably have been won by England but for the 'swerve' mania which has obsessed most of us since the war. Spin bowling has been despised here and in Australia. Geary, a new ball specialist, was preferred to Parker, at Leeds. The reluctance of average Australians to learn to turn the ball is comprehensible. Their custom, in Australia, of covering the wicket has, I think, cost them one rubber already. No cricketer is going to twist his fingers into vain knots on the flawless turf of Sydney and Adelaide. Whoever is responsible for the perpetual protection of wickets from Australia's occasional rain might conceivably be interested to know, on the authority of some of our best Test match cricketers, that if Australia had possessed one really good length spin bowler at the Oval on the Tuesday morning before lunch—then the 'Ashes' almost certainly would now be returning to Australia. In the old days, the rain was free to fall on Australian turf; our old enemy must get rid of the protected wicket rule and encourage her young men to spin the ball in the tradition of Hugh Trumble, Noble, Howell, and Saunders—to keep to our own times.

It was because we were aware that the modern Australian batsman did not know how to play the left-hander's turning ball that some of us argued the claims of Rhodes for the Test match at Leeds. Rhodes has *always* been a difficult bowler at Leeds, man and boy, these thirty years! But our Selection Committee looked to the seam bowlers to get the Australians out on a soft Leeds wicket; Rhodes, I believe, was reluctant to play in a Test match again. I am sorry that Roy Kilner, most charming of Yorkshire cricketers, has not this year trusted to his proper ability to spin and 'flight' a ball. It is against nature that a left-handed bowler of Kilner's gifts should ever exploit 'leg swingers'.

It will never be known how much cricket has suffered from this swerve and leg-theory obsession. Spin bowling would have won us the Leeds Test match—and perhaps Australia would have won at the Oval if, before lunch on the Tuesday morning, Richardson had pitched his off break on the off-stump instead of exploiting a leg-trap. The wicket was difficult, and Hobbs and Sutcliffe alone stood between England and defeat. If either got out, Collins must have known well enough, there would be an English collapse. (There *was* an English collapse, indeed, after Hobbs was bowled, despite that he and Sutcliffe had worn down the Australian attack, and batted until the pitch had grown easy again.) Why did Collins permit Richardson to aim his off-break on the leg stump and turn it time after time so harmlessly away from the wicket's danger zone that Hobbs and Sutcliffe frequently were able to play safely with their pads and decline the risk of a stroke with the bat? Every cricketer ought to know that on a turf where the ball is turning, a batsman is always likely to get out whenever he is compelled to play the ball *with his bat*. It was pathetic to see Richardson wasting a natural aptitude for spin—and all because of the period's craziness for 'theories' and its want of acquaintance with the authentic art of the breaking ball.

In the glorious Oval match we saw Rhodes ensnaring Australian batsmen with the old dodge—the tempting curve through the air, and the finger-spin break, away from the bat. Yet it is only last year that the modern seam bowlers were telling me, wherever I met them up and down the land: 'Take it from us—the old bowlers would never get wickets cheaply today. Batsmen know how to use their legs now—and you must bowl them out by swerve, while the ball is in the air.' As if the old batsmen (Arthur Shrewsbury, in particular) did not understand the art of pad play!

The Test matches had, for me, at any rate, no lesson better worth a cricketer's attention than this: Get back to the ancient trick of spin. And, for preference, let's have the ball that breaks away from the bat. (I do not, of course, mean the unreliable 'googlie', or the old-fashioned leg break.) Rhodes

confounded Australia's batsmen by means of the spinning-
away ball. And if Australia had possessed a bowler of the
Rhodes school, on that critical Tuesday at the Oval, England
might have lost the match as easily as she won it. The cricket
of Hobbs and Sutcliffe in that hour of stern challenge will go
down in letters of gold in the history of the game. Painful
experience in the past had taught Hobbs and Sutcliffe that, at
a pinch, 'the others' were scarcely to be trusted. And with
responsibility staring them in the face like a death's head they
achieved another great first-wicket stand, and, moreover, did
so by means of batsmanship so easy and stylish that the turf
might have been some hard, smooth stretch of Australian
earth! Shall we ever look upon the likes of Hobbs and
Sutcliffe again? 'I doubt it, said the Carpenter.'

1930

THE AUSTRALIANS

WE have heard a deal about the youthfulness of the Australian team, and in some places the term has been taken as a synonym for inexperience. The truth is, of course, that Bradman, Jackson, A'Beckett and Wall have each long since passed through the ordeal of searching and important cricket. In this country we must keep in mind the fact that an Inter-State match in Australia is far more crucial than the ordinary day-by-day county match over here; we have to think of a Lancashire and Yorkshire struggle to understand the challenging atmosphere of an Inter-State game. First class cricket in Australia is by no means as common as in this country; for that reason, it provides a stiffer test of a young man's ability and temperament. Many times in the past Australians have come to England while in their teens and have held themselves straightway like veterans. If Woodfull's team should fail, the cause will not be nerves or inexperience—unless the variable character of English turf bothers the younger players. We can be certain that stage-fright will not steal an ounce from their match-winning and match-saving powers.

It is significant of much that nowadays we refer to the 'youthfulness' of a Test match cricketer if he happens to be less than twenty-five years old. Our great players have since the war been older and older men, in every big match. Before the war, there were many cricketers who in their early twenties announced mastery to the whole world. All of these following players were famous and masterful before they reached their twenty-fifth year: Clem Hill, Victor Trumper, R. H. Spooner, A. C. MacLaren, F. R. Foster, Tom Richardson, Woolley, George Lohmann, Rhodes, Hobbs, and M. A.

Noble. I recollect the time when Bobby Abel, at the age of thirty-six, was affectionately known as the old man of the English team. Nowadays, cricketers seem to take longer than of old in coming to maturity. There is likely to be a call for new blood in the England eleven long before it is chosen for the first Test match at Trent Bridge, to be played in June. But when all is said about youth's right to an opportunity, can the Selection Committee do better than fall back yet again on the 'old indispensables'—assuming they maintain anything like true form? For the first Test match, at any rate, I would prefer to have on my side Hobbs and Woolley at 'half their best' than any two of our 'promising' young men at their *very* best. Some drastic and sudden changes in style and performance will be needed to keep out of the England eleven Hobbs, Woolley, Hendren and Tate. And I do not think you could pick a side of young English cricketers to beat a side of veterans of forty and over, composed in this way: Hobbs, George Gunn, Ernest Tyldesley, Woolley, Hendren, N. Haig, Smith of Warwickshire, Rhodes, Astill, Freeman and Emmott Robinson. If we had to match youth with youth, and put into the field an England eleven not older in bulk than Woodfull's eleven, I hardly think we could hold the rubber. A splendid chance was missed last summer by English cricket; we were afraid to trust our best youngsters even against a team of immature and inexperienced South Africans.

Woodfull's Australian team will make plenty of runs. The South Africans were able to achieve that much, in spite of training on matting wickets, and in spite of the absence from the team of a Jackson, a Woodfull, a Kippax, a Bradman. I fancy, too, that the Australians will get their runs in good style, and at a pace definitely leading somewhere in a four-day match. It is an error to suppose that Australian batting has always been slow and canny. Australian cricket is essentially opportunist. If the bowling of Grimmett, Fairfax, Wall and Hurwood should prove good enough, then the Australian batsmen will not loiter by the way. No Australian cricketer has ever been known to lose a match for want of energy to win. In 1926, the Australian batting became dogged only from the moment the truth became evident that there was no virtue in the attack of Gregory. In 1921, when Mailey, Gregory and

Macdonald guaranteed a great attack match after match, the Australian batting was dazzling; runs flashed over our fields at the rate of 90 an hour, from May to September.

Woodfull's chief problem will rise from his bowling. He cannot point to a Gregory or a Macdonald. Wall is a fast, but not a very fast, bowler. I imagine he will prove as effective as, say, Nichols of Essex. Hurwood has possibilities. Whether he takes wickets or not, his bowling will be interesting to watch. He tries to exploit all the tricks of a modern right-handed bowler of slow-medium pace. He possesses a 'googly', a leg break, and an off spinner. And he is not afraid to toss the ball into the air. Fairfax, too, will require careful watching. He has a stylish action—right arm well up and over. He gets pace from the pitch; his variations of speed and length are nicely shaded, and he causes the ball to 'runaway' fairly late from the bat. Fairfax may well turn out to be Woodfull's reliable 'stock' bowler. Our batsmen ought by now to have learned all of Grimmett's tricks—but they will probably be haunted by the knowledge that even in Australia, on flawless wickets, Grimmett's spin and low flight have persistently worried even Hobbs and Hammond. Australia's attack, though it can boast not one really great bowler, must *not* be underrated. It will not tire quickly and there will be variety and grim determination. The main difficulty likely to be suffered by the Australian bowlers in slow English turf, on which a length good enough for hard Australian grounds will pitch a yard too short, at least. If the summer should be at all wet, the Australian attack may discover that what is a dangerous length ball in Australia is, on English pitches, suspiciously like a long hop. The players in this year's Test matches will do well to get into their minds a single important fact. They are under an obligation to play for a finish, to see to it that all the hours which are to be devoted to the big games are not allowed to run to waste. There will be no fewer than four days in which to force a decision in each Test match. The English players engaged in them will be taken from their counties for two engagements every time. In short, the Test matches threaten to cut a big hole in our county cricket. The public will not tolerate, in the circumstances, a negative attitude to the Test matches. Something must be done to justify the twenty

and more days on which county cricket will be considerably
put into the background, all for the glorification of a fight
between England and Australia. Let it be a real fight—
bravely and imaginatively fought, to a proud, bitter end.

LEEDS

THE first day's cricket at Leeds opened as ominously for
England as for Australia. Jackson played too soon at
an inswinger from Tate and was caught at forward
short-leg. The jubilation of the crowd broke out quite voraciously as the score board announced Australia two for one
wicket.

But those of us who had watched Larwood's first over were
prepared for strong batsmanship, even though we did not for
a moment anticipate an innings of 309 from a single player in a
single afternoon.

The prophetic fact about Larwood's first over was that not a
ball rose to a greater altitude than half-stump high. Clearly
the wicket contained no fire at all; it was perfectly docile.

Bradman missed his first ball rather dangerously; then,
despite his own and Australia's tentative beginning, he did
not wait to play himself in.

But I must elaborate that statement, lest the impression be
given of a Bradman who lived dangerously and impetuously.

Bradman at every part of his innings was as watchful as
Woodfull himself; when a good-length ball came to him, after
he had reached 200, he put his head down and over the line of
the ball, and his bat was utterly canny, with the handle slightly
in front of the blade.

When I say Bradman did not pause to play himself in, I
mean that he did not, as most modern cricketers certainly do,
decide *not* to hit a four, whatever the ball's length, until he
had been at the wicket a long time. He began as though seeing
the pitch and direction of the English attack with the eyes of a
man whose score already stood at 150.

He began with a violent straight drive from Tate, but it was a defensive back shot. Then he knocked Larwood out of action by plundering eleven in an over, a drive through the covers, a square pull, a hit to leg, and a single to the off.

In fifty minutes he reached 50 out of 63 and then he had hit eight fours. Woodfull, at the other end, was as much forgotten by us, as much taken for granted, as Kreisler's accompanist.

Bradman never lifted a ball, never gave the faintest hint of a margin of human error. He was quick to see the overtossed and the short ball, and, more significant still, he was quick to see the ball which the bowler wanted him to hit. He never obliged!

His innings was unique in its perspicacity, its combined solidity and power, safety and speed.

He equalled the performance of Trumper and Macartney by scoring a century in a Test match before lunch on the first day of a Test match.

A remarkable fact of his innings which I have not yet seen pointed out anywhere, so far, is that he achieved his quickest rate of scoring in his first hour. He came to the wicket at twenty minutes to twelve and at twenty minutes to one he had made 70, including twelve boundaries.

Woodfull was out at three o'clock; the second Australian wicket made 192 in two hours, forty minutes, Bradman's share being 142. In the light of Bradman's brilliance, Woodfull had no objective reality for any of us save the scorers; but he was at his most obstinate. Yet, as a curiosity, it must be recorded that Bradman, despite the velocity, the range, and the energy of his cricket, seemed less likely than Woodfull to get out.

Kippax again played a suave innings and stayed with Bradman until after six o'clock. He was caught by Chapman when Australia's total was 423. The third wicket, held for two hours and three-quarters, was worth 229. Kippax's portion of 77 had the flavour of delicate culture.

At close of play, Bradman in five hours and three-quarters had hit 42 boundaries—showing us every stroke in batsmanship excepting the leg-glance; he had compiled 309, and Australia were 458 for three.

At one point of the historic afternoon, the score-board announced the glory of Bradman in these terms: *Australian Total*, 268; *Bradman*, 200.

Next morning, on a faster wicket, he was caught by Duckworth. In six hours, twenty-five minutes Bradman made 334, seldom hit a ball into the air, and gave no tangible hope to the field, with the exception of one hit to mid-on, off Richard Tyldesley, which might have been a catch had Tate got off the mark quickly enough.

This innings has caused something of a sensation in cricket. It has been described as the inauguration of a new era in batsmanship. And why? Bradman's innings was essentially orthodox; his strokes were all known to the game as far back as a quarter of a century ago.

Are we to acclaim him as sheer revelation because he uses his feet and possesses a rare range of strokes, and is capable of hitting very hard the sort of bowling which ties up the average county cricketer of these days, who seeks to bat from the crease?

Bradman's original contribution to batsmanship is not technical so much as temperamental. His strokes on Friday and Saturday might well have been photographed and used as illustrations to C. B. Fry's treatise on *Batsmanship*, written long ago. Bradman acts on Fry's principle—play back or drive.

Never is he to be seen lunging with his bat speculatively forward, and his right foot holding him back behind the crease. His stroke-play is clean, economic in energy—not an ounce wasted—but at bottom it is based upon a stance and footwork which allow him always to keep his head down and his eye on the ball. Where he differs from the great stroke-players of a quarter of a century ago is in the matter of his attitude to the game.

Whereas a batsman of the Trumper, Macartney, and the pre-war Hobbs class invariably went beyond his customary science and practised range of hits when he had reached, say, 150, Bradman brings to his longest innings the constant and unwavering mentality and vigilance of the modern record-breaker.

He is persistently playing every ball on its merits when his

score is beyond 200, hitting the loose ball unmercifully, but
never off his guard at the first hint of a serious challenge from
the bowler.

Bradman never goes divinely mad, as Trumper and Hobbs
did in the old days, when, having exhausted that part of their
skill which was rational, they became like men possessed by
romantic visions of wild and wonderful and new strokes in
cricket. Bradman is not a romantic ever; he is perpetually a
realist, with the oldest head a boy cricketer has carried on his
shoulders since W. G. Grace.

A great batsman—a phenomenal batsman for his age
—yes! But a 'new era', a creative force showing us arts never
dreamed of before—this is nonsense. I might employ a
Bradman as a beautiful example for a text book on the true
and lasting principles of batsmanship. And the tone of it, the
lessons and implications, would be quite conservative.

Australia's last wickets are never difficult to capture, and
on Saturday morning the side was all out for 566. Tate,
throughout the innings, bowled hard and well, if not subtly.
The other bowlers were pretty straight and unambiguous in
pace and flight—just the sort of stuff Australian batsmen are
nurtured upon.

Tyldesley, though far below his best in length or spin,
occasionally brought to Bradman's brow a faint line of care.
England can hope to get Bradman's wicket cheaply only by
aid of slow spin, and a flight through the air that puts a
problem.

England's innings began badly on a wicket yards faster than
it had been the day before. There was more than a hint of
dustiness on the pitch, but it needed Australia's spin bowlers
to find out and convince us that the turf was not entirely a
batsman's playground.

Hobbs and Sutcliffe allowed Grimmett to take the offensive as soon as he went on. 'Silly' point and 'silly' mid-on stood
on the batsmen's very doorstep.

England's opening partnership was without temper, without strokes; it was, in a word, defeatist in policy. Hobbs, after
promising twice to push balls from Grimmett to a'Beckett at
silly mid-on, at length did so.

A'Beckett rolled head over heels after scooping the ball up, closer to the wicket than I have ever before seen a fieldsman stand to any batsman on a hard pitch. There was a consultation between the umpires and then Hobbs was given out. Sutcliffe shortly afterwards tamely edged a ball to first slip as it was spinning away.

The philosophy of negation had now cost England two wickets for 64. Duleepsinhji hit his first ball for four and the stroke cleared the depressing air. Hammond, too, played well; in forty-five minutes Duleepsinhji and Hammond scored 59.

Then a beautiful ball from Hornibrook, worth 100 runs to Australia, pitched on Duleepsinhji's leg-stump and hit the off.

He had played, at any rate, like a cricketer whose main asset is a bat, a quick eye and foot—and a sense of style. Leyland, too, showed fight; he quickly hit Grimmett for two sixes.

A stand between Hammond and Leyland brought toughness of temper and some finish of technique to England's innings.

But England failed to save the follow-on by the narrow margin of 26 runs, being 175 behind the Australian total. The second innings opened disastrously, Hobbs being run out with only 26 runs on the board.

Hammond was caught by Oldfield when he had scored 35, and Duleepsinhji was caught by Grimmett.

When the score stood at 95 for three wickets, the umpires decided that the light was too bad for further play, and so the match was abandoned as a draw, and the honours are with Australia.

AFTER LEEDS

ALREADY it is clear that in the forthcoming Test matches there will be only two problems for our Selection Committee seriously to consider. Bowlers must be looked for who can get Bradman out, and batsmen must be discovered who can play Grimmett. To argue this much is not to disparage the other cricketers of Woodfull's team. I have no patience with the view that the Test matches are a simple case of England *v*. Bradman and Grimmett. Woodfull is a great defensive batsman; in three successive Test matches Kippax has made scores of 64 not out, 83 and 77. (No English batsman has been as consistent as Kippax; McCabe has shown rare style and promise; Hornibrook is a better left-handed bowler than most English examples; while Oldfield is still the most artistic wicket-keeper in the world.

The Selection Committee's strategy must concentrate on Bradman and Grimmett, because they are, so to speak, keys to the situation. Without their aid, Woodfull's team might easily give a fair account of themselves, but they would present no technical problems dissimilar to or more complicated than those which English players have to solve in county cricket every day. Bradman is an unique obstacle to England's prospects because he stands alone amongst contemporary cricketers in his ability to hit every loose ball for four and at the same time mingle with his rapid scoring the solidity of a defensive batsman. He has been compared to Trumper and Macartney by critics with short memories and little sense of style. Every great cricketer, like every great artist in any calling, makes for himself the standards by which his work has to be measured. The style is the original man himself. Bradman is Bradman, just as Trumper was Trumper. Let us admire the good things of the world for the essences of each of them. Bradman's originality consists in a power to score quick and hit hard, all round the wicket—without once lifting the ball into the air for hours, without ever risking a pennyworth more than Woodfull himself. When we think of other great brilliant batsmen we think of them as players who always lived dangerously—on the extreme edge of their resources. The bowler who had to suffer the ordeal of an innings by Trumper kept up his heart by telling himself that sooner or later he would bowl his best ball and that Trumper, in the throes of his rapture, would get out for want of thorough canniness. But Bradman never allows himself to be rendered drunk with his own fine rapture.

The moment the bowler sends him a really good ball he is as watchful, as circumspect, as the most inveterate stonewaller that ever lived. Bradman is a paradox—an aggressive defensive batsman, a quick scorer who never takes his eye off the ball. Where lies this genius's weak point? Let us think carefully. At Trent Bridge Robins bowled him—after Tyldesley had given him cause for thought. At Leeds, on the Friday, Tyldesley, though not at his best, kept Bradman on the defensive for a short period, during which time we saw a bat thrust forward which had no intention towards a scoring stroke, but was content to act as a checkmate. If Bradman has a doubtful part in his superb machinery, it is a certain tentativeness against the slow flighted ball which pitches on the wicket and spins away from the bat. I do not think he would try to hit boundaries off Grimmett's best ball—on English wickets. If there is any truth in these arguments, the conclusion is plain. England will do well to exploit against Bradman at least one bowler who can bother him more acutely and more consistently than Robins and Tyldesley were able to do at Nottingham and Leeds. In short, he must be a bowler of the Robins or Tyldesley category but must be better than either. One name, or at the most two names, spring to mind—Freeman and Peebles. The Kent player is the bowler of the day and perhaps Peebles is the bowler of tomorrow. For the Manchester Test match, Freeman or Peebles ought to be chosen. Neither may succeed in solving the Bradman problem; but it is pretty certain that Freeman at his best would give cause for a more than mechanical motion or operation of Bradman's technique. Straight fast-medium bowling does not trouble Bradman; against Tate, Geary, Hammond and Larwood at Leeds, Bradman, while he scored his 334, was free to bat as though he had left his brains in the pavilion; he was able to rely upon instinctive adjustments between his eye and the muscular organisation which controls his stroke play. Seldom did he need to consider questions as to what the ball might do in the air and after pitching.

The Grimmett difficulty can be more easily diagnosed but not more easily remedied. *It is impossible for any batsman, even a Hobbs, to play him safely from the crease.* Footwork, swift and reliant, carrying body and straight blade of willow to the ball's pitch and over it—here, surely, are the specifics for Grimmett. His chief danger is gone once he is compelled to bowl a short length. Throughout the Test matches so far, Grimmett has been allowed to attack with a 'silly' point and a 'silly' mid-off. The rubber will be won by the first English batsman who takes his bat firmly in his two hands, moves his feet in the Bradman way, and lambasts Grimmett for a few boundaries, each of them perilous to life and limb of the two fieldsmen standing close to popping crease on either side of the wicket. We need the Hobbs of the pre-war epoch to do this, but it is not unreasonable to expect someone to achieve it shortly.

THE FIFTH TEST AT THE OVAL

THERE seems a strange misconception going around about the fifth Test match. It is argued that because the game is to be fought to a finish the stonewaller will come into his own. 'Pack the England XI with batsmen who don't worry about runs but who can stay at the wicket for hours. For this is going to be a Marathon affair.' The simple truth is exactly contrary. There can be no virtue in stonewalling as such in a match played to a finish. Runs, and *only* runs, will count and decide the rubber at the Oval these next few days. Stonewalling has a competitive value whenever there is a clock to beat. But for the purposes of a game which is planned to go its ways regardless of time, the side that makes the most runs, *taking every chance to hit the loose ball*—that side will certainly be the victorious one.

Now there is a curious law of averages which, I believe, determines the life of any team's innings, no matter how carefully or how freely the batsmen behave themselves at the wicket. The canniest and most skilful cricketer is doomed to get out sooner or later; not many individual innings last longer than four hours. Woodfull himself must feel that the sand is running out after he has resisted the bowlers from noon to the tea interval. It is after a batsman has been on view three hours or so that he ought to realise his time is coming to an end, no matter how carefully he is playing. This, then, is the time for him to pick up every possible run. There will be no sense in a long innings during the Oval Test match if it does not possess a proportionate value in runs. Suppose, for instance, the Australians play normal cricket and make 400 in seven hours. What good would England's cause be served if we responded by stonewalling ten hours for 350? The Oval Test match will be won by the eleven which plays each ball on its merits; there's nothing like cricket—good honest bat and ball—no matter whether the match is bounded by three or thirty days. The span of every batsman's innings is limited; happy is he who hits all the bad balls that come his way before his predestined end arrives—perhaps in the shape of a veritable long-hop, because when the law of averages steps in and says 'Hold, enough!' why then, skill has nothing to do with the case!

I sometimes think that if only we could fathom the workings of this law, it would be possible for us to foresee the course of the events and the consummation of every cricket match. We would be able to engage a number of mathematicians, set them to work in the past performances of the players in any two chosen sides. The figures deduced would decide the issue—there would be no need for the match actually to be played; therefore the Press could concentrate wholeheartedly on the 'sensational' aspects, without the slightest necessity to worry over such distractions as those points of technique which call for close knowledge of the game. I certainly think our Selection Committees too frequently ignore the operations of the law of averages on the form of a great player. For example, they decide to leave a Woolley out of the England XI because he has, say, made only 7, 10 and 40 in consecutive innings. For my part, I should expect a century from any great batsman immediately after he had played three or four insignificant innings. Woolley is never so likely to achieve a big score as he is when for a week or two he has been doing badly. The only question to ask, when considering Woolley for the England XI, is whether he is in good health and in form. And 'good form' is not demonstrated merely by a big innings. You will often see a fine cricketer fail, even though it is obvious that he has been in the mood to display his skill; he has failed because it is his turn to fail. If Woolley plays for England this week-end, I shall look to him for a magnificent match-winning innings. Needless to say, I am writing this article before the team has been selected.

The man in the crowd recognises the influences of the law of averages when he talks of things 'going in cycles'. But not always do we need to dive into the mysteries of growth and change and decay to find out convincing reasons for all alterations in the performances of cricket teams. A few years ago, Australia won eight out of ten Test matches and lost none. Shortly afterwards, they were thankful to win a single game in five. But they could not blame anybody but themselves for this temporary loss of power. They were paying the price for too long a dependence on cricketers of established reputation. Since 1926 English cricket has been neglecting young talent, so much so, that whatever the result of the Oval Test match, the Australians will be free and able to emerge from the summer's rubber believing they have had the better of the tussle. For not only have they given us a good fight; they also have built up a team of players young enough to have years of splendid achievement before them. Meanwhile, we have been living—and rather precariously—on men whose best days are well behind them. In every eleven there should, of course, be the steadying presence of an old master or two—a Hobbs, a Woolley. But English representative cricket, this year and last, has been foolish to overlook persistently the ability and promise of such as Bakewell, Langridge, Gibbons, Nichol of Worcestershire, and Iddon —to name only a few of the potential young men of the moment. By the time the next England XI sails to Australia, Bradman, Jackson, McCabe and Wall will be hardened warriors and yet as young as our 'freshmen'. Which is a formidable thought!

REFLECTIONS ON 1930

Nᴏᴛ all the newspapers have taken the defeat by the Australians and the loss of the rubber with the smile of sportsmen and philosophers.

In certain places it has been discovered that a cricket match without a time-limit is against the interests of the English game.

Perhaps that is true, but there is a right time for the utterance of our various and contentious opinions. I do not recollect that any of us objected to the no-time-limit Test match in 1926, when we won at the Oval.

Some of the views expressed of this year's Oval game leave me astonished. I rub my eyes when I read that English batting is not adapted to 'timeless' cricket because it is naturally brilliant and unsafe. And I wonder whether I am waking or dreaming when I am told that the Australian batsmen, being born stonewallers, are bound to do better than the English in a match without a time-limit.

Bless me! I say to myself, is it true that these critics are discussing the same Test matches that I myself have seen this year?

Did I only imagine Bradman's brilliance at Leeds—his 304 in a single day, and his 30 boundaries between high noon and evening?

Was I the joyful victim of a delusion when, in the timeless match at the Oval, I saw Ponsford score a hundred dashing runs in two hours and a quarter, after he had gone in first against England's total of 405?

And then I consider the current argument that England lost the Oval Test match because our batsmen were not 'adaptable' to conditions which favoured long and cautious innings. 'Away with the no-time-limit match!' (so the cry goes). 'Let our batsmen get back to the gallant pace of the three-day county game, where the prize goes to the boldest'.

I suppose the sort of county match implied is, say, Lancashire v. Yorkshire, or Surrey v. Notts, or Leicestershire v. Northamptonshire, in which encounters, of course, boundaries are hit every day.

The very day following the end of the no-time-limit Test match we had a typical county engagement at the Oval; the first of its three days saw Surrey on a slow wicket scoring at a pace always below that of Australia in any Test match. Hobbs batted two hours and a half for 56; Ducat was on view an hour before he reached double figures. In four hours Surrey made 202.

And yet the Australians are being blamed for bringing into England the 'timeless' match with its temptations towards stonewalling! The solemn truth is that in all the Test matches this summer the Australian batsmen got runs quicker than the Englishmen did. Moreover, they got them by handsomer strokes.

I have not looked up the statistics, but I venture to say that, whether playing in their own country or in England, the Australians have usually made runs the faster of the two sides, and with a wider range of scoring strokes. How absurd it is to charge Australian batsmanship with congenital slowness and dullness in face of the cricket of Trumper, Macartney, Darling, Clem Hill, and Ponsford, and—choosing from the present eleven—that of Bradman, Kippax, Ponsford and McCabe!

There are good reasons why there should be a time-limit to a cricket match. But let them be discussed without prejudice to the Australian genius for the game under *all* conditions.

My view is that England contributed to their troubles at the Oval by a mistaken notion of the tactics needed in a match to be played to a finish. From the outset, over-much value was put on the length of an innings; the fact was overlooked that runs, and only runs, can possibly count in an engagement where time does not enter at all.

England's innings began at the rate of 22 an hour! Ponsford and Woodfull went in, confronted by England's 405—and in half an hour six boundaries were hit.

In each Test match the Australians showed a flexibility of technique quite lacking in the English sides.

They were obviously the younger and the fresher combatants; they had not been through the daily routine of county cricket. The trouble with English cricket today—if there is only one and not a hundred!—is excess of it, winter and summer. A Test match has become a habit with many of our players; no longer do they thrill, and see visions at the thought of a Test match.

It is just a part of the year's work. The Australian cricketer, with all his efficiency, does not suffer from any day-in-and-day-out routine that cheapens a great match for him. In his own country a great game is an event both rare and worth waiting for.

We must learn in England to put a value on our best players and on our best matches. There are too many unimportant games in a season, and too many winter tours that wear out the strongest and most enthusiastic cricketer.

The future of English cricket is not bright. For too long we have been depending in Test matches on middle-aged men. We had a chance last summer, when an untried South African team was here, to give experience to some of our promising young men.

We declined to take the risk, and as a consequence we find ourselves at the moment with several great players ready to pass out of big games—and no fresh talent hardened enough yet to come forward and take the places of the old masters.

*   *   *

The cricket match without a time limit is never likely to be popular in this country, especially if England cannot win under the conditions of it! No man who has played bat and ball, as the village and the school know these delectable instruments, will ever be able to understand how an Australian cricketer can find the heart to stonewall when his side's score is 500 for five. But while we, as a people, regard jealously the true traditions of the game, let us, as Cokane in Mr Shaw's play says, 'be just'. There is an unfair tendency at the moment to misunderstand Australian batsmanship—and to flatter our own for virtues it does not always possess. 'We lost the no-time-limit farce because the Australians are far more accustomed to playing cricket of this kind. . . . Most of the Englishmen still have some instinct for trying to get runs at a reasonable pace'. These lines, quoted from a leading critic of the game, may be taken as typical of the view held by hundreds of folk up and down the country. You would imagine from this view that, in the Oval Test match, Australia won by stonewalling and England lost by reckless hitting. The truth is that when England went in first they scored 76 in two hours, while when Australia went in first against 405, Ponsford himself got a hundred dashing runs in two hours and a quarter. In all the Test matches the Australians scored at least as quickly as England did. At Leeds, Bradman made 304 in a single day—and he went in with his side 2 for one wicket.

The Australians have nothing to teach us about slow scoring. Little use anybody in this country crying out, 'Away with no-time-limit games; let us get back to county cricket, where the clock compels a man to get runs or get out!' The pace of scoring of the Australians at the Oval was not slower than that maintained when Lancashire meet Yorkshire—in three-day engagements. The pot has not a vestige of right to call the kettle black. England, in my opinion, lost the rubber because they concentrated overmuch on defence—while the Australian batsmen played the bowling strictly on its merits. At the finish of the Oval match, we saw with mixed feelings a dazzling exhibition of hitting by Hammond, in spite of a 'sticky' wicket. Yet this same Hammond, on good wickets in the other four Test matches, gave himself up almost entirely to defence, holding in abeyance his true scoring strokes. The English batsmen, save Woolley and Duleepsinhji, have not attacked the Australian bowlers; they have generally come to the wicket with minds made up that whatever else happens they must keep their blades down on the ground. There is a fantastic theory getting about—Mr Fender shares the delusion—that England lost the rubber because the Australians batted in stonewall fashion, dour and canny, while England threw wickets away hitting out quixotically right and left. This is nonsense and untrue; I have not looked into the statistics yet, but I should be surprised to learn that in any of the Test matches England scored quicker than the Australians, or revealed anything like the same range of scoring strokes.

The case against the no-time-limit match is best made without a smug flattering of ourselves to the effect that English batsmen are too dashing for it. My complaint against the no-time-limit at the Oval is, indeed, that it spoiled the Australian batting—I was prepared for slow play for England in any circumstances, because I knew that, ever since the defeat at Lord's, our cricketers were feeling the weight of an inferiority complex. The absence of a time-limit reacted unfavourably on Bradman; he had no need to get boundaries quickly, therefore he didn't. At Lord's and at Leeds we saw him for the brilliant stroke-player that he naturally is. It is human nature for most of us to do what we *have* to do. Take away from cricket the spur of the clock, and even a Bradman will jog along as dully as Oliver Wendell Holmes's old horse. Cricket is bound to lose versatility of style, and also lose a flexible rhythm, if the clock is not in the game, to demand that here a batsman shall go fast, and there go slow. Again, there should always be a time-limit in any match, cricket or 'tiddley-winks', in order to make a true assessment of the skill of the combatants. As Mr Croome has put it so ably, neither team in this summer's Test matches possessed bowling that could be depended upon to finish a match within four days. Inadequate technique should not be allowed to get away with decision's prize because of some arbitrary interference with conditions of time, which in England, at any rate, may be said to comprise the ring of the game.

None of us doubts that the better team has won the rubber. Yet, as late in the summer as June 23, the Australians themselves had definitely come to the view that the best they could hope for was to achieve a 'good show' in the Test matches. I fancy that when the history of the tour comes to be written a quite heroic tale will be told of how Woodfull and his men won through from depression to abounding confidence. The recovery was probably one of the great spiritual victories in the history of cricket. I happen to know that in June at least one Australian cricketer of authority and experience had resigned himself to the worst.

BRADMAN, 1930

THE power of genius in cricket is not to be measured by the score-board, and not even by the clock. A Trumper, a Spooner, will reveal art and energy in one or two personal strokes or by some all-pervading yet indefinable poise and flavour. At Leeds Bradman announced his right to mastership in a few swift moments. He made 72 runs during his first hour at the wicket, giving to us every bit of cricket except the leg glance. But long before he had got near the end of his innings he was repeating himself; it was as though the sheer finish of technique was a prison for his spirit. He could not make a hazardous flight; he reminded me of the trapeze performer who one night decided to commit suicide by flinging himself headlong to the stage, but could not achieve the error because his skill had become infallible, a routined and mechanical habit not at the beck and call of anything so volatile as human will or impulse. When Bradman passed 200 at Leeds I felt that my interest in his play might break out anew at the sight of one miscalculated stroke. But none was to be seen. His cricket went along its manifold ways with a security which denied its own brilliance. Every fine point of batsmanship was to be admired, strokes powerful and swift and accurate and handsome; variety of craft controlled by singleness of mind and purpose. Bradman was as determined to take no risks as he was to hit boundaries from every ball the least loose—his technique is so extensive and practised that he can get runs at the rate of fifty an hour without once needing to venture romantically into the realms of the speculative or the empirical. The bowler who had to tackle Victor Trumper was able to keep his spirit more or less hopeful by some philosophy such as this: 'Victor is moving at top speed. Well, I'm bound sooner or later to send along a really good ball. Victor will flash at it in his ecstasy—and I'll have him'. The bowler toiling at Bradman cannot support himself by a like optimism. For hours he will see his ordinary balls hit for fours along the grass; then his good one will wheel from his arm, by the law of averages which causes every bowler to achieve one moment of excellence in every hour. But is Bradman ever likely to be so blinded by the radiance of his own visions that he will throw back his head at the good ball, confuse it with the others, and lose his wicket through a royal expense of spirit? Not he; he sees the dangerous ball with eyes as suspicious as those of a Makepeace. Down over his bat goes his head; the blade becomes a broad protective shield—and probably two pads will lend a strong second line of defence. It is not a paradox to imagine some bowler saying to Bradman, with strict justice, after Bradman has punished five fours in one over and cannily stopped the sixth ball: 'For the Lord's sake, Don, do give a fellow a chance and have a hit at her!'

The genius of this remarkable boy consists in the complete summary he gives us of the technique of batsmanship. In every art or vocation there appears from time to time an incredible exponent who in himself sums up all the skill and experience that have gone before him. It is not true that Bradman has inaugurated a new era in batsmanship; he is substantially orthodox in technique. Nearly all his strokes at Leeds could very well have been used as illustrations to C. B. Fry's thoroughly scientific and pragmatic book on batsmanship. But Bradman shows us excellences which in the past we have had to seek in different players; nobody else has achieved Bradman's synthesis. It is, of course, a synthesis which owes much to the fact that Bradman stays at the wicket longer than most of the brilliant stroke-players of old ever dreamed of staying. Perhaps he is marked off from the greatness of his predecessors not so much by technique as by temperament. It is hard to believe in the possibility of a more masterful stroke-player than Trumper was, or Hobbs in his heyday. But when Trumper and Hobbs were great batsmen it was customary for cricketers to try to get out when their scores went beyond, say, 150. How many times has Hobbs thrown his wicket away after reaching his century? Bradman brings to an extensive technique the modern outlook on cricket; a hundred runs is nothing to him; he conceives his innings in terms which go far beyond Trumper's or

Macartney's most avaricious dreams. He has demonstrated that a batsman can hit forty-two boundaries in a day without once giving the outfielders hope of a catch; he has kindled grand bonfires of batsmanship for us. But never once has he burned his own fingers while lighting them.

When I think of an innings by Macartney, I do not think entirely of cricket. My impressions of Macartney's batting are mixed up with impressions of Figaro, Rossini's Figaro, a gay trafficker with fortune, but a man of the world; hard as iron though nimble of wit; an opportunist wearing a romantic feather in his cap. And when I think of an innings by Trumper I see in imagination the unfurling of a banner. Not by Bradman is the fancy made to roam; he is, for me, a batsman living, moving, and having his being wholly in cricket. His batsmanship delights one's knowledge of the game; his every stroke is a dazzling and precious stone in the game's crown. But I do not find his cricket making me think of other and less tangible things; the stuff of his batsmanship is skill, not sensibility. In all the affairs of the human imagination there must be an enigma somewhere, some magical touch that nobody can understand and explain. You could never account for Macartney, Ranjitsinhji, Spooner, Trumper, in terms of even a marvellous technique. Bradman, as I see and react to him, is technique *in excelsis*. I could write a text-book on him with comprehensive and thoroughly enlightening diagrams. Could anybody have written a text-book saying anything that mattered about the batting of Johnny Tyldesley?

The really astonishing fact about Bradman is that a boy should play as he does—with the sophistication of an old hand and brain. Who has ever before heard of a young man, gifted with quick feet and eyes, with mercurial spirits and all the rapid and powerful strokes of cricket—who has ever heard of a young man so gifted and yet one who never indulged in an extravagant hit high into the air? Until a year or two ago Bradman had seen little or no first-class cricket. Yet here is he today, bringing to youth's natural relish for lusty play with a cricket bat a technical polish and discretion worthy of a Tom Hayward. A mis-hit by Bradman—when he is dashing along at fifty runs an hour—surprises us even as a mis-hit by Hayward did when he was in his most academic vein. How came this Bradman to expel from him all the greenness and impetuosity of youth while retaining the strength and alacrity of youth? How did he come to acquire, without experience, all the ripeness of the orthodox—the range and adaptability of other men's accumulated years of practice in the best schools of batsmanship? The cricket of Trumper at the age of twenty-one could not be accounted for, but we were content to accept it in terms of spontaneous genius. Besides, there was always the rapture and insecurity of the young man in Trumper. But while we can account for Bradman's batting by reason of its science and orthodoxy, we are unable quite to accept it—it is too old for Bradman's years and slight experience. The genius who thrills us is always unique but seldom abnormal. If Bradman develops his skill still further—and at his age he ought to have whole worlds to conquer yet—he will in the end find himself considered not so much a master batsman as a phenomenon of cricket.

As I say, the remarkable fact about Bradman's batsmanship is its steady observance of the unities. At Leeds he was credited with the invention of a new kind of hook. But there was no scope at Leeds for any sort of hook, ancient or modern. The ball never rose stump high on the first day; how can any batsman hook a ball that does not rise at a sharp angle from the ground? I have never yet seen Bradman perform the hook stroke, but I have seen him pull often enough. The pull, indeed, is one of his most efficient hits; it is timed to perfection, and the sound of it is as sweet as a nut. (This essay, the reader will bear in mind, was written of the Bradman who first astonished us in 1930.)

At Leeds more than half of his forty-six fours were drives in front of the wicket. His drive and cut, indeed, were much more frequently to be seen than his pull and leg hit. The secret of his stroke-power lies in his ability to move quickly backwards or forwards, making the length short or overpitched. The area of the wicket wherein a ball can be pitched that is a good length to Bradman is considerably narrower than that which is defended by all our county batsmen, Woolley excepted. He judges the direction of the attack rapidly; never is he to be seen lunging forward, stretched speculatively out; never does he fall into that 'two-minded' state which compels a batsman to make 'A-shaped bridges down the wicket feeling awry in the air for the ball', to quote C. B. Fry. Bradman clinches Fry's celebrated Fallacy of Reach: 'The Fallacy of Reach is fatal to true cricket. None but a giant by advancing the left foot and pushing out down the wicket can reach within feet of the pitch of a good length slow ball or within yards of the pitch of a good length fast ball. Why, the very thing the bowler wants one to do, what he works to make one do, is to feel forward at the pitch of his bowling.' Bradman plays back or else goes the whole way of the forcing stroke on punitive decisive feet. When he is as a last resort compelled to play forward, he actually goes back on his wicket to do so, and his legs are behind the bat, and his eyes are on the ball. So strong is his back play, and so quick his eyes and feet, that it is fatal to bowl a short length to him. Yet, so far, that is the mistake the English bowlers have made against Bradman. Frankly they have not 'stood up' to his punishment. Flattered by everyday batsmanship (right foot rooted behind the crease), English bowling has wilted at the sight of a bat that is busy and resolute; hence an attempt to take refuge in short bowling, a safe enough dodge in front of a cricketer who cannot cut. Bradman has thriven on bowling which he has been at liberty to see all the way, to see pitch yards in front of him. If he has a weak point, Robins, by accident or design, found it out occasionally at Trent Bridge. Every time (which was not often) that Robins sent a well-flighted ball to Bradman, pitched on the middle stump and spinning away, Bradman was observed to be thinking hard, entirely on the defensive. It is not, of course, for the pavilion critic to presume to know the way that Bradman can be got out cheaply. But it is surely not presumptuous for anybody to suggest that the short-pitched ball is about the last of all to send to a batsman with Bradman's voracious appetite for fours and his range of hits.

He has all the qualities of batsmanship: footwork, wrists, economy of power, the great strokes of the game, each thoroughly under control. What, then, is the matter with him that we hesitate to call him a master of style, an artist who delights us, and not only a craftsman we are bound to admire without reserve? Is it that he is too mechanically faultless for sport's sake? A number of Bradmans would quickly put an end to the glorious uncertainty of cricket. A number of Macartneys would inspire the game to hazardous heights more exhilarating than ever . . . But this is a strain of criticism that is comically churlish. Here have we been for years praying for a return of batsmanship to its old versatility and aggression; we have been desperate for the quick scorer who could hit fours without causing the game to lapse into the indiscriminate clouting of the village green. In short, we have been crying out for batsmanship that would combine technique and energy in proportion. And now that a Bradman has come to us, capable of 300 runs in a single day of a Test match, some of us are calling him a Lindrum of cricket. It is a hard world to please. Perhaps by making a duck some day, Bradman will oblige those of his critics who believe with Lord Bacon that there should always be some strangeness, something unexpected, mingled with art and beauty.

GRIMMETT

HE is an unobtrusive little man, with a face that says nothing to you at all; seldom is he heard by the crowd when he appeals for leg-before-wicket. He walks about the field on dainty feet which step as though with the soft fastidiousness of a cat treading a wet pavement. He is a master of surreptitious arts; he hides his skill, and sometimes, when he is on guard at cover, he seems to hide himself. He knows a trick of getting himself unobserved, and he darts forward to run a man out like somebody emerging from an ambush.

'Gamp is my name and Gamp my natur'.' That is a dark metaphysical saying; the meaning cannot be put into words, but none the less we can grasp it by the instinct for eternal substances. It is like that with Grimmett; the name penetrates to the quiddity, like 'curl', 'twist', 'slithery'; his name is onomotopoeic. I love to see him bowl a man out behind his back, so to say—round the legs; the ball gently touches the stumps and removes perhaps one bail. The humourous cunning of it reminds me that the Artful Dodger used to walk stealthily behind his master and extract the handkerchief from the coat-tails without Fagin's ever noticing it. Compare Grimmett with the wonderful leg-spin bowler he succeeded in the Australian eleven, Arthur Mailey. An Australian once said to me: 'Mailey bowled the googly stuff like a millionaire; Clarrie bowls it like a miser'. Mailey tossed up his spin with all the blandness in the world; his full-tosses were like a generous sort of fattening diet—before the killing and the roasting. Mailey did his mischief by daylight. Grimmett goes to work with a dark lantern; his boots are rubbered. Mailey's wickets were like a practised and jolly angler's 'catch'; Grimmett's wickets are definitely 'swag'. When he goes off the field after he has had seven for 57, I can see the bag he is carrying over his shoulder.

He is the greatest right-handed spin-bowler of our period. The comparison with Mailey was employed to stress not resemblance but difference; Grimmett is less a googly than a leg-break bowler. He uses the 'wrong' un' sparsely; he is content to thrive on the ball which breaks away and leaves the bat; that is the best of all balls. A straight ball, wickedly masked, is Grimmett's foil to the leg-break. He makes a virtue of a low arm; his flight keeps so close to the earth that only a batsman quick of foot can jump to the pitch of it. And then must he beware of Oldfield, the wicket-keeper who stumps you with courtesy; he does not make a noise to the umpire, but almost bows you from the wicket. Or he is like a perfect dentist who says when your heart is in your mouth: 'It's all over; I've already got it out; here it is.' To play forward to Grimmett, to miss the spin, and then to find yourself stumped by Oldfield—why it is like an amputation done under an anaesthetic.

Moments come to all of us when we are uplifted beyond the ordinary; we become touched with grace for a while; we become vessels of inspiration. Felicity descended on Grimmett at Trent Bridge in June 1930, on the first day of the Test Match. I have never seen cleverer bowling on a good wicket against great players. Hammond was batting; he made two of his own great forcing off-side hits, off the back foot. These strokes told us that Hammond was in form. Grimmett bowled him a straight ball which sped sinfully from the

beautiful turf. Hammond l.b.w. to Grimmett. Next came
Woolley. Left-handed batsmen love leg-spin bowlers; the
break turns the ball inwards to the middle of the bat. But
Grimmett did not send a leg-break to Woolley; he sent the
googly, whipping away. Woolley's forward stroke was
seduced by the fulsome length. Woolley was stumped by
Oldfield. A few minutes afterwards Grimmett drew Hendren
a yard out of his crease like a mesmerist; then, having got
Hendren where he wanted him, not far enough down the
pitch, but yet too far, he bowled him. Grimmett will remember in his old age how he spun and 'floated' the ball that day;
by the chimney corner he will babble of the way he turned a
batsman's smooth lawn into a 'sticky dog'. By sheer crafts-
manship he overthrew three great batsmen; nothing to intimi-
date, no brute force (as George Lohmann called fast bowling
of sorts); nothing but a slow spinning ball bowled by a little
man with an arm as low as my grandfather's.

The first sight of Grimmett bowling arouses mild laughter.
His action recalls the ancient round-arm worthies, or it recalls
cricket on the sands with a walking-stick for the wicket and a
father of six playing for the first time for years. A few steps, a
shuffle, and Grimmett's arm seems to creak. But watch his
wrist and his fingers; they are sinuous and beautiful. The wrist
twirls and swivels; the fingers seem to adore and caress the
ball, with the touch of a parent. Grimmett's fingers are always
light and wonderfully tactile; when he passes the salt at dinner
he imparts the ''fluence'.

He is, I believe, a sign-writer by profession. Can't you see
his right wrist at work, sweeping the brush along the orna-
mentation? Can't you see the fingers intimately putting the
finishing flick to a full-stop? Or can't you see the skeleton
key at work, finding the way through the locked door of
Sutcliffe's bat? He is, as I say, a master of surreptitious arts.
His countenance expresses no joy when he confounds his
opponents. But I imagine that long after close of play, as he
lies in bed and thinks about it, he laughs far into the night.
That apparent half-volley which Walters tried to drive; that
obvious long-hop that Hendren tried to hook. Confidence
tricks! O my lungs and liver, the wickedness of the world!

He seldom gets a man caught in the deep field. That is an

open and a brazen way to rifle the English house. Better by far a swift catch at first slip, or at the wicket; best of all l.b.w.; nobody knows anything about it away from the scene of the burglary. He is a great character, not only a great bowler. Sometimes he fancies himself as a batsman. He thrusts his left foot across and drives. Or he waits for it and cuts elegantly. Occasionally he plays late and sees his stumps all awry. Then, and only then, does he wear his heart on his sleeve. Everybody cherishes private ambitions; we all wish to be what we are not. Dan Leno sighed to play Hamlet; Henry Irving enjoyed himself best when he sat on his top-hat and pretended to be Jingle in a farce derived from *Pickwick*. Grimmett made fifty in a Test match at Nottingham in June; perhaps in his old age he will remember Trent Bridge not for his great bowling of 1930, but for his preposterously stylish and first-class half-century of 1934. The rest of the world will dwell for ever on his spin, learned in Australia, where a slow bowler must do his own work and not depend on nature and friendly wickets. For my part I shall think of him always as I saw him at Worcester in May, taking the county's last wicket and winning the game. A catch was missed from him, and in the same over another lofty chance was skied near cover. Grimmett would trust nobody but Grimmett this time; he ran after the ball himself, and when he caught it he put it in his pocket and glided from the field, concealed entirely amongst ten other victorious Australians. He had a high balding forehead which, in the sunshine, would appear to shine with the light of his cunning. He played and bowled in a period when the material environment of the game was so different from today's that cricket has become almost a *different* game. It was a period of grassless heavily-rolled wickets, with Test matches played to a finish in Australia, and limited to four days in England. (In 1926, Clarrie, on his first visit to this country, had to bowl for the first time in three-day Tests; and in the rubber took 13 wickets at 31 runs each.) On flawless pitches for the most part, a little bare in parts and a little dusty in England on the third fine day, and on the sixth in Australia, Grimmett had to cope with some of the greatest and most experienced batsmen cricket has ever known. In these conditions of a batsman's plenty, it was useless to depend on the 'seam'. Even the pace of a Larwood (before Jardine invented 'ways and means') was frequently more or less harmless. Bowlers who couldn't spin were usually doomed to vain sweaty toil. It was of no avail to bowl a good ball at Hobbs, Hammond, Sutcliffe or Woolley, if it was immediately revealed what kind of good ball it was going to be. These great batsmen knew all the technical answers. So, therefore, the bowler was obliged to practise deception—to confuse the judgment of Hobbs, luring him to perform the *wrong* right stroke. Bowling most of his days against great batsmen on wickets stuffed with runs, Clarrie in his career took 216 wickets in Test matches, at the amazingly low cost of 24.21 each. You will, I think, realise how much skill went into Grimmett's slow bowling if you compare his record with Trueman's in Tests, 284 wickets at 21.08 each, and Statham's, 245 at 24.96 each—the performances of these fast bowlers achieved not always against batsmen of the calibre of Grimmett's opponents. Grimmett, as I say, was under the necessity of using his intelligence to get wickets in dry weather. He had to scheme, hide his tricks for hours, send out decoys, lay in wait. Many years ago, in hot sunshine at Adelaide, New South Wales were scoring heavily. At the beginning of the day Clarrie had taken two wickets before lunch. Then Bradman began, in full and merciless spate. No more wickets fell. But Clarrie was still bowling at five o'clock. Then Victor Richardson, the South Australia captain, came up to Clarrie, saying, 'Well bowled—now put on your sweater, there's a breeze getting up.' And Clarrie expostulated, 'Are you taking me off?—*just as I was working out my plan.*'

BILL O'REILLY

WILLIAM Joseph O'Reilly ('Bill' for short) was one of the most skilful of bowlers, and very hostile on his day—which occurred too frequently for the liking of most batsmen. Off the field he would beam on the most prolific of run-makers. On the field he disliked all opposing batsmen at sight. His Australian colleagues called him 'The Tiger'. Whenever he was driven in front of the wicket for four, his Irish 'Paddy' would be seen almost visibly to rise. He would glower down the pitch, his attitude a whole vocabulary of invective in itself. His next ball would most likely be delivered with a view to rendering stumps, batsman and all, momentarily recumbent. He was, in fact, a bowler mainly of medium to slow pace, commanding extraordinary changes of flight. But without palpable alteration of action he could send down a really formidable fast ball—a catapult of a ball. He brought his right arm over quicker than the keenest eye or anticipation would infer from the rhythm of his action in general. You could not truthfully say his action was rhythmical at all. He ran lumberingly to the wicket, like a man going uphill in the face of a strong wind. He bent his right knee very much, and awkwardly, as the arm came over in a windmill swoop. Yet it was a strongly concentrated action at the moment of the ball's propulsion. The bent right knee allowed him to get a lot of flight, a lot of 'air', at his end. His slow (and disguisedly slow) 'googly' had a surprising bounce from the earth. This was the bait for a catch to the 'short-leg' trap, rapaciously led by Jack Fingleton. In his repertory was contained nearly every device known to the bowler's art. Bradman argued that the probability was that O'Reilly was a greater bowler even than S. F. Barnes, maintaining that O'Reilly was master of all the tricks known to Barnes—spin, flight, length and so on—and also he could bowl the 'googly', which Barnes didn't.

When I put this argument to Barnes himself he meditated a while, then said, 'It's quite true that I didn't bowl a 'googly'. I never needed it.

In Test matches O'Reilly took 144 wickets, average 22.59, 102 against England at 25.36 each. Barnes's wickets against Australia amounted to 106, at 24 runs each. We need to bear in mind, as we compare these two bowling geniuses—not to belittle but to glorify each—that O'Reilly had to get his wickets and his work done on pitches which were, over a long period, much more favourable to batsmen than those of Barnes's period, especially those in England. O'Reilly took

52 of his 102 Test wickets against England in Australia, at a time when pitches there were hard and without flaw for days. O'Reilly, in fact, was the product of cricket as it was played on heavily-rolled wickets and grassless. Also he was brought up in a period which, in Australia, insisted that all Test matches should be played to a finish. In short, O'Reilly learned his comprehensive arts against heavy odds to bowlers, against some of England's most thoroughbred batsmen enjoying heavenly conditions in which to make their strokes. In Test matches O'Reilly's opposition (and victims) usually consisted of such as Hammond, Sutcliffe, Leyland, Paynter, Jardine, Hendren, Walters and, at the close of his playing career, Hutton and Compton.

He had the stamina to support the heat and burden of the most scorching days. At Old Trafford in 1934, England batted first under a blazing sun, temperature 90° in the shade. In sixty-five minutes England scored 68, C. F. Walters magnificently cutting and driving 52 of these runs. Then O'Reilly actually dismissed Walters, Wyatt and Hammond in one over. Nonetheless, England's total reached 627—9 declared; O'Reilly bowled 59 overs for 189 runs and 7 wickets. At Kennington Oval in August 1938, as every schoolboy knows, or should know, England scored 903—7 wickets declared, Hutton 364. In this gigantic longitudinal innings of England's O'Reilly bowled 85 overs for 178 runs and 3 wickets. When Hutton passed the existing record of an individual total in a Test match the crowd rose to acclaim the hero. The Australians gathered round him shaking his hand—all except O'Reilly who, the first to see drinks being carried onto the field, made a bee-line for them. Years afterwards, when he was sitting in the Press Box at Sydney reporting on an Australia v. England Test match on a hot day, I asked him, 'Don't you ever wish, Bill, that you were out there in the middle again?' 'No,' he promptly replied, 'it's easier work here.'

For a great bowler he certainly gave the impression that he was often labouring and sweating. Sometimes he became curiously negative, pegging away on the leg stump, particularly on Hammond's leg stump, supported by the leg-trap. At such moments I would ask myself, 'Is he truly a great, as distinguished from an extremely good, bowler?' Batsmen also seemed to lull themselves with some similar quietist view of O'Reilly's attack. And, like dwellers on the slopes of Mount Vesuvius in a calm season, they would become easily complacent. Then the O'Reilly eruption would break out. No warning. A rush of blood to O'Reilly's head, plenty of it Irish. He would galvanise his run, his arms flailed the air, the swing over of the arm was convulsive, the ball delivered was an expletive. The batsmen, comfortable only a moment ago in the sunshine, were overwhelmed, uprooted, 'assaulted and—possibly—foxed out'.

O'Reilly's balding head shone in the burning light of day. In Australia I have seen him shaking off drops of honest sweat. He stood six feet two inches high, and was broad-shouldered. As I say, he didn't as a bowler make the most of all this height—at least, the casual observer of him said that he didn't. But many of his victims were lured to their ends because of the slower ball tossed up from the bent right knee. He had in him enough original Irish to know the uses of blarney. At bottom, though, he was a bowler of classic precision of length. He is wrongly put into the category of leg-spinners and 'googly' experimentalists. O'Reilly seldom served up loose or untidy bowling. His 'googly' was never overdone; he used it as bait. He is not properly to be described as a 'back of the hand' spinner. His leg-break was spun by the fingers mainly, with the wrist turned at the last point in the process of motivation—there wasn't a pronounced elbow turn. He liked a dry dusty pitch, as at Nottingham in 1934, when in his first Test match in England he took 11 wickets for 129. Other times, other manners—thirty years ago England batsmen of the calibre of Cyril Walters, Sutcliffe, Hammond, and Hendren regarded as good policy quick strokes while the Australian fast bowlers were getting the shine off the new ball; for they knew that soon O'Reilly and Grimmett would come on with spin, and also with flight asking twenty questions in the air. In the five test matches of 1934 O'Reilly and Grimmett accounted for 53 of England's wickets between them.

Australia's fast bowler 'Tim' Wall—and he was a very good and really fast bowler—had to be satisfied with 172 overs and

6 wickets. It was a joy to watch the skill, the allurements of flight, the varieties of spin and of length, sent along over and over by these two highly gifted bowlers—Grimmett, silent, stealthy and quizzical, a tiny man of sly humour, his arm as low as his grandfather's, a feline, 'pussy-foot' spinner—and giant O'Reilly, lumbering heavily into action, windmill and bulldozer, yet a wonderful combination of physical effort and well-thought-out strategy. At Sydney in 1936, England lost Arthur Fagg's wicket for 27, in England's first innings on a batsman's firm pitch. In came Hammond in all his majesty. The battle between Hammond and O'Reilly for an hour was as thrilling and as cleverly pointed and counter-pointed as any I have seen on the cricket field between two great players. O'Reilly onslaughted Hammond's bat. He attacked his leg-stump, he held back his 'googly', he hurled down his fast one, he exploited his dipper—he gave Wally no rest. At the end, Hammond conquered, 231 not out, his lion's share of England's aggregate of 426 for 6 (declared). But O'Reilly had the last laugh; he had found out during this nobly sustained and endured 231 of Hammond, that England's premier batsman could be tamed by a gnawing length on his leg-stump, or thereabouts. Hammond once again, in 1938, asserted himself in all his calm grandeur against O'Reilly; but, all in all, O'Reilly clipped Hammond's wings incisively enough from 1937 onwards.

Most of England's master batsmen of O'Reilly's heyday agreed that he was the greatest and most versatile bowler of their actual acquaintance. One day, though, at Brisbane, Maurice Leyland, in conversation with O'Reilly before the 1936/7 rubber began, said, 'Well, Bill, result of this rubber is in lap of gods. But there's one thing Ah can tell you, Bill, and tha knows it—Ah've got *thee* taped all right': O rare Maurice Leyland! O rare Bill O'Reilly, full of the milk of human kindness, a good son to his mother, friendly and considerate, a nature's gentleman, with Irish in him, wouldn't hurt a mouse—in domestic and private life, well away from a cricket field, a cricket ball, and from sight of an incoming batsman. The 'Tiger' and the lamb. Sometimes they lay down together, the lamb inside the tiger.

1932

SELECTION

TIME is running out: the cricket season is half over. And still the England team for Australia is 'wropt' in mystery; it is a problem the like of which no other Selection Committee in this country has had to tackle. Who is the batsman who will go in first with Sutcliffe? Who will be our fast bowler? What is wrong with Chapman as a captain? Is Jardine a born leader of men? Have we got a left-handed spin bowler—in case of a 'sticky' wicket at Melbourne? Will the wicket-keeper be Duckworth or Ames? Each of these questions is difficult to answer. The amateur selector of Test match teams seldom goes about the job in the right way. He is content to put down on paper the names of eleven cricketers who at the moment happen to be doing well. He does not realise that an England XI must be chosen with certain special functional ends in view. For example, even if, say, Tate, Allom and Bowes were all in great form, a Selection Committee would not choose the three of them—because each is dependent more or less on the new ball and they can't all use it at once. A point that is troubling authoritative judges of the game at Lord's at the moment is just one of those points which never occur to the layman. Are there three fine out-fielders in England who can be trusted to bat well: in other words, who do not bowl?—(because, of course, bowlers must field close to the wicket). I commend this conundrum to anybody who wishes an hour or two's innocent amusement in his club armchair.

Twenty years ago our Selection Committee was usually grappling with a perplexity exactly contrary to the one which this summer is causing wrinkled foreheads at St John's Wood. The trouble in those days was which men could possibly be omitted from the England XI. Once on a time, George Hirst and G. L. Jessop were left out—at Manchester in 1902. A cricketer, name of Albert Relf, used to score a thousand runs every summer and take a hundred wickets as well. But he never could get into the England XI in England. And he never had cause for complaint. Better all-rounders than Relf were available then! This year we cannot point to a single All-England cricketer who, in good company, is capable of scoring a thousand runs and taking one hundred wickets in a season. Here is a serious difficulty for our Selection Committee. For in the absence of great all-round players it is hard to choose a team which is not weak in batting at the end of an innings. No cricketer should be sent to Australia for his bowling alone unless he is a great bowler. But that is a counsel of perfection; there are no great bowlers in English cricket today.

Let us consider first things first. It is important that in Australia a solid foundation should be laid to an English innings. The choice of the man for Sutcliffe's partner is a terribly responsible matter. There is a notion that Woolley would do well in the position. I heartily agree that Woolley should be taken again to Australia; our greatest left-handed batsman will be needed to attack Australia's googly bowlers. But Woolley is not an ideal batsman to begin any innings; on the other hand, he is the very batsman to come in when the new ball is losing its shine. Why has not the name of D. R. Jardine been suggested as Sutcliffe's colleague? Obviously he is England's Woodfull. As a number five batsman, Jardine is capital in circumstances that call for a sudden stiffening of the defences—say, after a bad start to an innings. But it often happens that the bowling is tired at the hour of day when batsman number five arrives at the wicket. Jardine's lack of scoring strokes may sometimes allow half-volleys and long-hops to run to waste. Sutcliffe and Jardine ought to act well together in the important offices of wearers down of a fresh attack. Then Duleepsinhji must come in next with his felicitous bat, and after him, the incomparable Woolley. As a number five batsman, Hammond would receive encouragement to play soundly or forcibly, according to the state of the game.

And those are all the cricketers we can name with assurance as 'certainties' for the England team which will take the field at Sydney in December. As soon as we approach our bowling needs, we wander vaguely in the realms of speculation. But before tackling this riddle I will recommend Leyland and Paynter as swift out-fields who can get skilful runs. Leyland is revealing his old form again this season. The best fast bowler in England is Larwood; but he is not physically sound. Bowes is not a great fast bowler even at Lord's in dry weather; and if he is unable to take wickets in Australia he will prove a complete 'passenger'. Tate remains our most reliable stock bowler to keep one end energetic and fresh. Our best available leg-spin bowlers are F. R. Brown and Robins, both of whom can field well and bat tolerably. Voce, I suppose, will be given the chance of exploiting his left-handed swingers against Bradman—they do not really swing, but rather they go through the air direct to a place outside the leg-stump. The truth is that you could shut your eyes and put a pin's point in six places in the English bowling averages and by doing so pick as good an attack for Australia as any other. As to the claims of Chapman, well, I think I am right in saying that he would have had a hearty vote from most of our professionals had he been put before them as a candidate for the dual office of England's captain and England's best fieldsman near the wicket. But how can you get him into the eleven without disturbing the bowling and the out-fielding? This quandary becomes apparent as soon as we look at our eleven in the whole; Sutcliffe, Jardine, Duleepsinhji, Woolley, Hammond, Leyland or Paynter, Ames, Robins, R. R. Brown, Tate and Voce. In any case Jardine has already been invited to act as captain. And now that I *do* see my attempt at the England XI, I swear most emphatically that I do not enjoy the thought of anybody but Duckworth behind the stumps!

JARDINE

THE other day the cricketers playing in the match between Surrey and Yorkshire at the Oval offered a toast to D. R. Jardine: it was one of those impromptu touches of sportsmanship which are typical of the game—and very pleasant to think about by anybody who, like the present writer, is temporarily far away from England and cricket, lost in a foreign land where men sit in cafés and grow fat.

D. R. Jardine has gradually forced his personality upon the country. He is not exactly a man for the crowd; there is something aloof and angular in his aspect. And as he hates cant as much as anybody in the world, I will not mince words in this article and pretend that he has Chapman's power to win the hearts of an eleven by a single spontaneous human smile. Jardine does not suffer fools or folly gladly; he is a plain speaker and so keen on the game that he is not prepared to indulge in those nuances of terminology which usually win for a man the name of an artist in tact. If a cricketer serving under Jardine commits a fault of carelessness he will hear about it from his captain in direct and unmistakable accents.

He ought to prove the ideal captain against the Australians. In the past one or two England teams have suffered because they have been much too gentlemanly in leadership. The Australian is a realist; he has no use for talk about the 'best side' winning or about strengthening the Bonds of Empire. He is never prepared to make concessions, though he does not object to receiving them; Jardine should suit the Australian Realpolitik down to the ground. They will 'get no change' out of him, or if they do, it will be only just right—for D. R. Jardine is a true son of his own country.

The England team which shortly will sail the seas to the earth's other end is the best possible at the present time. Seldom has a side been chosen with nicer judgment; the Selection Committee for once in a way invite congratulations.

Not one English player is free to think he has been unjustifiably overlooked. The choice of Mitchell, after the defection of Robins, was a shrewd and enterprising stroke. I do not expect that Mitchell will ever 'run through' an Australian Test match team, but I expect him to get three or four wickets in most innings at a cost of thirty or forty runs each. If he does as well as that he will satisfy his friends. The spin bowler's job in Australia is to break partnerships; at the other end of the wicket, the medium-pace men try to keep a length and stop the scoring strokes. Tate and Voce ought to put a severe brake on swift runs, so much so that Bradman and his colleagues should be compelled to look for the boundaries from the tempting slows of Mitchell and Verity. And as soon as a player tries to hit either of these bowlers he is asking for trouble. If F. R. Brown is a success, Mitchell may not be wanted. But I fancy he will spin the ball in Australia to much more insidious ends than Brown.

I am optimistic about England's chances. The batting is handsome to contemplate on paper. There is only one danger —mistaken policy. The other day I was rather appalled to see Mr Robertson-Glasgow helping to perpetuate the notion that in Australia a batman's main job is to 'stay there and let the runs come'. Mr Robertson-Glasgow went so far as to assert that the typical Australian batsman cuts out a third of his scoring strokes in Test matches. Has Mr Robertson-Glasgow forgotten Bradman's forty boundaries in a single day in the third Test match, at Leeds, in 1930? Did he see Ponsford, in the 'timeless' Test match, at the Oval in 1930, flog the English bowlers for a hundred in just over two hours, after Australia had gone in against a total of 400 in a bad light? Has Mr Robertson-Glasgow never heard of the way Archie Jackson massacred Larwood in the last English tour to Australia? The typical Australian batsman hits the loose ball mercilessly—think of Trumper, Macartney, Clem Hill, Darling, Armstrong, not to mention Bradman, McCabe and the modern company.

The idea that cricketers of the stamp of Hammond will serve England's cause by 'staying there' passively is a ruinous one. Somebody must constantly be on the offensive, or at any rate on the look-out for the loose ball. We shall lose the rubber next winter if Grimmett is played by our batsmen from behind the crease. Once again I must repeat my old platitude: Test matches in Australia are won by the team that hits more loose balls than the other fellows.

Given the right policy, an even blend of aggression and obstinacy, England will bring the Ashes back to us next spring.

EVENLY MATCHED

I T is certain that the Test matches are going to be fought to the last over, with the combatants matched evenly, almost to a man. An England captain once told me that no team visiting Australia could hope to win a rubber unless it possessed a 30 per cent technical superiority over the enemy. Jardine's side will find the heat of an Australian summer quite as trying as the batting and bowling of Woodfull, Bradman, Grimmett, Ironmonger and company. We can only pray for cool weather and a fair share of the luck of the game—and good umpiring.

Bradman, I fancy, holds the key to the situation. If he is about to make his usual scores of 200, we may as well cultivate philosophical resignation. You cannot expect to beat the other side if they have a batsman who is supposed to fail whenever he makes less than 100.

I place no significance on the fact that Bradman has been dismissed cheaply so often by our bowlers. His little innings of 36 last Saturday read ominously, but then he treated the English attack as though terribly sure of himself. I wish, indeed, that Bradman had so far scored prolifically against us; the more times he falters before the first Test match, the more he will go into that crucial engagement with the law of averages working in his favour. When a great batsman has played a sequence of small scores his day is coming rapidly!

Leaving Bradman to the gods (for his genius is beyond the control of mortal scheming and skill), I think the rest of the

Australian batting is not likely to be better than England's. Woodfull, Ponsford, Kippax, McCabe, Fingleton and Richardson are not the technical superiors of Sutcliffe, Hammond, Pataudi, Jardine, Wyatt and Leyland, and if there is some hint of a 'tail' in Allen, Brown, Larwood, Verity and Duckworth, the Australians also will be compelled to carry more than one or two doubtful batsmen—Ironmonger, Wall, Grimmett and Oldfield, for example.

I am disturbed at the loss of Ames's batting form. For though I am aware he is not in Duckworth's class as a wicket-keeper, I fancy he would have been a safe enough stumper on perfect wickets, while, of course, promising us a score of anything from 50 to 100. I cannot understand his inability to get runs in Australia; his batting style was surely designed for true, fast turf.

Jardine has not yet solved the problem of his opening batsmen. At first, the Leyland-Sutcliffe combination looked excellent enough. But, for my part, I would rather see Leyland arriving at the wicket after the edge has gone from the bowling. Why cannot Jardine himself go in first with Sutcliffe?—obviously he is in technique and temperament England's reply to Woodfull.

On second thoughts, though, I would prefer not to have Jardine as Sutcliffe's partner. Two stonewallers, at an innings' outset, tend to let the attack get on top. What would Hammond do if he were sent in first? He can defend *and* attack. My confidence rises at the thought of Hammond and Sutcliffe opening an England innings. But I doubt if he will do so; the solution is more likely to come from Wyatt, a good sound artisan and at all times a man of courage.

The sad illness of Duleepsinhji cruelly spoiled the balance of our batting. Jardine must find *two* batsmen to compensate for the loss of a genius. Also, Duleepsinhji's absence will weaken the slip fielding. I hope we have had exaggerated reports from Australia about poor fielding in Jardine's team. If runs are given away and if catches are missed by our cricketers, Australia will win all the five Test matches.

Every lover of the true sport of the game will be glad that Allen has shown admirable form so far. He had few friends up to a week or two ago; it was being taken for granted that Allen

would not get a place in a single big match. But he is a young
man of immense tenacity. He really can bowl fast, and
moreover, he is capable of a gallant innings. His promising
form so far more than makes good the comparative failure of
Bowes. Obviously, if Allen can gain his place in the eleven as
a fast bowler, instead of Bowes, the batting and fielding will
become strengthened into the bargain.

Jardine's difficulty will be to find room for Larwood and
Allen and Voce, yet each of these three seems indispensable.
Verity, I take it, has staked a firm claim; we cannot risk
leaving him out of the side, if the Australians deploy Ironmonger against us—as they will. Given a night of rain, a
left-handed slow bowler can win a match in an hour in
Australia, where sticky wickets are the most vicious in the
world. I wish the reports from Australia would tell us whether
Brown is spinning the ball. This is an important point.
Bradman's weak spot is still the ball that pitches well up to
him, drops on the wicket, and breaks sharply away.

Where the technical balance between two cricket teams is
more or less even, the deciding factor is usually tactics. I am
not easy in my mind about Jardine as a tactician. His grit and
earnestness are superb; he would perish in the cause of laying
low the Australians. But he overdoes the policy of 'ca-canny'.
He is inclined to believe that it is possible to beat the
Australians by passive resistance on the part of his batsmen.
The truth, on the contrary, is that there is no special virtue in
staying at the wicket in Australia simply for the purpose of
consuming time. Runs and *only* runs, settle the issue in
matches fought to a finish.

And the best way to make runs on Australian wickets is to
play strokes all over the field—from the bad balls. The
victorious team in Australian Test matches is the one which
hits more loose balls than the other team. There is a danger
amongst English batsmen at the present time to imagine they
are playing the Australians 'at their own game' if they defend
for hours and score slowly. A remarkable fallacy! Australian
batsmen have always mingled attack and defence in proportion. Bradman never spares the loose ball. Ponsford doesn't
—or McCabe, Richardson or Kippax. If Hammond plays in
the Test matches as he did last summer at Lord's in the

Gentlemen *v.* Players match, I imagine that neither Grimmett nor Ironmonger will know where to pitch the ball. Both of these bowlers thrive on batsmen who play with the right foot rooted behind the crease.

Jardine's team has reason to be confident. Let the batsmen look out as keenly for the bad ball as for the good ones, and all will be well, unless Bradman behaves phenomenally, in which case we must face the inevitable and—try to run him out.

MELBOURNE

WHEN Jardine's team sailed for Australia last September, it did not carry everybody's confidence. Some of us were convinced that the bowling lacked distinction and match-winning stamina. Larwood especially was 'suspect'.

And now today, the England bowlers are sweeping Australia's batsmen out of their way, right and left. Hardly once, yet, has Jardine's attack been held up. The stand at Sydney between McCabe and Richardson was a momentary piece of obstinacy, but once it was removed, the breakthrough sent Woodfull and his notables stampeding ingloriously. What has happened that Larwood, Voce and the others should today be upsetting Australian wickets with an ease and alacrity beyond the powers of any English bowler save Barnes and Frank Foster?

Obviously Australian batsmanship is below standard. The illness of Bradman has changed entirely the prospects of the England team. With Bradman in his best form, Jardine would have needed all of Mr Warner's optimism to help him envisage victory. It is hard to beat the other side if they have a batsman who most days can be trusted to get a score of 200.

Bradman may regain his true form, but he has before him a psychological problem to solve. He has never before been on a 'bad patch'; he is not accustomed to a thin period. He has now to think himself into a category of normal performance; a vulnerability in him has been exposed in the sight of his own eyes. He may take some time getting used to it.

Then there is the suspicion that Bradman does not like fast bowling. True, he scored 334 at Leeds against Larwood in 1930, but the wicket that day was of a lifelessness which it is difficult to find the equal of on fast Australian earth. Macdonald once told me he preferred to bowl on the best Sydney turf than on a 'doped' English wicket. 'You *can* bounce them out there!' he said. I have in mind an occurrence at Liverpool at the beginning of the Australian tour of 1930. Macdonald 'set himself' to get Bradman out. He bumped the ball at a terrific pace. Bradman hedged a few strokes—and then ran *towards point*, and allowed a straight ball to uproot his leg stump.

Bradman today is in a difficult position; he has to 'lay' the fast-bowling spectre and at the same time put to flight the mocking spectre of his infallibility of yesteryear. Yet I believe, at bottom, in his greatness—on a true pitch.

The fate of the rubber, I think, rests with Bradman and Larwood. If Bradman masters Larwood at Melbourne, I am certain the other English bowlers will suffer severe punishment for the rest of the tour. If Bradman continues to fail, none of the other Australian batsmen will be good enough to beat us. And I am convinced that only Larwood is capable of getting Bradman out, time after time. Jardine's duty is clear then—and he has already shown to us that he knows what that duty is—to keep Larwood fresh and sound in energy and limb.

We must bear in mind that the England side has yet to encounter their worst enemey—the heat of an Australian summer at its height, and the wear and tear of scorching activity on earth hard as concrete. When Larwood was last in Australia he began bowling as masterfully as on the present tour. But he could not keep it up; before long, Bradman and Archie Jackson were cutting and driving him ruthlessly. And Larwood is a bad bowler when his luck is out—as we have frequently seen for ourselves at Lord's in the last summer or two. Tate will be wanted at Melbourne. And it is rather disquieting to learn that Brown is not spinning the ball.

We need not fear the ability of England's batsmen to make

heavy runs—so long as Sutcliffe and Hammond maintain good form. But I would not trust the others too far, if the Australian bowlers 'got away' with a flying start. Fortunately for England, Australian bowling at the present time cannot boast a Mailey, a Gregory or a Macdonald. On the Australian grounds, Grimmett seems unable to spin the ball with that abruptness which in England left one or two England batsmen the pictures of helpless, straddle-legged immobility. Given a sticky or a wearing wicket, I fancy Ironmonger would be unpleasant, but with rain or dust about either side is as likely as the other to be batting—and Verity can spin the ball as skilfully as Ironmonger. For the life of me, I cannot 'see' the Australian bowling breaking through the defence of Sutcliffe and Hammond, save by some incredible loss of ability on the part of both these great batsmen. And Wyatt has already proved himself a reliable partner for Sutcliffe.

And if the England eleven should cultivate a 'tail'—which they might easily do—after all, it could not possibly be longer than Australia's. Our attack will need to be worn out by long toil against Bradman not to find a swift way through the defences of Oldfield, Wall, O'Reilly, Ironmonger and Grimmett.

Jardine has wisely warned us not to be too eager to count our chickens. Still, the team that wins a first Test match in Australia (where all games are played to a finish) ought to feel 'on clover', for they have left their opponents with the terribly stiff job of winning three matches out of the remaining four. To perform such a feat, a lot of luck is necessary, and a technical superiority of roughly 30 per cent. The luck may smile on Woodfull, but where is the 30 per cent superiority to come from?

ENGLAND'S ASHES

WHEN Jardine's team sailed for Australia last autumn, the confidence of all cricketers in this country was not altogether behind him and his men. The fact that Bowes was rushed into the side at the last minute was, in a way, a vote of no confidence in Larwood. And to say the truth, Larwood did not look like a great fast bowler in the representative matches played at Lord's and Manchester last summer. On these occasions, though—as I fancy I pointed out at the time—Larwood did not exploit the methods which Trent Bridge knew; methods which are now known in Australia and, apparently, all over the world.

Some day, when the history of modern cricket is written, the name of A. W. Carr will be mentioned as that of the man who first saw the possibilities in persistent leg-theory, practised at great speed, with a magnificent regard of the consequences.

There is no doubting that the bowling of Larwood has won the rubber for England. And it is as certain that the method of his attack has been the means of solving the Bradman problem. It is true that several of the Australian batsmen were clean bowled at Sydney, Melbourne, Adelaide and Brisbane. But it was Larwood's attack that unsettled all of Australia's champions, so much so that they could seldom concentrate upon stroke-play; at the back of their minds (or in the front!) was the knowledge that any moment they would be called upon not only to protect the stumps but also their heads and chests.

Larwood's achievement can be called creative. He has altered the entire face of Australian Test cricket. He has conquered the perfect wicket, which only yesterday, so to say, was the lazy hunting-ground of any cricketer with two good eyes and a bat. Bradman's colossal scores for years have occurred like acts predestinate and inevitable. Woodfull gained the name of the 'unbowlable'; Ponsford smashed the records of all the mighty scorers of the past. All last summer we were asking ourselves, 'Where are the bowlers to get Bradman out?' Day by day we visited English cricket fields, searching for the deliverer. None of us could discern him in the aspects of Larwood, Allen, Voce, and Hammond. A few optimists hoped that F. R. Brown might give Bradman and Woodfull trouble; but really the hope was depressing.

Larwood in Australia is obviously a better bowler than he is in big games in England. Or maybe, the Australian batting is today abnormally weak. I think it is. For one thing, no team could reasonably hope to win a Test match with four or five men on the side incapable of some show of expert batsmanship. Has Australia, in all the annals of cricket, ever had a 'tail-end' as frail as the one which has ruined her chances this season? Australian cricket is momentarily short of the all round player—a strange thing to say of Australian cricket, which in the past has bred an Armstrong, a Giffen, a Noble, a Macartney, a Gregory—to name only a few instances. England's batting often had its unreliable periods; but right down the order-of-going-in there was somebody who could be trusted to keep his bat straight or busy.

Even the authentic batsmen of Australia were not to be trusted. Woodfull for a long time apparently could not 'see' the ball; Bradman, as I say, found the mechanism of his technique disturbed by Larwood's leg-theory. McCabe and Richardson are both dashing rather than sound batsmen. There were really only two problems for the English attack seriously to ponder in an Australian innings—Bradman and Woodfull. And in the crucial match at Brisbane, after Richardson had helped Woodfull to give Australia a great start to their first innings, Bradman and Woodfull at last settled down together.

In the equatorial heat of the afternoon of the first day at Brisbane, Australia's total arrived magnificently at 200 for one wicket—with Woodfull and Bradman apparently well set. How remote England's chances of victory seemed then; how our perspiring bowlers and fieldsmen must have fought hard to maintain hopefulness and philosophy! I shall always believe that the Australians lost the rubber at Brisbane when on the first afternoon Mitchell bowled Woodfull; and in the opening half hour of the second day, when Larwood bowled Bradman.

And the irony of it all is that Woodfull, after hours of defence, ran out to drive Mitchell, and missed (Australia 200 for two)! Grimmer irony still, Larwood most likely would have been taken off by Jardine for a rest the over after he sent down the ball which accounted for Bradman when he was in the seventies. The way the English bowlers and fieldsmen 'won through' from Australia's superb position of 200 for one, in scorching, scourging heat, must go down into the golden book of cricket. And Paynter's plucky innings must go with it.

Inspired by Larwood's fires, which were never subdued, the other English bowlers added inches to their stature. But with Larwood out of the way, or with Larwood bowling as he did in 1930, Bradman would have enjoyed himself as usual. All the same, we are bound to give praise to Allen, Voce and Hammond, who were quick to seize the advantages offered them.

But unless Jardine had co-ordinated his attack, and the strange methods of it, Bradman and his colleagues might easily have prevailed after all. Jardine led his men to victory according to a deliberate plan. In all the cricket displayed by his team, in batting as well as in bowling, you can trace the Jardine *realpolitik*—a canny mechanical scheme, with no room for romantic moonshine or sentiment anywhere.

And we must remember that at the present time few folk in this land seemingly want anything else out of Test cricket but victory for England. They do not think that too high a price is being paid for it when Hammond bats two hours and forty minutes for 34 (which he did at Brisbane), or when Jardine bats an hour for nine, or when on an Australian wicket against a limited Australian attack, an English innings lasts ten hours for 356.

Every man to his taste. I love liberty and would not force my ideas unreasonably on others. If the crowd wishes to see fast leg-theory bowling disturbing the poise of batsmanship, making lovely strokes impossible, creating a situation in which a Palairet and a Spooner could not exhibit their beautiful arts—very well then, let the crowd encourage such bowling, not only when it is practised by Larwood against Australia, but also when it is practised by Bowes at Kennington Oval.

And if the crowd wishes to see a strokeless play perpetuated for hours in an England innings, with a Hammond faithless to his true genius—and all for the 'Ashes'—very well, then, let the crowd flock in their millions to see this sort of cricket. But I shall stay at home; and likely enough the crowd will stay at home, too; because you can enjoy strokeless cricket well enough by looking at the accounts in the newspapers. The virtue of an innings of 40 made in three hours becomes apparent in a report of a cricket match. To enjoy a Spooner, a Hobbs, a Woolley, a Trumper, attendance on the field of play is necessary and desirable.

Jardine deserves the highest praise for his independence of mind, his superb resolution in circumstances which would have unnerved softer temperaments. He never budged from his purpose. And in modern Test cricket, which is 'followed' by millions of newspaper readers, many of whom have seldom seen a first-class match, a cricketer is compelled by pressure of public opinion to regard the 'result', the victory, as the be-all and end-all of cricket.

For my part, I do not care for cricket that lacks beautiful strokes. The modern captain of cricket has his point of view, and I can understand it. But I myself would not, if I were a captain of cricket, encourage any of my bowlers to practise an attack which did not 'face up' to the challenge of a Bradman's scoring strokes; I would discountenance any attack which caused a great batsman to believe that he was under a necessity to think first of protecting his body *four balls an over*.

And I would not allow a Hammond to hold in abeyance his own incomparable strokes all round the wicket. But I am old-fashioned in my cricket standards; when I learned the game, Trumper and MacLaren were my Test match heroes. Moreover, I must confess that I am not in the least interested in sport as an affair of competition, of winning and losing. I watch cricket because it can be the most beautiful and the most gracious game of all.

I would not cross the street to see leg-theory exploited over after over, with the field crowded round a batsman's legs, taking simple catches from a batsman who momentarily does not know where he is.

I remember Tom Richardson, who once apologised to Johnny Tyldesley after he had accidentally pitched a ball short and hit Johnny on the arm. With his next ball, Richardson sent Johnny's off-stump flying yards through the air.

The useful work of Ames behind the wicket has not been given the amount of praise it has deserved. Most of us have regretted the absence from the Test matches of the best wicket-keeper in England. Ames committed only one blunder; against the fast leg-theory bowling he must have had to work hard and dexterously. Ames has come through his ordeal with honour.

Another pleasing point in the rubber was the advance of Verity as a batsman. He was equal, on more than one critical occasion, to holding up an advancing Australian attack. Maybe Verity will repeat the miracle of Rhodes, who was chosen while a young man to play for England as a slow left-handed bowler, and went in last or last but one in an England innings and then conceived an ambition to go in first for England, and in time saw his ambition realised.

These Yorkshiremen are never satisfied. Lancashire and Yorkshire, as usual, have reason to think well of their darlings —Sutcliffe, Verity, Leyland and Paynter. But the rubber was really won by the experiments made on quiet afternoons at Trent Bridge last summer.

When Larwood failed to impress us in the trial matches last year he did not, if I remember well, bowl leg-theory. Next season should prove interesting and diverting here. My sense of humour visualises a great scene at the Oval—Larwood attacking Jardine with his 'bumpers', and the crowd rather embarrassed! But we can be certain of this: Jardine will not protest.

HAROLD LARWOOD

I N the Australian summer of 1932–33, Larwood, acting under the unflinching generalship of Douglas Jardine, threatened to split in twain the Commonwealth of cricket. To reduce the runs and moral ascendancy of Bradman the attack called 'body-line' was invented, and put into brilliant and devastating execution, mainly by Larwood. But back in England Larwood was frowned on whenever he gave our own batsmen a taste of Jardine's medicine. Certain county clubs broke off relations with Nottinghamshire. Photos were taken and exhibited of the bruised empurpled anatomies of English batsmen, lately colleagues of Larwood in the land of the barbarians—meaning Australia—photos of English ribs tickled by Larwood, who could not make the proper British compromise and realise that what was good and fair for Bradman could not possibly be served up to our own thoroughbred gentlemen!

Larwood, one of the fastest and most accurate of fast bowlers, needed no Jardinian theory of the survival of the fittest and quickest to achieve his dominance over batsmen. It was his bad luck, though, to have to bowl in a period of perfect wickets, lifeless most times, with Trent Bridge a stuffed cushion of runs. In Test matches in England he was obliged to cope with turf flattened by the heaviest rollers and anaesthetised by all sorts of groundsmen's dope.

In 1930, Bradman's first onslaught on English bowlers on England's green and pleasant turf, Larwood bowled in three Test matches—at Nottingham, Leeds, and Kennington Oval. In these three engagements Bradman scored 8, 131, 334 and 232. In 1950 at Melbourne, England and Australia each could not score 200 in an innings on a good wicket—the totals were 194, 181, 197, and 150. Larwood watched the wickets falling as he sat next to me in the press box. After a long silence he spoke, 'Look at 'em,' he said, 'getting out as soon as they come in'. Then, after a pause, and straight from the heart, he added, 'Eh, dear; when I thinks over mi Test match career I seemed to have spent all mi time bowlin' at Bradman'.

He came to fame swiftly. Unknown in 1924 he was bowling for England in 1926, his first Test match at Lord's, but he was not too formidable then, with 2 for 99 and 1 for 37. He was dropped from the England XI of that summer until the fifth Test—Chapman's famous victory—and he took 3 for 82 and 3 for 34. But batsmen all over the land agreed that he was the fastest bowler seen—or hardly seen—in our cricket fields for years. He had to wait until 1928 before he could show what he could do on Australian turf. And, at Brisbane, in Bradman's first Test, he shot out Woodfull, Ponsford, Kelleway, Hendry, Ryder and Ironmonger for 36. He could not, naturally enough, keep up the pressure throughout the rubber. Indeed, he could not definitely claim an immovable place in the England XI until the so-called 'body-line' plan was put into operation. Then, alas, injury to a foot contributed to the sudden ending of his career altogether. In 1935 he bowled at a pace not much above medium. He was thirty-two years old now, and sad it was to see the familiar gallop checked. At his best he made a glorious sight. He was not tall, far from it, a mere 5 ft 7 in., weighing 10 stone 8 pounds, perhaps, as he matured, adding a little of muscle. He was square-shouldered and proportionately built. He ran to bowl with a splendid stride, a gallop, and at the moment of delivery his action was absolutely classical, left side showing down the wicket, before the arm swung over with a thrillingly vehement rhythm. He could bring the ball back from the off, an action-break, not inswing that could be seen all the way. But it was his pace that demoralised. His length was beautiful to watch. Only in the 'body-line' campaign did he pitch short. His bouncer, by the way, was terrifying; compared with it Trueman's is amiable, good-natured. At Larwood's pace not much in-or-out swing is possible. I once asked J. T. Tyldesley how did Kortright bowl. 'Fast', said J.T. 'I know *that*', I replied, 'but what did he do with the ball?' 'He bowled it fast', said J.T., 'there was no time for the ball to do anything else.' Occasionally I would watch Larwood with a feeling of relief that I hadn't to go out to bat against him—even granted that my ability had been topclass. I have not experienced this sort of apprehension watching Trueman or Statham.

One afternoon at Old Trafford I saw a sort of rehearsal of the 'body-line' method. Rain had prevented cricket before five o'clock. Then, on a 'flying' pitch (and hardly any on-lookers present), Larwood struck terror into Lancashire's batsmen. This was the occasion on which E. A. Macdonald, playing for Lancashire then, retaliated fearsomely, after advising the Nottinghamshire players to ring up the nearest infirmary and reserve beds. He was frustrated by George Gunn, who walked out of his crease cutting and slicing velocity right and left—*with leisure*. In his short span Larwood took a hundred wickets in a season eight times. And he was a superb close-to-the-wicket fieldsman—and a first-class batsman, really first-class. He missed his century in a Test match at Sydney by four runs, caught by Ironmonger, his only historically recorded catch. This innings was played during the 'body-line' rumpus; and the Sydney crowd cheered Larwood in their thousands.

If ever a cricketer wore himself out in the service of his country it was 'Lol'. For Jardine, in the 1932–33 Australian Tests, he bowled some 1,320 balls. In 1958–59, also in Australia, Trueman bowled 696 and Statham 812 balls. When Larwood bowled in Australia the pitches there were para-disaical for batsmen, prepared from Bulli and Merri-Creek soil. Australia, in fact, had for years been known as the fast bowler's graveyard. These following figures served as their epitaphs: Tom Richardson, average a wicket, 30; J. M. Gregory, 31; E. A. Macdonald, 65; Fielder, 27; Ernest Jones, 27; Cotter, 30. In 1928–29 Larwood's bowling analysis for Tests in Australia was 18 wickets for 728 runs, average 40.44. On English wickets in 1930, against Bradman, Larwood had to be content with four wickets at the cost of 73 runs each. The cruel pitches frustrated him, so Jardine found the remedy. 'Body-line' temporarily lowered Bradman's batting average from 100 to 58. And Larwood in this rubber took 33 wickets for 19.51.

A breed of Larwoods, armed with eight or so fieldsmen on the leg or onside, would no doubt have put an end to cricket altogether. But Larwood's deeds in Australia were none the less wonderful. They were not much less superb as performed for Nottinghamshire, when A. W. Carr was captain of one of the most fascinating of all county cricket teams to watch. I asked George Gunn one day to give me his opinion of Larwood as a fast bowler. George was the greatest of all players of fast bowling of his day. 'Well', he said, 'I haven't to bat against him myself, so I can't rightly say—but I should think he's fast all right.' We can leave it at that.

1934

THE AUSTRALIANS

THE advent of the Australians has been heralded by loud and disproportionate trumpets. Day by day we have been told exactly where the team has found haven on their voyage to us from a distant land—for all the world as though sailing the seas in the 20th century were a venture of peril and anxiety.

In the old days Darling, Noble, Trumper and the other immortals came to us with no clatter and clamour to make them seem preposterous and stale before setting foot in England. It was a sad moment when the popular Press decided that cricket could be counted as 'news'; I can remember the time when Fleet Street generally held the view that cricket deserved only a small 'show', usually without a single 'crosshead'. If we are not careful, we shall live to see the summer game spoiled by the Press.

Already some of us are feeling that we have tasted the Test matches in advance, so to say, and tasted them to the sickening point. It is necessary that we should see to it that all this 'stunting' is rendered ridiculous. No doubt the influence of Fleet Street is overrated; the public surely is not entirely gullible. But it is not easy to get away from the atmosphere of headlines, with their hectic announcements of another sensation.

This year, more than ever, we need a good atmosphere for the Test matches. All lovers of true sport must endeavour to create and to sustain a feeling of good sense and proportion. The two teams will come together with the frenzies of last winter-but-one not altogether forgotten. Is it too much to ask of Fleet Street that every journalist might be allowed to write on the Test matches with sanity? Let us, for heaven's sake, give the players a chance.

This time the main issue at stake in the Tests is not the rubber, but the goodwill which for years has endured between the cricketers of England and Australia. Anything like a repetition of the trouble of last winter-but-one will certainly put an end to the matches for a long time to come. The players can be trusted to 'get on with the game'. Any newspaper that endangers the atmosphere should be 'warned-off' all cricket fields.

I am in a position to say that the Australians are determined to show to all of us that they are intent chiefly on cricket for the game's sake. They will, of course, try hard to 'recapture the ashes'. But that ambition comes second to a desire to give pleasure to English crowds by keen and skilful and beautiful play.

Woodfull is a magnificent sportsman; Australia has never sent to us a cricketer of finer ideas. And a splendid team has been chosen to serve under him. The celebrities of the 1930 conquerors will be seen again: Woodfull, Bradman, Oldfield, Ponsford, Kippax, McCabe, Grimmett and Wall. And the newcomers promise to be the most interesting that Australian cricket has discovered for years; I am led by good judges of the game to look for exceptional batting from Darling, Bromley and Brown. The Australians never visit us without introducing to us at least one new master; they have a genius for unearthing genius at the right time. Bromley and Darling are left-handed batsmen, both able to hit handsomely all round the wicket.

Darling is expected by Australian critics to develop into another Vernon Ransford; he played against Jardine's invincible team, and in the second Sydney Test match, the last of the 1932–1933 rubber, he scored a superb 85. Bromley stands 6 ft high, is only 21 years old, and though he is an 'experiment', the Australian Selection Committee have reasons enough for their faith. Brown, I am warned, might easily score 1,500 runs in his first English season; he is a defensive batsman who waits patiently for the loose ball, then thumps the life out of it.

All in all, the Australians should make vast numbers of runs, given a tolerably dry season. Bradman is a greater player today than ever he was; his strokes from Larwood's 'leg trap' bowling were described by all cricketers who saw them as the strokes of genius. It is a slander against a beautiful player to say that he ran away from Larwood. What Bradman did against Larwood's leg-theory attack was to move away to the leg side of the ball so as to be in a position to hit brilliantly to the uninhabited off-side. Bradman has been a victim of that lurid 'publicity' which I have mentioned before; a less balanced head than his would have been turned completely by the racket made about him a year or two ago by the catch-penny ghouls.

Given a summer of dry wickets, Australia will indeed be terribly hard to beat. If the weather favours spin bowlers, and if England gets a fair share of the 'luck', Verity should be able to turn the issue in our favour. The Australian attack is causing some anxiety, even amongst the Australian critics —who invariably are optimistic at a tour's beginning, for they are born propagandists always. O'Reilly did not add last winter to the great reputation he won in the Tests against Jardine's team. But if it is true that he can spin the ball from middle stump to the off stump on a Sydney pitch, he is bound to cause trouble on an English turf, whatever the weather. I confess I have not yet been able to obtain from any Australian critic a satisfactory description of O'Reilly's bowling; if he is as clever with the 'going away' ball as he is said to be, why does he so often place two men close up on the leg-side? O'Reilly ought not to win Test matches in England if he is only an off-break bowler. But we shall se.

Fleetwood-Smith and his left-handed 'googly' might well give us the really intriguing cricket of the summer. I remember that poor dear Roy Kilner once told me, in his own gorgeous Yorkshire, that the next development in the game would produce a left-handed 'googly' bowler. 'We're stuck for bobbins just now', said Roy. 'These doped wickets have helped t' batsmen to larn all th' owd tricks. I'd like to see somebody a-bowling t' wrong 'un left-handed. I've tried it misel', but t' Yakshire team calls it t' "Chinaman" contemptuous like'. Even Emmott Robinson, fielding at silly-point, used to watch Roy in some suspense. 'Now doan't thee bowl t' "Chinaman" whatever tha does, Roy', he would say.

Fleetwood-Smith, like all 'googly' bowlers, is prone to lose his length. Hammong once hit his spin unmercifully, to the dismay of the Australian crowd. But it is by punishment that the true 'googly' bowler is made. B. J. T. Bosanquet was never so dangerous as he was a few moments after he had pitched a ball half way down the wicket, and had achieved what the incomparable A. C. M. Croome once called a polyhop.

Grimmett is a far better bowler on English turf than he is on the cast-iron grounds of his own land. He will, we may be sure, tackle our batsmen with his usual tenacity; he is good to watch—a little terrier of a bowler, the batsman his bone! Ebeling is another stranger to us; he is a steady fast-medium bowler who should find an ally for his outswinger (while the ball is new) in a 'green' English wicket and an English air.

The fast bowler, Wall, has usually been underrated; he can achieve real pace. In the match at Melbourne, in December, 1932, he bowled Hammond with a ball quick and good enough for W. G. Grace, who, of course, has never been excelled as a batsman against fast bowling (Percy Perrin was his closest rival). Chipperfield, another young and 'un-baptised' Australian, is a useful batsman and bowler—and one of the great slip fieldsmen of the day.

The Australian attack, then, will depend on O'Reilly, Wall, Grimmett, Fleetwood-Smith, Ebeling, Wall and Chipperfield, with McCabe as a utility man. It is a fair combination of various paces and spins, and our batsmen are not likely to make the mistake of holding it in too slight esteem. But the English attack will be as good, to say the least, even if Larwood fails to recover soundness of limb. If I were Woodfull, I should today be confident to know that on my side were Verity and Clark.

The loss of Jardine is not to be measured or easily repaired; our greatest tactician since A. C. MacLaren. I hope to see Wyatt as England's leader at Nottingham; he is a student of the game, and a sportsman. He and Woodfull will be a guarantee of keen but chivalrous play.

The season waits for us like a lovely lane right down the summer time. We are all eager for the sight of our old favourites, eager for our first walk down St John's Wood Road in the May sunshine, eager for the sound of the bell calling the players to action, eager for the stop-press news, eager even for the tidings that Bradman is 157 not out. None of us will be as young as we are today. 'Play', gentlemen, 'play!' And please, Fleet Street, remember that this is cricket; the meadow game with a beautiful name!

THE FIRST TEST

As I write these lines the England eleven for the Lord's Test match has not been chosen. It is devoutly to be hoped that no consideration external to true cricket will keep Larwood out of the engagement. He is the greatest fast bowler of our time, one who has never, when fit and strong, needed to employ tactics not known of old by Tom Richardson, Lockwood, N. A. Knox, Brearley, Gregory, and Macdonald. If the so-called leg-theory rumpus should deprive us of Larwood the irony of the tragedy will be acute. For the acid joke of it all is that the present Australian batsmen's main weakness is *against fast bowling which flashes from a good length just outside the off-stump!*

This weakness was revealed at Trent Bridge by Farnes. I shall never believe that it was ever necessary for Larwood to exploit a leg-trap against Ponsford, Bradman, Woodfull, McCabe, Kippax, Chipperfield, and the rest. Each of these batsmen is seldom able to resist a more or less speculative stroke at the fast ball near the off wicket. I cannot remember any Australian cricketer who was content merely to watch fast bowling go by the off-stump. Time after time, at Trent Bridge, the Australians put their bats towards the off side bowling of Farnes as impulsively as the moth that flickers into a candle. I shall die in the belief that Larwood could this year beat the Australians by bowling with the length and direction which were honoured in the past by the classical fast bowlers.

The pity of it, if a theory unwisely driven to the extreme should mean the end of Larwood's career as a Test match cricketer! For here we have a beautiful fast bowler good enough to hurl his speed at W. G. Grace—hurl it on the good-length spot which was the mark of classical fast bowling, the spot that threatens the middle and off wickets, and stimulates great expectations in the bosoms of four slip fieldsmen. Even yet I trust Larwood will be persuaded that he is a successor in the line of Lockwood and Richardson.

Without Larwood's aid, England will be hard put to it to win at Lord's, unless they bat first. I trust the Selection Committee will not overdo the fast bowling plan: two bowlers of speed will be enough. So far, the fact has been generally overlooked that it was not England's bowlers who lost the match at Trent Bridge. Australia were put out twice for reasonably moderate scores; we shall be lucky if ever again this summer we see Bradman, Woodfull and Ponsford dismissed six times in one Test match as cheaply as they were dismissed at Nottingham. I agree that the Australian batsmen are apparently happier against medium-paced and slow bowling than they are against quick bowling. None the less, I get a sense of panic in the notion that England will be able to win the rubber by a wholesale 'barrage' achieved by three fast bowlers—if, indeed, there are as many as three fast bowlers at the present time in the universe!

A Test match attack should always be chosen proportionately, with pace and spin nicely blended. Suppose that England has to bowl at Lord's on a 'dead' wicket which, in the absence of sun, does not become 'sticky'? What, then, will be the use of three, or of two, fast bowlers? Before the summer is done England will badly want a spin bowler of the 'googly' type. Why is the name of Freeman never mentioned when we are occupied in the nation's job of picking the England XI?

But, as I say, England lost at Nottingham through no fault of her bowlers. We were beaten because too few of our batsmen could play with confidence the slow spin of Grimmett. It was Grimmett who laid the mine; he was the sapper that patiently prepared the upheaval which in England's second innings overwhelmed our batsmen. Is there no safe way of tackling Grimmett? On the Tuesday, at Trent Bridge, he and O'Reilly were helped by a slightly worn wicket. But on the second day of the match, when the Trent Bridge turf was a

batsman's restful bed, Grimmett put his spell awfully on
Pataudi, Hammond and Leyland. I admire Pataudi's batsmanship in county cricket, and I refuse to believe that he did
himself justice at Nottingham. I imagine that he will 'stand
down' at Lord's, and that some day he will return to Test
cricket and conquer.

Hammond also was a complete failure at Trent Bridge; in
this country he seldom plays in his free, masterful Gloucestershire style. He is entirely unlike Sutcliffe, who bats for
England at his best, and for Yorkshire at his second best.
Hendren, too, made the mistake, in England's second innings
at Trent Bridge, of departing from the quick-footed methods
which in the first innings enabled him to master Grimmett's
length and spin.

If England win the toss at Lord's, some English batsmen
must be given orders to attack Grimmett, *regardless of the
consequences*. But mere slogging does not constitute offensive batsmanship. I fancy that J. T. Tyldesley would put
Grimmett out of successful action by a bold combination of
the drive, the cut, and back-play in front of the pads of the ball
difficult to reach. But it is not (thank goodness!) the critic's
job to tell our heroes how to play for England. All that the
critic can do is to point out, from the experience of watching,
the way where failure lies. Timid footwork, with the right toe
rooted to the earth, contributed towards England's thrashing
in the first Test match.

Something will be done, I hope, to bind England's fielding
together. Sutcliffe is a slow runner; this weakness should not
be unnecessarily exposed. And, frankly, I was not at all sure
about the wicket-keeping of Ames at Trent Bridge. He would
not be considered for a moment as England's stumper were he
not a good batsman in county cricket. But it was not the
individual parts of England's fielding that invited criticism at
Trent Bridge; rather was it a collective slackness when things
were running Australia's way. Adversity seems to sharpen
Australian keenness; and seems to blunt England's. This
must not be. Losing or winning, a cricketer should constantly
feel the honour he gains by playing for England. He is a poor
spirit who will not play hard, to the last gasp, for his country.

When the match at Nottingham was finished on a lovely

summer evening, the crowd gathered in front of the pavilion and cheered victors and vanquished alike. Here was the dear true spirit of the game. The old unhappy battles of 1932–1933 were forgotten. Some despicable efforts have been made—by people who cannot endure a beating—to stir up the mud again. Every lover of cricket will do his best at Lord's to create the atmosphere of the game and to scotch at birth any irrelevant discontents. It does not matter so much this time who wins the rubber; the great thing is to get Test cricket back again into the old chivalrous temper.

SECOND TEST—VERITY'S MATCH

AT the end of the second day the general impression was that the Lord's Test match would be drawn. England's score of 440 had been answered by 192 for two wickets.

So far 'honours were even'. England, thanks to Leyland and Ames, had achieved a total which in most cricket matches would spell security. And the innings taught one or two lessons for the Selection Committee's edification. The Australian attack is terribly dependent on Grimmett. He was handicapped, Friday and Saturday, by a strong wind, which blew most of his spin away. The crafty little bowler tried to defeat the breeze by exploiting a flight even lower than his customary trajectory. But, as a consequence, he was guilty of a lot of long hops.

O'Reilly was disappointing in England's first innings; he did not spin his leg-break. He looked full of heavy toil, lumbering away with fast-medium pace on the leg stump. I imagine that O'Reilly is always bowling untrue to form when he is bowling beyond slow-medium. England's batting in the next Test match must be strengthened in offensive stroke-play. The Selection Committee must make up their minds about Hammond. His form against Grimmett in this country is poor.

Walters on Friday batted himself into the England XI for the season; he showed us style, courage and skill. I liked the way he used his feet to Grimmett; and I think he was mainly responsible—apart from the wind—for causing Grimmett for once in a while to suffer the influence of an inferiority complex. Leyland and Ames came together on Friday when the pessimists were at their most cheerful. Five of England's wickets were down for 182, three of them taken by Chipperfield's childlike and bland leg breaks. (Yet Chipperfield is no inconsiderable bowler; he gives 'air' to his spin.)

Leyland and Ames held the sixth wicket for England while 130 were added. Both scored centuries, Leyland in his lusty Yorkshire way and Ames in his commonsense way—competent, clever and sometimes handsome. Ames is a godsend to England; he can be relied on most times to stiffen the middle of an innings. Maybe he would not be chosen for a Test match purely on the strength of his wicket-keeping. But if he is not an Oldfield, who is incomparable, he keeps a solid wicket, and has yet to miss a crucial catch for England.

When Australia's innings began at ten minutes past three on Saturday afternoon, Bowes and Farnes attacked. Here was the much-advertised fast bowling of England, here was the assault by force which for weeks had been advocated by critics as the one and only way in which England could hope to overthrow Australia's batsmen. Bowes, strangely slothful in his general deportment, caused one or two balls to rear; he hit Woodfull on the body, and so did Farnes. But Woodfull is not 'seeing the ball' well this season; he contrived to stay in with Brown 80 minutes only because he is a man of intense character and willpower. Technically, his innings on Saturday, was weak; spiritually it was strong and noble. Bowes bowled him at last by his really fast ball.

Then came Bradman. Farnes was put on at once to exploit the alleged dislike of Bradman for fast bowling. And Bradman hit fourteen off the first over he got from Farnes—a square-leg-hook, savage and grand; a glorious pulled-drive, off the back foot; a two hooked late from a good ball; and an off-drive of sculptured rhythm and poise. Bradman then attended to Geary; he cut him and drove him quick as a panther. Verity was called into action, and Bradman pierced the crowded offside field thrice, to the boundary, off consecutive balls.

I have never seen greater batsmanship. The crowd was sent into a delirium of delight. What a game this cricket is, in England on a June day, that it can exorcise partisanship from the breasts of men and women—women especially!—and make thousands of English folk kin with Australians in love and admiration of cricket shot through and through with genius. Bradman's batting was not wild or reckless this time, as I am afraid it was at Nottingham; he hit seven fours in forty minutes, all along the grass; he hit practically every ball offensively, but always with the middle of the bat.

He was out rather unluckily; a ball from Verity 'popped' on the good wicket and Bradman could not check his stroke. He sent a return catch to Verity, who held it avariciously. In the same over, a ball or two earlier, Bradman had hit precipitately at a beautiful 'hanging' ball from Verity and had escaped a 'c. and b.' by inches. Verity was the only bowler on Saturday who looked to be in the Test match class. He gave to his bowling the virtues of length, flight and spin.

Bradman's 'new' mood is fascinating; he is easily the world's most delightful batsman and the world's greatest stroke-player. But from Australia's point of view he is too much the artist and not enough the practical utilitarian. Perhaps he will shortly find the happy medium between the Robot of 1930 and the man who has just discovered the soul of a great cricketer, a cricketer fit to wear the mantle of Victor Trumper.

Brown, aged only twenty-one, scored a century in his first Test match at Lord's. He is a cool-headed batsman, straight and easeful in style, a pretty player, who is destined to score thousands of runs against England. He gets into position rapidly, with few movements; he could bat in the old top-hat of Hambledon.

England's 'fast' bowlers on Saturday were both sad failures. I have, as my readers may know, been no supporter of the idea of using wholesale fast bowling against the Australians. One fast bowler is ample if he is good enough. At Manchester the English attack must contain a leg-break bowler.

During the week-end the weather broke; rain softened the wicket on top and the ground underneath remained hard. Australia were trapped on Monday at the mercy of the finest living left-handed spin bowler—Verity by name, Yorkshire by nature. The pitch probably never became unplayably 'sticky'; none the less, it helped Verity's spin, and also helped that curious 'bounce' of his from the ground, from a good-length ball. From the moment he bowled his first over on Monday morning, I prepared myself for an England victory before close of play.

I am at a loss to understand why many good judges of the game, watching from the pavilion, could not see at once that the pitch was made for Verity. The ball that got McCabe out in the opening half-hour was evidence enough; it spun across venomously. Wyatt even failed to realise how potentially Verity was bowling; Verity himself seemed scarcely to realise how ideal the conditions were shaping for him—so long as he bowled from the pavilion. He actually went over to the nursery end after he had taken three wickets in an hour for next to nothing. Fortunately, Wyatt realised the miscalculation in time. But not before Chipperfield and Oldfield had held Australia's seventh wicket a dreadfully long time and had scored 40. Australia failed to save the follow-on only by seven; I think they would have saved, even won, the match had England batted again on Monday afternoon. The turf developed into a 'glue-pot'; and Verity was superb. Grimmett and O'Reilly might have bowled dangerously in circumstances that favoured 'going-away' spin.

In the match, Verity took fifteen wickets for 104, fourteen on Monday. He bowled not more than six loose balls all day; and he bowled for hours, lovely to see, grace concealing his deadliness. He kept an alluring length, and his break pitched on the middle stump and whipped across. Only Chipperfield exploited the correct technique; he played back most times and put a straight bat to the ball, with his body behind it. The other Australians were guilty of fast wicket forward hits at the pitch of the spin!

Bradman hit wildly across the break; his innings, at the crisis, was unworthy of his genius. Woodfull, though out of form, stayed in for two hours, when all was lost for Australia.

It was a noble example of courage and will-power. Technically, Woodfull was unequal to the occasion; but he persisted by sheer character. Australia lost eighteen wickets in the day; in her first innings, Yorkshire, represented by Verity and Bowes, took the whole ten. Had Mitchell been fielding, Verity's analysis would have been even more remarkable than it was. A great victory, for if England had the luck, they also had the bowler!

LEEDS

To the end of time the first day's play of the Test match at Leeds will remain 'wropt in mystery'. On a beautiful wicket, England struggled five hours for 200. Every batsman stayed in long enough to obtain a 'good look' at the Australian bowling; nearly every one of them played his first ball confidently and seemed to be settling down when he got out.

The Australian bowlers and fieldsmen were as astonished as the rest of us. Woodfull told me that as English wicket after English wicket fell, he and his colleagues on the field simply could not believe their eyesight. O'Reilly and Grimmett bowled well, but the perfection of the Leeds turf stole all venom from their spin. True, the Australian bowlers are cleverer than English bowlers at variation of flight; Chipperfield was exceptionally skilful with the changes he rang on his curve through the air. But the collapse of England, after the total had promised big deeds, was one of those chapters of accidents which defy explanation, and make cricket the very darling of caprice amongst games.

Walters began England's innings magnificently. He hit three fours straightaway. Wyatt was very lucky to win the toss again. Keeton, acting as deputy for Sutcliffe, played a capital little innings, even if the slow bowling of Grimmett did trouble his sturdy Nottinghamshire bat. He was out to O'Reilly's quicker ball at 43, and though Walters 'slowed down' and was out at 85, Hammond and Hendren settled easefully after lunch. Surely it was all Lombard Street to a China Orange that England's score would go as far as 400, at least.

A good straight ball by Wall bowled Hammond at 135. That was the beginning of England's end. Hammond was guilty of an indolent stroke; his innings never announced that mastery which Hammond is showing this year in county cricket. Really, there is an enigma about the batsmanship of Hammond. His performances against Australia in Australia have been strong and vast; his performances against Australia in his own country have been tentative and small. He is forcing the Selection Committee to a reconsideration of his place in the England XI—whether he should any longer be entrusted with the important functions of No. 3 in the batting order; and whether it would not be wise to look for some other batsman to fill the position, and for the Committee to regard Hammond as an indispensable all-round cricketer.

Hendren tackled the Australian bowlers shrewdly for a considerable period; his bat looked as wide as a church door when Chipperfield beat and bowled him by means of a change of speed. Leyland and Wyatt then 'dug themselves in', only to succumb unexpectedly; Wyatt stone-walled for more than an hour, then allowed Grimmett to draw him yards down the wicket! Leyland irrationally drove across a quick half-volley from O'Reilly and was leg-before. O'Reilly has a positive genius for disguising a good ball as an indifferent one. There is no doubt that the Australian attack is far more strategical than any we can gather together in England. The Australian bowler is compelled by everlasting wickets in his land to use his brains; English bowlers trust to wickets which in wet weather help the spin, and in dry weather often crumble on a third day.

England's third wicket on Friday fell at 135; seven wickets proceeded to topple for 65. No attempt was made to drive O'Reilly or Grimmett or Chipperfield off their lengths. The batting accepted the parlous situation on slow, doubtful feet. There was excitement in the afternoon's closing half hour; Brown and Ponsford made 37 comfortably enough for the first Australian wicket. Bowes changed ends, and in quick sequence he dismissed Brown, Oldfield and Woodfull. The crowd departed from Leeds in elation—Australia 39 for three.

In the papers the next morning, some of the experts told us that Bowes had bowled magnificently, that he would crash through the Australian innings, that the Leeds wicket was not above suspicion. The foolishness of optimism—most depressing of human vanities! Bowes, frankly, took his three wickets by the help of fortune. He defeated Brown by a respectable ball that made pace from the pitch. Oldfield, sent in to bat out time, slashed at a ball he could only just reach, and fell to a catch by Ames. And Woodfull played a ball into his stumps! I could see no particular technical merit in Bowes's attack; indeed the bulk of it rather depressed me, because of its lack of real speed.

*   *   *

The Australian is a naughty animal; when it is attacked it defends itself. Thirty-nine for three, 494 for four. England suffered and received in the pit of the stomach the heaviest blow of retaliation known in the history of Test matches. The vast crowd came out to Leeds ready to witness an Australian collapse; false prophets had betrayed trustfulness on Friday; those depressing people the optimists had descried in the attack of Bowes terrors that did not exist there. The easeful wicket, even, was transformed in hopeful imagination into a dusty track leading to the ruin of all Australians.

The day began with two balls by Bowes left over from the evening before; Bradman drove the first straight for four and the second to the on, also for four. These hits were ominous; they lacked the rhetoric which many times this summer has told us of a Bradman strangely different from the Bradman of six years ago, a Bradman in rebellion against his own mastery and driven a little beyond proportion to that intemperance which hath been the untimely emptying of thrones. Bradman once again entered his own domain, conquered himself as well as the enemy, and conveyed to us his pleasures in spacious plenty. Those two preludial boundaries off Bowes were executed over the line of the ball with the body in control to an inch; the strokes were fundamental; I saw them like grim, purposeful stanchions fixing to the earth a great innings.

Bradman drove another four from Bowes, a drive to the off swift and beautiful. Then he batted half an hour and scored only 11; every defensive sound of his protective blade was doom striking for England's bowlers. At the crucial moment Bradman put his genius into discipline for a while, sent it back for a term to the sound yet brilliant school of which he himself is headmaster. Throughout the present season it has been my belief that Bradman would make two hundred in an innings the first time he played the good-length ball off the pitch consistently for half an hour, avoiding a single hit across the ball's flight. Not once did Bradman slash the off-side ball round to long-on with his right foot across the wicket in an attitude excessively belligerent.

His genius was his good slave; his innings wedded art and utility, style and honest service, personal pride and devotion to his team. It was the Bradman of 1930 with a difference; the batsmanship was organic, not mechanical. Four years ago on this same comfortable Leeds wicket Bradman scored three hundred runs in a Test match in a day, and he scored them as though moved by wheels and levers cunningly hidden from us, driven by a lifeless machinery simulating life. This wonderful innings had the vitality of brain, blood, and nerve; every part of it throbbed with a consciousness that was of the spirit; it was a creative innings which took its shape hour by hour, according to the will of a cricketer playing for Australia; the design of it was political as well as handsome. First the base was well and truly laid; 100 runs in three and a quarter hours; then the infantry of batsmanship went into action— another 100 in two hours. And at last, when the moment was ripe, the cavalry put the routing, finishing touch; 70 runs in seventy-five minutes, the bat a piercing quick lance. The precision in the three periods of Bradman's masterpiece was the precision of fine art, not that of mechanical rotation.

But all this as though we were forgetting Ponsford, who with Bradman played his part in the biggest stand ever achieved in a Test match, 388 in five hours and a half. The finest praise that could well be given to Ponsford is that he was never out of the picture; his cricket boldly invited comparison with Bradman's, and survived it. He was no mere bass fiddle in the orchestra of the day's batsmanship; his innings was a solo part, too—in a double concerto of classical cricket. The skill of Ponsford, different in pattern and inspiration from Bradman's, was woven like a superb counterpoint in the texture of Australia's innings; few other batsmen living at the present time could have played in Bradman's company and not seemed to live unseen in the shade of Bradman's grandeur. Ponsford's innings reminded us that there is one glory of the sun and another of the moon. He exhibited a magnificent defensive technique, directed mainly by a forward push that smothered the length ball at birth. His on-side play was a model of economical propulsion; his bat circled round his wrists, and no daylight was to be discerned between the wide blade and his body. Every stroke spoke of experience and common sense.

Ponsford is experimental only against the really fast ball; in this match England's fast bowling is unmistakably slow.

Once and once only during the long day did Ponsford and Bradman reveal that like all humans they are prone to error and irrational impulse. Just before lunch Bowes was driven by desperation to the exploitation of a few short, bumping balls; Ponsford wavered and retreated Dolphinwards; he made a sandbag of the rounded part of his anatomy. His poise was momentarily disturbed, so that when his score stood at 70 and Australia's at 166 he slashed at a rising off-side ball and sent an ideal cover-point catch to Mitchell, who missed the chance because he started much too late. A few moments earlier than that Bradman's bat clove recklessly at a kicker and crashed the ball violently between square-leg and mid-on rather deep; Hopwood stuck one hand out and never looked like holding the catch, if catch it really was. Hopwood could scarcely be blamed; it is not the recognised duty of cricketers to hold sudden thunderbolts.

Ponsford himself broke the stand; he hit Verity to long-on for four, a glorious stroke, and trod on his wicket ever so gently while doing so! Wyatt twice tried to catch Ponsford at 'silly' mid-off, but even great pluck and determination cannot work miracles. Ponsford amassed his 181 in six-and-a-quarter hours.

When the England team walked wearily off the field on Saturday evening, Bradman was 271 not out, at the end of six hours and a half of consummate batsmanship; it was not only a victory over technique and a dangerous position—39 for three *is* a dangerous position, after all! Also it was a victory over that delightful but mischievous imp who this summer has led Bradman one or two reckless, brave but ruinous dances. This was the true Bradman, playing for Australia, putting his art and his temperament under discipline, serving the occasion's need and the game's science and beauty with an equal diligence and devotion. Thirty-nine for three—494 for four; that was the wonderful tale of Saturday!

On Monday Bowes thwarted Australia's intention to make runs more and more gaudily and so force a vast and condescending declaration. With a wind behind him, he achieved real pace, and he made the new ball swing beautifully. He bowled McCabe and Bradman with balls that kept surprisingly low. Bradman's 304 was amassed in about seven-and-a-quarter hours. Six Australian wickets fell between eleven o'clock and half past twelve for 90. Yorkshire, once again, took all of Australia's ten wickets; the Leeds crowd rejoiced greatly. I do not think the average Yorkshireman worries overmuch about anything in cricket but the glory of his own county.

England went in at one o'clock, needed 384 to save the innings defeat. Keeton was bowled by Grimmett's leg-break when 28 runs were promising a good opening stand. Soon after came the day's bitter pill. Hammond at last showed his true gold; he made four regal boundaries. He looked to be enthroned for the day. Suddenly, devils of indecision seized him; he played a ball to mid-on. Walters ran—and apparently Hammond said nothing. Seeing Walters more than half way down the pitch, he decided also to run, but he did so with no conviction. He was out easily, a wicked waste of a great batsman.

The rest of the afternoon was austere. Hendren achieved a martyr's crown; three hours and a quarter for less than 50! He was terribly unsafe to begin with, but he would not be put down. Wyatt and he resisted for two hours and scored only 65. Then Leyland and Ames played through the closing hour, cool and skilful, with an eye on the weather. When rain stopped play England with four wickets in hand, were in a hopeless state. The match has demonstrated beyond argument Australia's superiority, and her claim to the prize of the rubber.

AFTERMATCH

EVERYWHERE I turn, I hear people crying out, 'Thank goodness the Test matches are over!' I seem to be the only man in the land who enjoyed the Test matches—and indeed I *did* enjoy them, immensely! I revelled in the challenging occasion; in the great batting of Bradman, Leyland, and Ponsford; in the lovely rippling innings of Walters; in the subtle spin and flight of O'Reilly and Grimmett; in the big-hearted endeavour of Farnes, Bowes, Allen and Clark.

There was nothing the matter with the Test matches, except the horrible dust raised by the cheap Press—a dust that obviously blinded many people to the many skilful and beautiful deeds performed on the field of play. Those folk who talk of the Test matches as events dreary and unpleasant either did not witness them, or they allowed vulgar journalism to come between their vision and the true deeds. I have been watching Test cricket for more than thirty years; I have never seen more interesting Test matches than those of this year; seldom seen finer bowling than Grimmett's and O'Reilly's, or pluckier batsmanship than Leyland's, or prettier bowling than Verity's at Lord's, or more fascinating cricket than Bradman's, who began the season like a man bewitched out of his senses and then, at the crucial moment of the rubber, recaptured his usual fine and complete mastery.

Before we are much older, the howls of irrelevant controversy will die down, and the Test matches of 1934 will receive their due—will be seen for what they really were, matches big and alive with doughty deeds. Naturally, the Test matches would have appealed more vividly than they did to the popular mind if England had won the rubber. I am afraid that some of us, here and in Australia, are losing the knack of accepting defeat handsomely.

When did the opinion first get abroad this summer that the Test matches were not true sport, that the atmosphere and temper of them were unpleasant? Not after the gallant game at Trent Bridge; all the English newspapers agreed that the game there was fought superbly, in accordance with the grandest traditions of cricket. And indeed it was: I shall never forget the scene at the finish, when on a lovely June evening, the crowd gathered in front of the pavilion and cheered victors and vanquished alike. No raving for leg-theory then!

At Lord's England won, and all lovers of the game were unanimous that Test cricket was itself again, chivalrous and magnificent. Nothing happened in the stalemate at Manchester to disturb the peace; we all sympathised with the Australians because of the illness that temporarily crippled Bradman and Chipperfield. Even after the game at Leeds, where Bradman found true form, and where England were a beaten side but for a cloudburst, nothing was said or written to suggest that the Test matches were foul, iniquitous and offensive to the taste of sportsmen.

Then how did it come about that by the time the Oval match was half way through, countless tongues were slandering Test cricket and the Australians? I can say confidently here and now—nothing was done on the cricket field to cause a change in the atmosphere; the players played the game and enjoyed the rare rigour of it all. It was the cheap Press who ruined the Test matches of 1934; it was the cheap Press who poisoned the air. Body-line and leg-theory had nothing to do with the change of atmosphere; the cricketers were helpless to prevent the spreading of the filthy fumes. Nobody bowled body-line in the Test matches, and when leg-theory was employed at the Oval by Clark and Bowes, the Australians played it and Bradman hit it. Those people who at the moment are saying 'Put an end to Test matches!' are really playing into the hands of the cheap Press; they are recognising the influence of a pernicious 'stunt'.

There was nothing wrong with the cricket of the Test

matches of 1934; only the Press was wrong, or part of it. Next year, cricket in this country will miss the fine stroke-play of the Australians, and the beautiful spin bowling of Grimmett and O'Reilly. The country will miss the big occasion; instead, there will be the county routine—50 runs an hour, frequently made by batsmen as ready to protest as any Australian when a bowler exploits persistent bumpers to a packed leg-side field. Let the fact be kept in mind that one or two English counties have protested against the so-called leg-theory of Larwood; nobody wants it, certainly not the playing cricketers of England or Australia.

The future of Test matches is not in danger if only we will ignore the 'stunt' journalists. Cricketers know well enough that little or nothing is at issue between the MCC and the Board of Control. The difference between legitimate fast leg-theory and 'body-line' based on the persistent 'high kicker'—this difference is recognised by all responsible participants in cricket, in England, Australia, New Zealand, the West Indies and South Africa. The Press-fed man in the street does not understand the difference; moreover, the difference is not known to many well-intentioned *literateurs*.

POSTLUDE

A USTRALIA deservedly won the rubber. At all points of the game England's cricketers were outclassed. There were non-technical explanations, but not by the players. Much was made of the unfortunate circumstances that kept Larwood and Jardine out of the Test matches. The suggestion was circulated that England's fast bowlers suffered embarrassments not caused by cricket. All these apologies were irrelevant to the main issue, which was the form displayed by England's batsmen since the first engagement at Trent Bridge.

England's defeats were primarily caused by bad batting. In every Test match a fatal collapse ensued. On the second day at Nottingham England lost four wickets in little more than half an hour on a perfect pitch after a good start and after the bowlers had done well enough to dismiss Australia for a moderate first-innings total. England won the toss at Lord's, and five wickets fell for less than 200. At Manchester, before lunch on a beautiful turf, three England wickets surrendered in one over. At Leeds, on a wicket described by the England captain as a 'feather bed', England were all out for 200. Then in the most crucial game of the lot came the débâcle of the Oval. Even with a Larwood in the side, England could scarcely expect to beat Australia if the batting were thoroughly and consistently unreliable. Leyland, Walters, and Ames several times demonstrated that O'Reilly and Grimmett could be hit; unfortunately, some of their colleagues, notably Hammond, preferred to play clever spin bowling tentatively from behind the crease.

Students of the game not blinded by that partisanship which afflicted a few Southern spirits observed one interesting fact of technique in the rubber. The Australian attack conquered by trusting faithfully to the great and ancient principles of length, flight, and break. Many times the England attack concentrated on the modern 'shock' methods, legitimately, but none the less with a pathetic trustfulness in what George Lohmann called 'brute force'.

An unintelligent shout for fast 'leg-theory' played into the hands of Bradman, Ponsford, and McCabe. Good fast bowling, accurately pitched, is one thing; erratic short stuff, hoping for mis-hits to a leg-field is another. The wisest comment on England's fast-bowling tactics, fair but foolish, was written by Mr C. B. Fry: 'All that was necessary to incommode this Australian team was straight fast bowling, at or over the stumps. Most of them would have supplied the leg-theory for themselves. That is, by the way they play.' Excepting Bradman and McCabe, the Australian batsmen all revealed an inability to play the quick ball that goes past the off-stump or keeps straight on it.

The wretched England fielding at Manchester and the Oval was, of course, inexcusable. England, in fact, never found a unified team, never welded good spare parts into an organic machine. Performances in county cricket were constantly proved to possess no value. English county cricket is deplorably slack; there is too much of it week by week. The visit of the Australians exposed weakness of technique and weakness of point of view of the game.

Contrary to the general opinion, the Australian batsman is usually a finer and freer stroke player than the English batsman, especially in a Test match. The reason may be that in this country natural ability to drive and cut is ruined by too much coaching by unimaginative professionals. There is next to no coaching in Australian cricket; an English 'pro' would have put a quick end to many of Bradman's audacious hits.

Patriots who took England's defeat badly advertised the 'farce' of the game at the Oval. Would they have called the match a farce if England had beaten Australia in a little under four days after scoring 475 for two wickets brilliantly on the first day at the rate of eighty runs an hour, and after following up that performance by decisive and fascinating bowling? There is no dull cricket when O'Reilly and Grimmett bowl; both are artists of the craft of varied flight and break. There was nothing farcical at the Oval save the inability of England's attack to prevent an aggregate of 700 runs by Australia in an innings.

Whether a cricket match without a time-limit is an idea acceptable to English notions of the game is another consideration. The point is that England agreed to play one Test match in the rubber to a finish, and that Australia batted with beauty and spirit for a good portion of the time and bowled and fielded magnificently for the rest.

Something must be done by the legislators of the game to get 'leg-theory' defined. But the moment for that necessary work is not while the victors are being cheered and the vanquished are being chastised and consoled. So easy would it be to seem to be making excuses.

1938

THE AUSTRALIAN SIDE

SATURDAY, May 7th, was one of the coldest days I have
ever known on a cricket field. I was reminded of a
drawing made by Phil May to commemorate the Jubilee
of W. G. Grace. Phil depicted the 'Old Man' standing on
guard at the wicket in the familiar aspect—whiskers and
M.C.C. cap, and the left toe up. But also he depicted cover-
point wearing wicket-keeper's gloves. Phil sent the original of
the drawing to 'W.G.', who thanked him for the honour, but
added: 'Why is cover-point wearing the wicket-keeper's
gloves?' And one night soon afterwards 'W.G.' was pulled
out of bed by the arrival of a telegram which said, simply and
succinctly, 'To keep his hands warm.'

All the Australian spin bowlers must have felt the need of
gloves or something during the first few perishing days of
May. Our summer—as Charles Lamb once remarked—has
set in with its customary severity. But the dry weather has at
least given the Australian batsmen the firm wickets which suit
their strokes. The side is bound to be powerful in batsmanship. Last week at Leicester, Bradman was not playing,
and McCabe was out for a 'duck', and Fingleton scored only
34. Yet, at close of play, the Australians, as usual, were 243
for two wickets. Badcock and Hassett performed a brilliant
partnership of 183 in an hour and 50 minutes; it was unbeaten
at half-past six, and I think it must have been nearly the finest
exhibition of stylish cricket achieved by two young Australians since Victor Trumper and Clem Hill made their names at
Lord's some 39 years ago.

The impressive fact about the batting of Badcock and
Hassett was the mastery of technique displayed by each.
There is usually the hint of inexperience in the most gifted

young man's batting—for instance, it is possible to see, or to sense, where a shrewd bowler would find out the immaturities of a Compton or an Edrich, no matter how brilliantly these two promising cricketers happen to be playing at the time. But Badcock and Hassett last Saturday, for all their brilliance, did nothing that was not experienced.

Badcock was 40 minutes making six. Then he smashed the Leicestershire attack to the tune of 100 in two hours. He is a dynamic batsman who, in some way, reminds me of Hendren, just as Hassett reminds me of Sandham. Badcock, even when he is merely defending against a good ball, suggests a scoring stroke somewhere at the back of his mind. He is always busy. Hassett is a batsman of poise, of balance. He plays in an invisible top hat. He is never awkward. He can drive powerfully without obvious effort—simply a free swing and a follow-through. On good wickets he is likely to score many delightful hundreds.

The Australian batting is certain to be strong, but, so far, there is a doubt about the bowling— though in these early and frigid days spin-bowlers have scarcely been able to use their fingers. The interesting point is that most of the wickets taken by the Australians have been taken by the spin bowlers— Ward and Fleetwood-Smith. Cold weather cannot be blamed for the mix-up in McCormick's run to the wicket, or for O'Reilly's poor form up to the moment of writing. McCormick will probably have got his action in order, more or less, before these lines are printed—if he has not, there will be trouble, for habit breeds habit. McCormick at his best is the fastest bowler of recent years; in an inter-State match last year his pace left even Bradman with no time for any but a stroke done by reflex action. The Australian attack will suffer if he is unable, in the Test matches, to prepare by bombardment a way for the infantry led by 'Sergeant' O'Reilly.

At Leicester, O'Reilly's bowling, as at Worcester, was ludicrously harmless. It possessed little spin and no accuracy of length—O'Reilly, of all men, inaccurate in length! I could not believe my spectacles. He was thumped in front of the wicket for fours by mute but not altogether inglorious Watsons, Dowens, Armstrongs and Jacksons. In Australia recently, O'Reilly kept Hammond quiet for hours, tied up his strokes, reduced him to fretful inactivity.

When I was in Australia a few weeks ago, a rumour went round that O'Reilly was not bowling as dangerously as he bowled a year or two ago. 'He is losing his leg break'. I could obtain no support for this view from players in a position to judge, and from what I saw of his bowling in the nets, it seemed as masterful as it was in 1934. He is a curious bowler—I fancy, like all great ones, he is temperamental. He needs plenty of work—an occasional and a quick wicket. O'Reilly is not likely to strain his energies in day by day cricket—because he is Australia's spearhead for Test matches. But the rubber probably hangs on whether O'Reilly is able to assert his old mastery during the next week or two.

The present form of the Australians is not striking dismay into the hearts of the young hopefuls of England. There never was, surely, such a season as this for centuries by aspirants to a wider fame. Every day we hear of fine play by Compton, Edrich, Hutton; and, best news of all, the master—our one and only 'old master' maybe—is in form; I refer, of course, to Hammond. The England team should be strong enough in batting, if there is a confident and bold policy, with no nonsense about 'staying there'. Unfortunately, no great bowler emerges from the mass, no Tate, no Johnny Douglas, no spin bowler half as clever as Fleetwood-Smith or Ward. There are plenty of honest medium-paced men, like Phillipson, Cornford, Perks, Pope (A.), Pollard, Nutter—a new Lancashire lad who bowls a rasping inswinger. But the leg-break artists are scarce—and it is the ball that spins away from the bat that is sorely needed against Australian batsmen. Medium-paced stuff is 'jam' to them if it 'comes in *to* the bat'.

Mitchell of Derbyshire can spin a ball with any cricketer living; but he seems to lack organisation. Sims is good at Lord's when the wicket is slightly worn. And there is a promising leg-spin bowler in Lancashire, his name Wilkinson. But the Australians are so quick-footed that none but a great 'googly' artist is of the slightest use against them. There is, of course, no excuse for pessimism; the Australians are not 'invincible'. No team was ever that. We will give them a severe game by not underrating them, by admitting and studying their strongest points, and by backing-up our own technical points with a confident attitude of mind.

Faint-heartedness, as much as anything else, lost the rubber at Adelaide last year, after superb bowling had given our men a great opportunity. A bad ball remains a bad ball even after it has been bowled by an O'Reilly, a Fleetwood-Smith, or by any other mortal and, therefore, fallible human being.

1938—TRENT BRIDGE

THIS week-end, at Nottingham, we shall begin to know where we are with Bradman and his company. It was cheering at Lord's the other day to see the Australians rendered temporarily vulnerable on a damp but by no means a sticky wicket. England might be able to win the rubber easily in a wet summer—'might', I say, because in a wet summer you are just as likely as your opponents to get trapped on the wicket when it is at its worst. Still, I am fairly certain that the Australians need a fast ground for a full exploitation of their all-round strength. Bradman has yet to prove that he can play a long innings against a turning or a 'popping' ball. Moisture in the turf does not improve the attack of Fleetwood-Smith—and I fear him more than I fear O'Reilly.

But we must be warned about O'Reilly. We have not yet seen him this season really on the war-path. He will, I am sure, be a different O'Reilly at Trent Bridge today. He is a baffling man. Most good judges of cricket agree that he is the best bowler in the game at the present time. None the less, he can dwindle any day to a toiling, lumbering mediocrity. At his fiercest, he suggests a wicket every over, as he whirls his arms and thunders to the crease, like the windmill in *Don Quixote* coming to life. I find the most extraordinary variations of opinion amongst cricketers about O'Reilly's methods.

I have heard one famous England cricketer arguing with another upon the question of O'Reilly's spin from leg. 'He doesn't spin it an inch; he only "rolls" it; and you should play as though it were coming straight'. 'Not —— likely!' said the other; 'he bowled me last week with one that pitched on the leg and hit the top of the off-stump.'

Both of these players were members of Allen's team in Australia; both had faced O'Reilly many times, and often —and yet they could not agree that O'Reilly turns the ball from leg.

O'Reilly, I suppose, disguises his tricks cunningly; he does not cause a wide break which any fool could see. But most batsmen tell me that his chief assets are length and subtle variations of flight. I have watched him at work for hours, here and in Australia, and I am satisfied that he thrives upon timid or diffident batsmen. He should be attacked, not recklessly, of course, but by some player who can use his feet and drive straight. O'Reilly serves many half-volleys. It is 'all up' with us if he is allowed to take the initiative, and to set his field with a couple of men almost on the batsman's doorstep, crouching at 'silly' mid-on and 'silly' short-leg, like body snatchers.

Fleetwood-Smith is a law unto himself. His best ball is almost unplayable. And the 'new' leg-before-wicket law added vastly to his power. He also waxes prosperous on slow-footed batting. For the rest, the Australian attack is mediocre—though I thought, at Lord's last week, that McCormick was gradually recovering true form. He has not shown us more than a third of his proper speed yet. All in all, this Australian team is not strong in bowling; perhaps, indeed, it is the weakest bowling team sent to us from Australia since the time when Frank Laver, the manager, was obliged to don flannels—and capture a hundred wickets by his 'baseball' swervers. Think of the attack commanded by Armstrong: Macdonald, Gregory, Mailey (the greatest and the only graceful 'googly' bowler), Armstrong—and, if wanted, but he never was wanted, Macartney—not to mention Hendry and Ryder, both of them better with the new ball than Waite or McCabe. If England loses the rubber by batting, then our batting will be exposed as deplorable in technique and spirit.

The problem we have to tackle, the really complicated

problem, on a good wicket, is to get Bradman out—and a few others, such as Fingleton (who is a better batsman than Woodfull was), McCabe, Hassett, Badcock and Brown. It is almost inconceivable that in any Australian innings we shall not suffer from one century at least from one of the aforesaid. The prospect of dismissing Bradman ten times in the rubber is an austere prospect. Short bowling on the leg-stump by any Englishman should be indictable, if not certifiable. Better far to bowl for run-outs. Frankly, I think the attack of each side will be incapable of winning a match in dry weather within four days—that is, if not assisted by defeatist batting. And if we should witness this summer the spectacle of four draws and the rubber won by a 'snatch' victory in the fifth—well, then, consolation would emerge, for a rubber so unsatisfactory as this would mean the end of the four-day time-limit in a Test match between England and Australia.

Before I saw Test matches played to a finish in Australia, I was 'against' the no time-limit Test match—as pigheadedly against the idea as any crusted old die-hard of the Lord's Long Room. But I know now that a played-out Test match is great sport. You realise as soon as the struggle begins that one side or the other is doomed—no means of escape! This is a dramatic thought, and it endows every ball with doleful significance. There is no dull play, no dreary air of stalemate. Every ball is a nail in somebody's coffin. On English turf, five days would be ample for a decision. The present rubber must be the last of the four-day limit—which is a foolish anachronism, not wanted by the public.

I can only hope again that Bowes is chosen, and given firm instructions not to try to bowl too fast. The issue of the rubber will be settled, I think, at Nottingham; for if the Australians can win there, they will be able to subsequent matches to keep the advantage by the strength of their batting. The rule in warfare, I believe, is to attack the enemy on his weakest flank. Well, the Australians are not strong in bowling. But what happens if both of the enemies have the same sort of weak flanks? In that event, I take it that providence joins sides with the fellow who gets his blow in first.

I may be old-fashioned, but I confess that I should like to see a backbone of North of England character supporting this year's England teams. Lancashire and Yorkshire, admittedly, no longer can give us MacLaren, Spooner, Tyldesley (J. T.), Brearley, F. S. Jackson, Hirst and Rhodes all in one dazzling galaxy. But the tough nerve of the North prevails yet, and in a crisis at Nottingham I would prefer to have on my side a Mitchell, a Leyland, a Paynter, even a George Wood—no matter how lowly a position these warriors might be reduced to at the moment in the averages, where ability so frequently is misrepresented by 'damned dots'.

McCABE'S INNINGS

TODAY McCabe honoured the first Test with a great and noble innings. At one time Australia was only 263 for seven, with no survivors to help McCabe except McCormick, O'Reilly and Fleetwood-Smith. McCabe changed the gravest situation with the ease of a man using a master key; in an hour he smashed the bowling and decimated a field which for long had been a close, keen net. He pulled his side out of a terrible hole and gave Australia a chance to save herself. Today he scored 213 out of 273 in three and a quarter hours while seven wickets fell. The dear valiance of his play won our hearts. And, believe it or not, when Brown and Fingleton began an uphill job of work a large portion of the crowd actually barracked because Brown and Fingleton played safely and declined to betray McCabe's skill and courage, which they would have done had they attempted indiscreet strokes. Never before have I heard barracking of more stupidity than this. McCabe gave the crowd their money's worth and snatched the match temporarily at least out of England's almost certain grasp. Fingleton and Brown would have been traitors to McCabe had they batted in any but a sound defensive manner; runs now were a secondary condition. Brown and Fingleton possibly carried caution to excess, but the ironical part is that during the period in which they were jeered at they scored only some fifteen runs fewer in two and a quarter hours than England scored in two and a quarter hours after lunch on the first day of the match when Barnett had landed the lunch score at the vantage point of 169 for no wicket. Fingleton no doubt incensed the crowd by sitting down on the grass, perhaps an unwise gesture. But an appeal against the light was not probably justifiable. But let me get away from paltriness and tell the tale of McCabe's masterpiece. And I will try to describe it in the rhythm of its occurrence, and I hope that my narrative will give the faintest idea of the grand crescendo which crowned all.

Warm sunshine blessed the scene at last this morning, and we now had reason to thank Heaven that Bradman got out in Saturday's darkness; this was his own weather and the wicket still contained runs for the picking, even though marks made by Australia's heavy artillery had slightly roughened the surface. McCabe at once drove Farnes effortlessly through the covers for four; then Farnes bowled Ward. The day began now with Hassett in, small and immaculate as Quaife; he almost played on to Farnes forthwith; the ball gyrated from his bat like a kitten seeking its own tail. Trent Bridge looked handsome; bunting and coloured flags suggest royalty or a fairground with cocoanut shies at Australia's batsmen two a penny. Wright bowled with Farnes straightway, and Hassett tried to drive a quick leg-break on the half-volley; spin caused him to slice the stroke, and Hammond held the inevitable catch at slip. Wright dropped the ball in the rough stuff high enough up the wicket; it would have been impossible to cause as much spin as this on Friday on any part of the pitch. Australia 151 for five, and, I imagine, much distress in the Anthenaeum Club, Melbourne, in the lordly mansions of Toorak, in Castlereagh Street, Sydney, in Wagga Wagga, Bondi, Southport, which is near Brisbane, Adelaide, Perth and Kalgoorlie; in all these places the time would be evening at nine o'clock and the people would be listening, incredulously to the wireless, men and women and boys and girls, even the babies allowed to stay up late for the occasion. And patient ships moving without seeming to move through the blue water of the Pacific on the long way from Colombo to Fremantle would be listening too; cricket girdles the earth nowadays; but I must cease or I shall sound like a cricket dinner at Lord's with Sir Pelham in full song.

McCabe was a great player all the time; he has been out of form, but now, in a severe hour, he held himself calmly, masterfully. But he inspected the pitch once or twice and stabbed late at a ball from Farnes which kept low. The situation became one in which a logical policy of batsmanship was difficult to shape; noon on the third day is too early for defence without runs, yet Australia's position chastened a free swinging stroke. Badcock endured for a while an unnatural life; he reached forward to play back. The English bowling seemed merely steady; I thought to myself now, 'Heaven protect this attack the day Bradman and the others get off with a flying start.' Things continued to go awry with Australia; Badcock tried to cut a potential half-volley, and like Fingleton he played on.

The innings was rent in twain now; McCabe was left standing on a solitary rock of sound technique; between him and the rearguard yawned a chasm. He proceeded to play the cricket of heroic loneliness; he hit Farnes for six to square leg with the serenest sweeping movement. He cut late with the touch of intimate art. Impending disaster did not ruffle him; even a snick through the slips off Farnes was tranquil and graceful. Farnes bowled keenly, accurately, ominously, and fast; Wright at the other end turned his leg-break now and again and avoided too much short stuff. Sinfield's off-breaks had an amiable aspect, but he more than once troubled even McCabe; clearly the turf was now not entirely insensitive to spin. In one other point, too, the English attack at the moment excelled Australia's, a point which had nothing to do with winning the toss; the length was never, or seldom, loose. Barnett defended while McCabe took charge; it is the sure sign of a great batsman that he can at a challenge take charge; what does the term master mean if it does not mean mastery? With his team cornered McCabe played the innings of the match and to make him this compliment is not to forget our Barnett's courage and skill on Friday. But McCabe was so sure an artist, so ripe and, with all his aggression, so stylish and courteous. Australia's Barnett ably put the straight obstructive bat to the ball until after lunch he decided to drive

Farnes, in spite of the new ball; ambition was his undoing, but he served Australia well in a last-minute stand of 67.

Now came the death and glory, brilliance wearing the dress of culture. McCabe demolished the English attack with aristocratic politeness, good taste, and reserve. Claude Duval never took possession of a stage coach with more charm of manner than this; his boundaries were jewels and trinkets which he accepted as though dangling them in his hands. In half an hour after lunch he scored nearly fifty, unhurried but trenchant. He cut and glanced and drove, upright and lissom; his perfection of touch moved the aesthetic sense; this was the cricket of felicity, power and no covetousness, strength and no brutality, opportunism and no meanness, assault and no battery, dazzling strokes and no rhetoric; lovely, brave batsmanship giving joy to the connoisseur, and all done in a losing hour. One of the greatest innings ever seen anywhere in any period of the game's history. Moving cricket which swelled the heart. Not once but many times McCabe has come to Australia's aid in a crucial moment and has played gloriously when others have lost heart; he is in the line of Trumper, and no other batsman today but McCabe has inherited Trumper's sword and cloak.

When McCormick was bowled McCabe was 160; he now scored fifty in a little more than a quarter of an hour. He blinded us with four fours in an over from Wright; his innings became incandescent; he reached his two hundred and received worthy acclamation. He passed Paynter's score with a gesture of magnanimity. The English bowling suffered demoralisation; length and accuracy vanished. A majestic on-drive sent Australia's total beyond four hundred. With consummate judgment he kept the bowling; Fleetwood-Smith was almost as much a spectator as I was. This gorgeous sirocco had a calm pivotal spot; McCabe's mind controlled the whirlwind; his shooting stars flashed safely according to an ordered law of gravitation. He scored 72 out of 77 for the last wicket in half an hour; after lunch he scored 127 in eighty minutes. In all, he scored 232 out of 300 runs in 230 minutes, and hit a six and thirty-four fours.

Brown and Fingleton made, or declined to make, more than 89 in two and a quarter hours; a wonderful left-handed catch by Hammond then accounted for Fingleton amid universal rejoicing. At the evening's misty fall Bradman was as dour as Brown himself; tomorrow he will move heaven and earth to express his gratitude for McCabe's lifeline; and England will move heaven and earth to overwhelm him and all. Another famous day.

THE LORD'S TEST

A T the end of the second day the Test match was in the balance. Against England's 494 Australia had scored 299 for five wickets, during one of the most multitudinous afternoons ever known at Lord's. The gates were locked at a quarter to eleven; the crowd gathered everywhere, sweeping over the boundary-line like a tide. They saw play which is already historic; they saw Hammond's majestic innings come to a proud burgeoning end; this was an innings with a ground-swell and a reverberating full-close. Hammond has never before exhibited a more easeful and comprehensive technique. It was all fit for the throne-room. He made most of the strokes of the game after the manner born. He came to the wicket, on Friday, with England on the edge of crisis: the score was 31 for three.

Paynter was his brave, patient armour-bearer; the little Lancashire man put his canny bat to the ball. Sometimes his feet contradicted the direction of his hits; but that is Paynter's way. He has his humour as well as a quick eye and an ability to play extraordinarily late. The king and his henchman scored 222 for England's fourth wicket; then Ames batted splendidly in the shadow cast by Hammond's radiance. But all of us could see the precise technique of Ames; we are fortunate to possess a wicket-keeper who can make 83 in a Test match against Australia, and make them in a model manner.

England's total at one time on Saturday stood at 457 for six. Another hundred runs were needed to force home the good cause, and to honour the superb salvage work done by the captain (and what a captain!), Paynter and Ames. Wellard batted like the blacksmith on the village green; he clove the stratosphere and was easy game for O'Reilly. England's last four wickets fell on Saturday for 37.

After lunch came the day's irony and drama. Seldom before has fate so sardonically mocked Australian cricketers as now. The wicket seemed easy and hard when Fingleton and Brown scored 69 for the first wicket, scored them at will, without a wrinkle of thought. Then, suddenly, Wright bowled almost the only difficult ball he achieved all day, a pretty leg-spinner which lured Fingleton forward and at the last second whipped away to the bat's edge. Hammond's slip catch was as decisive as it was decorative. Bradman then came forth, and the Australian innings again emerged into full flowing and prosperous seas. A ball or two from Wright gave Bradman cause for second thoughts; but he attacked Farnes, and seemed ready to smash the steady but not difficult English attack. At a quarter past three Australia reached 100 for one; Bradman not out. Resignation came over the crowd like veils. Hammond at this point took Wright off and put Verity on instead.

'A mistake', said the critics, and in theory it was a mistake. 'But grey is all theory, my friend', said Mephistopheles to the student. The material world goes by results. Everything came off for England at Lord's on Saturday, June 25th. Verity sent a widish ball to Bradman, who attempted a cut. To our amazement he chopped his stroke into his stumps. The mighty roar of the crowd must have sounded terrible in his ears.

Then McCabe joined Brown who went his way unperturbed, guarding one end of the wicket safely, waiting for somebody to come in and massacre bowling which he, for the most part, frustrated at leisure. McCabe was in his most hostile mood—charming because he is supple, but with the iron hand under the glove of velvet. He hooked audaciously. He sent a ball from Verity soaring for six, defying the fieldsman at deep square leg. He threatened to put the English attack to the sword again. He lay back to Farnes and cut him with a bat vehemently aimed. We heard the fierce crack of it; we saw the ball, or only just saw it, flashing to

Verity in the 'gully'. Verity hurled himself forward and caught the catch of his life. Australia 152 for three, and the master batsmen out of the way! The crowd beamed on the sunlit world.

Half an hour afterwards, even in less time than that, we tasted the ashes of disillusionment. Brown at last found his partner; Hassett was excellent, steady in defence but quick to belabour the loose ball. He has little height, but he can add to his stature by wonderful footwork. For an hour and a half Brown and Hassett batted together as though sauntering down a pleasant avenue. The English attack seized the new ball, after Australia had gone beyond 200. Farnes for a while troubled Brown with a series of vivid out-swingers. But the power of Farnes suffers curious rises and falls. Brown scraped through the 90's, reached a hundred, and then, like a born Australian, began to begin again. At ten minutes to six Australia were 272 for three. Hammond asked Wellard to swing his arm once more. Wellard so far had bowled with nothing more about him than enthusiasm and a willing heart. Hassett cut him at once, which made Australia 276 for three. The next ball but one, simple and straight, somehow got past Hassett's bat, and Hassett departed l.b.w. And in the same over, Wellard bowled Badcock, for a duck—because Badcock inexplicably played back to a half-volley! I confess I was almost terrified to see these 'accidents' occurring in the Australian innings. There comes a time when luck swings round, when it is the other side that finds that nothing goes right and all goes wrong. At close of play, Brown was still there: suppose Bradman had not chopped that ball into his wickets! But it is these little vagaries which make cricket the game of caprice.

On Saturday evening the wheel of the match swung England's way. The question now was, what of the Lord's wicket? Verity was England's cleverest bowler, and it was significant that he used two slips. Early in the day, O'Reilly and Fleetwood-Smith had both spun the ball. Thus did the week-end leave hope and expectation on tip-toe.

The third day was, for England, ironical. At the morning outset, our bowlers got to work at once; Barnett and Chipperfield were put out unmercifully, and now Australia were

308 for seven. Hammond probably would not have sent Australia in again, even if they had not saved the follow-on. But the stand achieved by O'Reilly and Brown was exasperating and important, because it stole much from England's advantage at a crucial moment. Rain fell later, just before lunch. O'Reilly helped Brown to add 85, and made 42 himself. As a consequence, when England batted again on a rearing pitch, their lead of merely 72 was no sort of reassurance against a turn of fortune caused by the weather. At close of play England had lost Barnett and Hutton for 39, and the match, after all, was anybody's.

O'Reilly drove Verity for two sixes and a four in an over. He was missed off Verity at deep long-off, but Paynter would have needed to jump like a performing monkey to hold the catch. It was, I thought, a mistake of Verity, to bowl from round the wicket to O'Reilly. From over the wicket, he might have forced O'Reilly to reach to the off side—and O'Reilly does not like to reach. It strains his anatomy. We could understand the difficulty experienced by England's bowlers against Brown. He is a proper batsman—a model of uprightness and straightness. He carried his bat through the innings, was undefeated at the end for a double century. He took charge of Australia's position with remarkable command after Bradman and McCabe had fallen. He is only a young man; but he has a shrewd old head. As I say, we could understand *his* mastery. But O'Reilly!—well, he is a great bowler and a vulnerable defender of his own stumps. Yet nobody could apparently pitch him a quick 'yorker', or a quick ball short of hitting length. Even Fleetwood-Smith was able to stay in with Brown and hold Australia's last wicket for 45 minutes—until the grass had dried and spared Australia's bowlers the handicap of a greasy ball at the beginning of England's second innings.

We left Lord's on Monday evening hoping for the best, yet ready for anything. And we knew, more than ever, that England's bowling was not much better than Australia's. I doubt if poorer bowling than this year's has ever been witnessed in Test matches between England and Australia. No wonder that, already, four double centuries have been scored by batsmen in the first two games of the rubber. Shortly, if this goes on, a batsman will be dropped if he gets merely a morsel of a seventy or an eighty!

AFTERMATH OF LEEDS

THE sudden end of the match at Leeds has set many people arguing hotter than ever against the idea of extending time for Tests in England. But there is an old saying—it was, I think, Huxley's: What a pity that a plain fact should ever upset a beautiful theory! Besides, it is not simply a theory that four days are not enough for the finishing of a game between England and Australia. The conditions at Leeds were not normal; not once in a blue moon could they occur at Trent Bridge, Manchester, or at the Oval. There was a peculiar atmosphere at Leeds, peculiar even for Leeds, an atmosphere which helped the swing bowlers. On the Saturday darkness fell upon the scene. Moreover, the batting on both sides suffered inexplicably from nerves. At any rate, though we might grant that four days would probably bring in a decision to a Test match at Leeds most seasons, the fact remains that all the other grounds, with the possible exception of Lord's, would not favour a summary end in dry weather.

What are the arguments against an extension of the time limit? Let me be frank and give an account of the change in my own views on the subject. Like most middle-aged Englishmen, I was brought up on the three-day Test match. And well do I remember the farcical rubber of 1899, in which Australia won the second and drew the remaining four. Until as recently as the autumn of 1936, I clung obstinately to the conviction that the played-out Test match meant certain dullness. I had no logic to support this conviction—it was an Englishman's conviction; that is to say, it was based on nothing but habit and prejudice. Then, in 1936, I went to Australia and witnessed a rubber played under no-time-limit conditions. I was delighted. As soon as the first match of that rubber began at Brisbane, as soon as the first ball was bowled, my imagination thrilled at this thought: 'Heavens, one of these teams is doomed; somebody must lose; nothing can save one or the other. The match is a trap; there is no escape!'

At once I realised that where there is no time limit to frustrate destiny, *there can be no slow play*. Every ball is a nail in somebody's coffin, in a match fought to the finish. Slow cricket is exasperating only when we know it is wasting time, leading to stalemate. It is absurd that the nation's sporting instincts should be stirred by the advent of a Test match between England and Australia; that thousands of enthusiasts should flock to see the play; that all over the Empire people should hang on to each moment—only at last to see all the skill and contriving rendered null and void, because of the interference of the clock.

Now I am not about to agitate for the played-out Test match in this country. There are clinching objections against it. I do not refer to the inroads which the played-out match would make on county cricket. Without Test matches between England and Australia, county cricket would be in the bankruptcy court in next to no time. Once in every four years the county season could well afford to take a second, even a back, seat to Test matches. (And there should be Test matches only between England and Australia and England and South Africa in this country.) The case against played-out Tests here goes beyond the momentary interests of the counties, who, as we have seen, profit in the long run. The main point is that most games between England and Australia would run their course *within* five days. Even the match on the feather-bed at Nottingham in June would have reached a decision on a fifth day. And if the Test match at Manchester had been a played-out affair we might have waited a fortnight not only for a finish but for a beginning!

The English are a people who thrive on compromise. The clash of opinions upon the duration of Test matches in the future will merge into an amenable policy of give-and-take. The Leeds holocaust must not be used as a red herring. Let us agitate for six-day Tests in this country, knowing that by asking for six days we shall be granted five. But even with a five-day limit granted, there must be a certain proviso. The groundsman must curb his zeal for a wicket built not for five days but for all time. Here we arrive at the old difficulty—no set rules can be laid down for the treatment of soils of different localities. Still, there are the teachings of experience —a groundsman who knows his job at all knows when to stop, knows when he is preparing a turf which will unfairly, or unreasonably, handicap the bowler.

But we are here discussing the future of Test matches merely as affairs governed by the material circumstances of soil, clay, manure, dung. There is surely the spirit, the will to play the game. If a good batsman deliberately puts aside all scoring strokes, there is no reason why, on a good wicket, he should not stay in all day. I can foresee that under a five-day limit batsmen may set themselves for 200 or 300; that a score of 600 all out will be the general aim.

If cricket is to be allowed to degenerate into a mechanical matter, then there is no telling what robots the game may not evolve for us. But a cricket match should never become a sequence of automatic adjustments between the players and their material environment. *Captaincy should determine the issue*; stalemate can be avoided, in all circumstances, by the will to win. A few years ago our county cricket was perishing for want of enterprise and purpose. The Lancashire and Yorkshire match, for example, seldom reached a decision; the uninitiated blamed the wickets, but the draws occurred 'on principle'. Mind you, they were not always the dreary draws that folk in the South imagined they were; there was humour in the determination of both sides not to do anything at all for three days. Rhodes used to pitch a run-saving length, rather wide to the off—pitch it to dear old Harry Makepeace, who would not have dreamed of hitting a ball, not before lunch anyhow—no, not if it had been offered to him on a plate.

But the custom staled. A new attitude entered the Lancashire and Yorkshire match, and now they come to an end—sometimes. A game, like any other activity in life, is controlled by the will of those engaged in it. Five days would guarantee conclusive Test matches in this country, would provide against a blank day because of weather, and would challenge the ambition of the combatants, and give scope for putting ambition into force.

BEFORE THE FIFTH TEST

U NDOUBTEDLY the fifth and last Test match of the rubber will not, whatever happens, cloud our eyesight to one or two important facts which have emerged since the engagement at Trent Bridge in June raised hopes that at last we were about to witness an overthrowal of Australian cricket.

It seemed then, surely, that our batsmen had laid the old 'bogy', and had escaped from a sense of inferiority against O'Reilly and his colleagues. The fact was widely advertised that this Australian team lacked collective greatness; it was a one- or two-man show. And since the month of June events have emphasised the lack of all-round distinction in the ranks of our ancient foemen; at any rate, several of them have sadly failed to reproduce in this country the skill which in their own country brought them into prominence. McCormick has been a shadow of himself; Badcock, Fingleton, White, Ward, Fleetwood-Smith and McCabe have all sadly disappointed their admirers.

The team, indeed, has been a two-man show. But, if it comes to that, *Othello* is a 'two-man show'. It is easy to say, 'Take Bradman and O'Reilly out of the Australian XI and it would be pretty poor.' Maybe; take Othello and Iago out of the play and it would not be as good as it is. Take only Hammond out of the England team . . . !

We live in lean days. When people claim that Bradman is the greatest batsman of all time, do they pause to ask if Bradman has ever had to face great slow left-handed bowling on soft pitches, season after season, or great fast bowling most days? At the present time there is not a single great fast bowler to be found anywhere. And Verity, the only slow left-handed bowler of any account, does not spin the ball as cunningly as Blythe did, or Rhodes, or Parker—not to go back to the legendary Bobby Peel. I have watched cricket for more than 30 years, and I cannot remember the time when bowling in first-class cricket in all parts of the world was as bad as it is at the present time. O'Reilly is the only living cricketer who would stand a chance of getting a place as a bowler in the Australian team of 1902—nay, in the Australian side of 1921.

A few years ago, England's attack consisted of Tate, Larwood, Geary, J. C. White and Robins (when he really could spin a leg-break). Bowlers of the calibre of Kennedy, Newman, Freeman, Mercer, and Astill never received invitations to play for England against Australia in England. This year Leyland is near the top of the English bowling averages! C. B. Fry once captained an England eleven which possessed something like the following attack: Barnes, F. R. Foster, Woolley, Dean, J. W. H. T. Douglas, and Hearne (J. W.). Maurice Tate in his form of 1924 was worth two contemporary English bowlers at least. These are facts which must be borne in mind when we enter on the indivious job of making comparisons between Bradman and other great batsmen.

I find that most players now in the game agree that nobody in modern cricket has equalled Hobbs on all pitches, in all parts of the world, and against all sorts of bowling. I think the position of Hobbs as the greatest since 'W.G.' is an unassailable one. The three greatest, on all wickets, were 'W.G.', Hobbs, and Arthur Shrewsbury—I speak of Englishmen, and do not forget Victor Trumper and Ranjitsinhji.

Lean days we live in, surely, when we cannot beat an Australian team which includes several players who would not make a great noise in the world if they played for an ordinary English county. It boils down, no doubt, to Bradman and O'Reilly. Yet why? Bradman we can all understand; on a good wicket he is the master. Of O'Reilly it must be admitted that he commands a technique, that he knows where he is pitching the ball, that he can spin a 'googly' and suggest a leg-break, and best of all, can keep a length and vary his flight. But in Test cricket, these qualities have been common enough always.

I decline to believe that the collapse of the English batsmen at Leeds was entirely a triumph of technique—'Was it scare?

Kangaroo-land's demon bowler, or our own lack of courage, nerve, backbone?' At Leeds, irresolute footwork was discernible throughout England's second innings; our batsmen took up paralytic attitudes confidently assumed to be those of self-defence. But I do not believe that first-class cricketers, taking them as a whole, lose representative matches by what the average man calls 'the dithers'. 'Temperament' is a vague matter, and is governed considerably by skill.

At Trent Bridge the English batsmen suffered no qualms against O'Reilly. But at Trent Bridge the wicket was so perfect that O'Reilly could not spin the ball. His success at Leeds was, I think, due in part to the fact that he could turn the ball there. More important, though, was the psychological effect of the spin on the English players' minds, because as a class English batsmen are, nowadays, not trained day by day to cope with spin pitched with unerring accuracy. At Leeds, in England's second innings, at least half-a-dozen of our best batsmen played back to balls from O'Reilly, which invited forward strokes. Hardstaff's stumps were shattered as he stabbed late off the back foot to a potential and quick half-volley, which broke after dropping. But it should not have been allowed to drop.

An O'Reilly is rare in cricket of the moment, simply because he seldom bowls rubbish.

HUTTON AT THE OVAL

Monday, August 22nd

THE crowd was immense for the final Test match here today, congested to acute discomfort on the stony popular side, and at half-past eleven nearly everybody not in one of the stands received a slight drenching from a shower which held play back until five minutes to twelve.

In O'Reilly's first over Fingleton misfielded, and as the batsman hesitated I thought that the Australians were at once resorting to attempts at run-outs as the most likely way of dealing with their problem—trying to persuade Leyland and Hutton to 'linger out a purposed overthrow'—which is not a quotation from a cricket book but from one of the sonnets of Shakespeare. Hutton got to work immediately with a glorious off-drive from Fleetwood-Smith, and then a roar of applause recognised the fact that the partnership had become the most prolific in all the history of Test matches. Fleetwood-Smith settled into a length of extraordinary steadiness for a bowler who tries as hard as he does to spin, and Hutton played him with an exemplary forward method. O'Reilly, too, needed careful scrutiny; the bowling was less harmless hereabout than it ever was on Saturday. But Leyland drove O'Reilly straight for four, a quick and impertinent hit, late and power-ful, a real smack in the face.

At twenty minutes to one Fleetwood-Smith beat Leyland by means of a lovely spinner which flashed inches over the stumps; Leyland was not half as startled as Fleetwood-Smith. Fifty runs only were scored in the first hour, too many of them from absurd short ones, with Leyland responsible for the risk; he probably wished to keep himself and the crowd awake, but a better way was a brilliant cover-drive, which he thumped from Waite and sent up to 400. Fleetwood-Smith's bowling in this first hour was beautiful; on a fair pitch he would have taken wickets; his fine art was abused by the groundsmen's drowsy syrups.

Then, at ten minutes past one, the partnership ended in the way, the only way, it had ever seemed likely to end. Hutton pushed a ball to the off from O'Reilly, Hassett misfielded, and Leyland went for a second run comically dangerous and unnecessary. He was out easily, and so we shall never know how long it would have taken the Australian bowlers to break the stand by their own devices. It put on 382 in some six and a quarter hours—which, of course, was the duration of Leyland's innings of 187.

Hammond came in with the score 411 for two and banged Fleetwood-Smith for four straight and pulled him round for four and rifled the over for a dozen. Next over he again pulled Fleetwood-Smith for four, a great scythe of a stroke; he scored twenty in a quarter of an hour before lunch and suggested the cavalry charge after the infantry's sturdy preparation, if one may use obsolete military language, probably incorrectly. But after the interval the plan of campaign was reconsidered, and another dour piece of sapping was undertaken, slow and industrious. Hutton reached 200 after eight hours of incredible accuracy. Then, like a proper Test match batsman, he proceeded to play himself thoroughly in and did nothing perceptible for half an hour, until the green light shone once more in his mind and he hit Waite through the covers for four—as perfect a drive as any connoisseur could wish to see. All in all, though, no risks were taken; so far the only risk taken in the innings was the risk of a short run. Fingleton left the field because of cramp—I wondered that O'Reilly did not leave the field because of Hutton. The Australians stuck to the hopeless toil philosophically and Bradman changed his bowling, and the umpires counted the overs, and the runs mounted, and the clouds rolled on, and the gas-holder went up and down, and the trams went by the ground, and the hours waxed and waned, and somewhere even the weariest river wound safe to sea.

When Hutton was 215 Waite twice beat him, or rather, got a ball past his bat, which in this match meant the same thing. Hammond after lunch compiled 16 in an hour to Hutton's 24. The cavalry had gone back to the stables, while the sky threatened plenty of rain and a pretty wicket for Australia's innings. I wondered what Waite and O'Reilly were thinking about as they bowled and bowled, and also I wondered what Hutton and Hammond were thinking about as they batted and batted. And I could not guess at all why, when they struck a four, they did so off one kind of ball rather than off another of much the same kind. Drinks were served on the field when England were 485 for two, then Hutton made another of his glorious drives to the off. He was, for all his slowness, always pretty to see in the eyes of the close student of batsmanship; technically he is easily the best of our young batsmen; he knows the grammar backwards. His defensive play is elegant because mostly he moves forward. And he never, needless to say, wastes energy.

Hutton at 228 snicked Fleetwood-Smith to leg for four when he was trying to drive. The mishap was a faint proof that we were watching human and fallible batsmen. Five hundred was reached at twenty-five minutes to four, after the innings had lasted for more than nine hours, in which time the Australian bowlers had taken a wicket. Hereabout Fleetwood-Smith beat Hammond twice in an over, which was an achievement. Australia's only two bowlers were noble in their faith and persistence, and a question which may now have occurred to some spectators was whether O'Reilly was bald before the game began on Saturday or had gone bald since then. Hammond added 27 after lunch in an hour and a half. Hutton outpaced him, passed Hammond's score of 240 made at Lord's, and then stopped another good ball from Fleetwood-Smith with the side of his bat. Fleetwood-Smith enjoyed not the slightest luck and scarcely seemed to expect any.

The crowd did not find the slow batting objectionable. They were revelling in their heart's desire, but I tremble to think what they would have said if the Australians had stone-walled with their grand total 520 for two. The press would have been husky with letters about it tomorrow. Hutton, at 246, cocked a ball from Fleetwood-Smith to the off side. It was a capital ball, too, which actually spun. Few bowlers have bowled as well and for so long as Fleetwood-Smith in this match and for such scant reward. The batsmen continued to take risks with short runs, but nobody would risk a catch in the unguarded acres of the outfield. Hammond's 50 occupied him for two hours, in spite of his busy prelude before lunch. The batting since lunch had become rather unchivalrous. At four o'clock England had increased Saturday's total of 347 for one to 530 for two—183 in three hours and three-quarters. I cannot remember that any Australian team in the same strong, not to say impregnable, position has batted as slowly as this. A pretty late cut by Hutton came as gushing water in a desert.

A quarter of an hour from the tea interval two wickets suddenly fell, to the general bewilderment—it was as though the Gorner glacier had leaped forward. Hammond was leg-before to Fleetwood-Smith, and justly to Fleetwood-Smith. And at 547 Paynter also succumbed l.b.w. to O'Reilly; he made a duck, which was clever of him on this wicket. So far three wickets had fallen l.b.w. and the other was a run out, after ten hours' play for 550. The stumps were a survival from a distant epoch in the game's development; they were like a little toe on the human foot. During the afternoon there was faint evidence that the turf was beginning to take spin a little; at any rate, Fleetwood-Smith caused Hammond to stab late, and, as I say, Hutton once got a ball on to the side of the bat.

During the tea interval rain again descended gently, so that cricket was delayed until five o'clock, when the Australians returned to the field leaping and gambolling like spring lambs. Bradman tossed the ball about and played a sort of 'tick' or 'chase me' game with somebody. You would have thought that they were beating England easily. In Waite's first over after tea Compton played forward and was clean bowled —the most extraordinary occurrence of the match; I wonder that the bails came off; they might well have been fossilised. England were blotting their innings; three wickets had fallen while nine runs were scored—Hammond's, Paynter's and Compton's, and the total was the beggarly one of 555 for five at five o'clock.

Hardstaff forced Waite to the square-leg boundary, one of the best strokes of a generally strokeless day, a stroke quick and supple at the wrists. And slowly Hutton went his way towards passing R. E. Foster's 287 amassed in 1904 in Australia, the highest innings until today by an English batsman, and made because J. T. Tyldesley batted a sticky wicket dry before Foster went in. Hutton reached 288 out of 600 at twenty minutes to six, a remarkable performance.

The cricket grew in style and animation, thanks largely to Hardstaff, whose strokes possessed lustre. An off-drive by him put cricket's clock back nearly half a century—left leg forward and the flashing bat. And this time he played Fleetwood-Smith forward with some confidence, not back, as usually he has done, with the air of a man gulping down a beating heart. At his best Hardstaff is an artist, a spreader of delight, not one of the bricklayers and hod-carriers. He nearly lamed McCabe at silly mid-on with a terrific drive off O'Reilly; McCabe we glad to turn his back on the terrific missile which he saw coming at him. Somebody will (and should) be killed some day fielding in that position of bluff.

One of the sights of the evening was O'Reilly and

Fleetwood-Smith chasing a hit to third man, running a race—with both of them I take it, conceding weight. All day the Australians fielded well, and Bradman placed them thoughtfully.

Barnes bowled leg-spin towards six o'clock and Hardstaff's cricket now suffered the familiar bend at the knees. One ball kept low, and Hardstaff was nearly leg-before. This sign of quick, low spin probably disconcerted Bradman as much as it disconcerted Hardstaff; it may have been a sign of wrath to come, and just as we were proclaiming Hutton's 300 the rain came once more, still gently, but with a sky that probably caused the ghost of a smile to appear on the face of Verity, who as a rule is not given to smiling at small things.

*   *   *

Tuesday, August 23rd

This afternoon just before tea Bradman was bowling and England were 887 for seven, which was the equal of the highest score ever made in a first-class match in England. Suddenly Bradman fell to the ground in utter collapse. He had severely sprained an ankle and was sent from the ground to be X-rayed. For hours Bradman had worked hard and tirelessly, always leading his men, never slackening effort, always cheerful and inspiring. He was carried from the field, and the crowd stood up in silence, as though at a valedictory ceremony. With Fingleton also out of the match, through a strained muscle, Australia's cup was 'bitter full. As Bradman is unable to bat at all the match has been ruined as a contest, which is wretched luck for England as well as for Australia, because England will be deprived of full credit for victory, after a remarkable, not to say relentless, exhibition of batting.

For seventy-five minutes this morning Hutton kept the great crowd on a rack of suspense, we were all waiting for him to beat Bradman's record of 334, the highest in a Test match between England and Australia. When he was 311 a beautiful ball from Fleetwood-Smith nearly bowled him; Fleetwood-Smith's luck in the English innings was sinful. Slowly the minutes went by, Hardstaff was often uneasy and doubled up against the slow bowling, and though he occasionally made a glorious stroke, we could not enjoy them. Everybody ached for Hutton's sake; we trembled to think that on the verge of achievement he might fail, get run out, or die, or something. At half-past twelve Hardstaff drove a no-ball from O'Reilly straight for four, and the Fleetwood-Smith came on again, with Hutton's total 326. Hutton pulled his first ball to the boundary, and in the same over got a single, which took him opposite O'Reilly, who proceeded to bowl a no-ball, which Hutton missed entirely, while the crowd groaned disappointment. O'Reilly attacked fiercely to keep the record in Australia, but Hutton obtained another single, then against Fleetwood-Smith he made a grand late cut and his score became 336.

The scene which now occurred moved even the hardened critics. Thousands of happy people stood up and cheered. Somebody with a cornet began to play 'For he's a jolly good fellow' and the crowd took up the refrain in that evangelical tone which the British public invariably adopts when it lifts up its heart to rejoice in song. Moreover, the voices and the cornet did not keep together—but in the circumstances I admit that to say so is a piece of pedantic musical criticism. Bradman shook hands with the hero, all the Australians shook hands with him, journeying to the wicket from the remoter parts of the Oval—all except tired Bill O'Reilly, who lay prone on the grass until he saw a man coming out with drinks, when he got up at once and made for him, in a hurry. The cheers broke out again as soon as Hutton went beyond 336 and exceeded Hammond's innings against New Zealand. Hutton took the occasion with a charming modesty. He raised his cap in acknowledgment of the honours done to him, and bent his head. But what a moment for him!—the moment of his life.

1950–51

THE AUSTRALIAN TEST SERIES
THE BATTLE OF BRISBANE

THE remarkable fact about cricket in Australia—where from a population less than London's teams are easily assembled year after year as good as, and often better than, our best—is that little first-class cricket is played in Australia. The great grounds of Sydney, Melbourne and Adelaide lie empty day after day; the amount of cricket involved by the Sheffield Shield competition could be fitted into a month of an English summer. Australian Test match players emerge mainly from Saturday afternoon engagements in the 'grades'. And owing to Australia's rapid twilights—it is dark at seven o'clock or thereabouts—evening practice is out of the question.

At the earliest opportunity I saw Lindwall bowling against Queensland. He was not fast, but the easy rhythm of his action seemed in my eyes terribly potential. A week later he was still holding himself in check against the MCC, excepting one sudden and sinister spurt with the new ball.

Opinion here is divided about Lindwall, but Arthur Morris, the New South Wales captain and a close friend of Lindwall, said to me the other day: 'He'll be all right when we get to grips . . .' Keith Miller, whose fast bowling in 1948 was as much respected by the English batsmen as Lindwall's, doesn't wish to bowl much nowadays. 'I think I'll go in for batting,' he told me the other week; then proceeded to score a double-century against the MCC.

There is usually a thunderstorm at Brisbane. When Hammond's team played there in 1946, the thunderstorm that struck us was really awe-inspiring. Strong men battle-scarred in the war just over then, quailed as the sky became pitch-black, and the lightning forked and the heavens exploded, and hailstones big as cricket balls descended, and the field was flooded, and furious winds removed the roofs from wooden houses. But next day, when we went to the ground, the waters had subsided—nay, vanished. The earth sprouted green in the burning heat. Palm trees displayed primary colours. It was a Test match as though played in Joseph Conrad and the Old Testament.

Weather, of course, was the villain of the piece at Brisbane during the first Test and again England the victim. It was all ironic and eccentric, the larger lunacy of cricket. I must first point out that sticky pitches in Australia and sticky pitches in England are as different as the ravening tiger from the subtle rattlesnake. English turf after rain and sun does not render scientific batsmanship inapplicable and impossible: in Australia the behaviour of the ball after it has dropped on sticky turf suggests that it is entering another dimension, a dimension not yet suspected by Einstein. A good length delivery may suddenly rise straight up and remove the batsman's cap: or it may skid like a stone thrown over ice.

On Monday, December 5, twenty wickets fell for 130; England scored 68 for seven and declared, Australia scored 32 for seven and also declared; then England, in again to try to get 193 for victory, lost six for 30. The declarations of Brown and Hassett were both sensible in the circumstances, even if governed by the sort of logic that persuades a man to attempt to get out of a burning building by a window on the eighth floor when the fire brigade and escape have gone home by mistake. The bitterness of the pill which Brown and his men had to swallow was intensified by the fact that on the first day England bowlers and fieldsmen achieved a really brilliant piece of work by dismissing Australia for the very poor total of 228 on a wicket excellent enough for good batsmen. An additional flavour of acidity was contributed by a superb innings by Hutton at the death on the closing morning, after the turf had lost one or two fangs: and Hutton was twice not out in the match, heroically invincible, but with no survivors to help him as he was obviously storming to triumph. Waste, waste. In the second innings Hutton was held back in England's batting order to strengthen the dubious middle regions, in the belief that the pitch would diminish its venom. But in the wild and whirring Monday evening his emotions are best left to imagination, as he watched Bedser, Bailey, McIntyre, each throw his innings away thrusting for runs, when close of play was near in a shocking light and when the plain policy was to endure until tomorrow's better opportunity with Hutton, and possibly Compton, England's main hopes.

As far as speculation at cricket can ever pretend to be demonstrative and conclusive, we may safely argue that the Brisbane match was thrown away in less than twenty minutes through most culpable carelessness on the part of three players whose duty it was to nerve themselves, nose down to the ball, as sturdy obstructive helpmates of Hutton. Compton failed badly first ball at the crucial moment, but even than, and in spite of the weather, the chances are that Hutton would have cut and driven his course through to a victory second to none, if somebody could have stayed with him for just another hour. The pity of it! I have for long opposed the argument put forward some weeks ago that Hutton should be sent in to bat for England 'to stiffen the middle'. A dangerous expedient at most times: a desperate expedient if your reserves of batsmen are weak after the fall of the third or fourth wicket, for obviously you will expose your Hutton to want of opportunity to finish his innings: in other words he might easily be left stranded not out. In certain circumstances there is a surface case in favour of withholding a great batsman from the attack: for instance, as at Brisbane, if there is a prospect that the wicket will get easier. But when all is said and done, I find it difficult to lend approval to any move of tactics that involves waste of the world's greatest sticky wicket player. And it was for fear of a sticky wicket that Hutton was sent in number eight.

There's the humour of it. Another laugh on the wrong side of the face is provoked by the fact, or the thought, that throughout this Brisbane match England bowled and fielded better than Australia, and contributed the one and only unmistakably great example of individual batsmanship. On the sticky wicket Australia at one period were no runs for the loss of Moroney, Morris and Loxton. At the finish, when

England were in the throes and only Wright retained from the
wreck to stonewall while Hutton attacked, the Australian
bowling visibly faltered in the face of Hutton's withering but
finely concentrated and controlled power: he drove and cut
Lindwall vehemently yet with the utmost ease: there was no
hurrying. Every stroke, though rapid and merciless, was
perfect in poise: it was an innings that showed us the cool
pivotal spot at the heart of the storm: it was one of the most
classical innings of our time in execution, and one of the most
romantic in spirit. I wonder why Hutton does not oftener take
the offensive when wickets are good and the wind is in his
team's favour. He is the most versatile stroke player of our
day as well as the most thoroughly organised in defence. (His
beautifully timed back play in this match to Iverson's spin was
a model for all students of cricket, Compton not excepted).
Maybe like most of us he is inspired to his best visions and
deeds by lost causes and the feeling that what he is now risking
will hurt nobody but himself.

As I left the Brisbane cricket ground on Tuesday, December 5, to the recuperation of the groundsman and the record-
ings of overworked historians in the press box, I tortured
myself with the memory of Edrich's stouthearted resistance
on this very same battleground four years ago, on a wicket
even more difficult than this of England's latest undoing. He
would have made a pleasant sight for Hutton had he come to
the wicket when England in their second innings were 46 for
seven.

The rubber is already half in the grip of Australia; and there
are likely to be heartbreaking pitches waiting at Sydney,
Adelaide and Melbourne, to test faith, philosophy and
physical staying power on the part of Wright, Bedser and
Bailey. The Australian batsmen are already smacking lips in
anticipation: it is also possible that they wish to eliminate
from their minds every impression of their fallibility, not to
say futility, on the fantastica, comica, illogical, and diabolical
bowlers' paradise of Woolloongabba.

MELBOURNE AND SYDNEY

T HE second Test Match, played at Melbourne, will long be remembered—worth a journey across the world, if ever a game was. For the Englishman, the issue of it all had a quite sickening irony. I have known no other match of which you might say, as might safely be said of this one, that the victory and the defeat hung on and was decided by a single ball, by a single false step by a great batsman. England wanted 179 runs to win. When the fourth and closing day arrived, England had scored 28 of these 179 for the loss of Washbrook's and Bailey's wickets. Everything depended on Hutton. And there's the sardonic rub: he, Hutton, a Yorkshireman compact and composed of patience, succumbed at the pinch, at the turning-point, to an impatient impulse . . . England 92 for four: 87 behind, every run a milestone on a road of travail; but we were 'making it', Hutton the master of all he surveyed. Then Hutton suddenly drove with a spasm of belligerent opportunism across the length of a ball from Johnston pitched well forward and not too quick. At the last second's last fraction he apparently tried to check the swing of his bat—too late. The ball went straight up, a 'skier' close to the square-leg umpire. Lindwall was obliged to wait a little for the easy catch to fall into his hands . . . The crude 'skier' beggared England's opportunity to win and caused immediate bankruptcy. And there was another dish of acidity for our palate at the 'death'; Bedser not out 14, played the Australian bowling, for all its access of voracity after Hutton's downfall, with the utmost confidence, moving forward where others had remained behind the crease. I decline to believe that Bedser would not have accompanied Hutton to an English victory.

It is pretty certain that if England's task on this bodeful afternoon had been to score 179 in two hours and a half, the match would have been won by England, probably by three wickets. As it was, England batted four hours twenty minutes for 150, on a wicket very much in the batsman's favour.

Ian Johnson and Iverson exploited their off-spin without a deep field in the straight on-side. The match was lost by batsmen who would not leave the crease. The accurate Australian attack was 'giving nothing away'. And Brown, the hero of England's first innings, batted 42 minutes for 8; Evans 9 minutes for 2; Parkhouse 102 minutes for 28; Hutton 124 minutes for 40. England missed a main chance. F. R. Brown might well have felt an acute lowering of the spirits when once more he lost the toss, but he has a John Bullish determination not to bow before circumstances if he can help it; and he and his men went into action with visible eagerness and appetite. In this first day there was nothing for the connoisseur better than Bedser's bowling. In a world governed more by justice than this one, he would have been rewarded by four wickets at least before lunch; and not only was his attack a challenge to the finest skill in contemporary batsmanship but also it was beautiful to watch and, surely, a pleasure to play and counter.

The first ball of Bedser's second over veered from the off-stump, as Morris found himself stretching forward more than he really wished to go; a catch at second-slip was a clear case of effect following from cause. Harvey, in next, enjoyed —or did he?—a charmed life during his first overs from Bedser. Beautiful bowling indeed, making us recall the un-paralleled performance of Barnes years ago, also at Mel-bourne. Harvey, though, missed no opportunity to display a glorious stroke or two, he cut Wright's loose stuff with the swordsman's clean flash of decision. And Archer pluckily put his nose to the grindstone; he looked vulnerable all the time, but somehow he hung on and persisted. A brilliant catch by Evans accounted for Harvey from a leg-glance, executed very late. A taste of blood quickened Bailey's zeal; he bowled with rare and renewed gusto, and received compensation for a few frustrations when Bedser, at second-slip, held one-handed a mishit by Archer travelling swift as a bird on the wing. Miller was beginning to look dangerous when he was adjudged l.b.w. He is one of the few batsmen of the present day always, or at most times, swift to attack and reluctant to fall back on passive resistance. He is refreshing to watch, tossing back the black mane of his hair, tall, athletic, aquiline. But he is not so much a great batsman as a brilliant improviser of strokes. There are holes in his defence, and he cannot check an impulse even when his reason steps in just in time.

It was when Miller was out—Australia now 93 for four wickets—that we were given to understand that yet again a Test Match was being fought on a pitch fair to good batsmen and good bowlers alike. To the surprise of one and all, Australia's innings was all over and done with before six o'clock—close of play in Australia ('stumps', they laconically call it), the total a mere 194, Hassett top scorer with 52. The Melbourne crowd, one of the most generously 'sporting' I have known or seen in a lifetime, expressed a huge satisfaction at England's astonishing advance. 'Now's your chance!' they roared to F. R. Brown. And the least optimistic of England's supporters (in the Press Box) believed that at last luck had turned England's way and had delivered the enemy into our hands. Sleep on this Friday night was disturbed only by pleasant dreams.

The awakening was rude and disillusioning. Next morning England's major batsmen were deplorable on a wicket still not unfriendly to purposeful forward strokes. Six wickets fell for 61; then F. R. Brown made a leonine retaliation in an innings of John Bullish and Johnsonian girth, blood and authority. Brown received gallant aid from Bailey and the irrepressible Evans; but as we looked on and admired a rearguard action of pluck we could only regret, yet again, a wasted opportunity. Simpson faltered at the morning's outset, caught in the slips off Miller from an ordinary quick, not fast, outswinger, the sort of ball Sutcliffe invariably disdained to have anything to do with. Dewes promised to stay at the crease by sheer adhesiveness, a sort of figured bass to Washbrook; a wonderful catch got him out. Miller dived low at rare speed, his movement as beautiful as swift, and held a mishit of extraordinary velocity. A moment afterwards Washbrook was leg-before to a not particularly vivid ball from Lindwall. O, these contemporary batsmen of ours!—they will take the most grave risks in cricket, especially in Australia, by putting legs in front of the stumps, leaving themselves at the umpire's mercy: they prefer to endanger themselves this way than employ a bold straight bat full face forward! This was a nasty enough pill to swallow; but soon another one stuck in the throat of every Englishman present; and not a few Australians could not stomach it. Hutton went back correctly to cope with an off-spinner from Iverson; as far as I could observe he decided to play no stroke, and the ball struck his pads or some part of his lower body, bouncing high above the wickets. 'Catch it!' cried Iverson, and Tallon, the wicket-keeper, obeyed with glee and leisure. Hutton did not think he was out, but the umpire decreed Hutton's bat had made fatal contact.

Parkhouse hinted of a liking for hits of culture to the off, though his general aspect recalled the old hymn: 'Brief life is here our portion'. Brown demonstrated how old-fashioned folk consider a cricket bat, and its uses, by swinging it aggressively; Bailey defended while 65 precious runs were added for the seventh wicket. A superb ball from Lindwall bowled him; Lindwall nowadays seemingly smoulders for an hour then erupts, a sort of Mount Etna of fast bowlers. Brown drove a mighty six to the straight boundary, a little to the on, a rubicund blow, infused with his own nature. He was belligerent but not indiscreet until he misjudged when he was 64; and Evans batted like a cheeky cockney, hopping on his feet down the pitch. A drive by Evans to the off from Miller was faultless. A 'bumper' from Miller didn't disconcert him in the least; he put up his nose as though smelling it. A tumult of applause announced that England, after all, had just got in front of Australia's 194; and the reception of Evans back to the pavilion—caught trying to hit the ball out of sight—was, like Brown's, of the warmth that fills the heart and makes the lover of cricket love the game more than ever. The crowd was worthy of the match and a great ground. I gathered that nearly everybody was wanting England to win.

No cricket pitch could be expected to behave itself soberly if left alone for two days, least of all an Australian pitch at Christmastime. So on Tuesday, December 26, when the struggle was resumed, it was not as most folk expected it would inevitably be, a batsman's holiday on a turf now dry and purified of all the acidity in its system the previous days. From noon to six o'clock, the fight was bitter indeed, interrupted only by the usual and, this time, necessary intervals for lunch and tea. It was indeed one of the most astonishing and enthralling days in all my experience of cricket. But not immediately did a cloud appear in Australia's azure heaven. Morris not out 10, Archer not out 15 continued Australia's second innings; three runs only behind England, ten wickets in hand. From the first ball Bedser and Bailey counter-attacked from the position to which England had been thrown on Saturday. A great crowd attended, breathless every ball, now silent, now explosive. Now and then a ball did not rise very much after pitching, though never did we see an authentic shooter. For an hour or so I resigned myself to long slow attrition, while Morris and Archer laboured to reduce Bedser, Bailey and Brown to moist, unpleasant and ineffectual bodies. Only one wicket fell before lunch and in 90 minutes only 50 runs were made, with menacing deliberation. Morris abruptly got out by making no stroke at a well-flighted length from Wright, whose bowling as a whole in a low-scoring match was fatally bad and expensive. None of us foresaw the wrath soon to come, not even when a clever slip-catch accounted for young Archer, who has the root of solid attractive batsmanship in him, straight with 'nose to the ball'. The fever and fun set in when Harvey was run out by a throw in a thousand. He backed up impulsively to a hard defensive stab by Miller at a surprisingly quick ball from Wright; Washbrook, running to the right of cover, picked up swiftly, and as Wright had not yet recovered from his ponderous windmill energy of action, Washbrook had virtually to aim at one stump. Harvey, yards out, threw his chin up, expressing misfortune and philosophy.

Miller showed desperate fight; his aggression hinted of some mental unease, as though he were instinctively realising that Australia after all were not to voyage in calm seas all on a torrid afternoon. And, moreover, he wore a cap to protect himself from the sun. Miller with his hair invisible is as though W. G. Grace were to appear unwhiskered. He performed two formidable strokes off Wright, a sweep to leg and a vehement drive to the off, both strokes mingling grandeur and rapacity while there's chance to plunder. Bailey clean bowled him with a ball to which even so quick-sighted a

cricketer as Miller could not change his stroke quickly enough
from offence to defence. This was another mighty step forward for England—and once again I was compelled to suspect the temper of the wicket under the sun, burning like
toast. A stroke to the off-side, which was nearly Hassett's
undoing as soon as he came in, took him as much by surprise,
probably, as it took myself. F. R. Brown now lumbered into
action to help rest panting Bedser and Bailey until the new
ball was available. He proved rather more than a substitute;
in fact he broke the back of Australia's second and crucial
innings by ridding us of Loxton, Lindwall, Tallon and the
gallant and always challenging captain, Lindsay Hassett.
Bailey caught Hassett incredibly from a rapid slash to back-
ward point. Bailey flung his heart and soul at the chance and
held the ball stretched out so far on the grass that after he had
grasped his prize we could almost see his body contracting.

Glorious cricket by England, all this: nothing to do with the
wicket. Every run invaluable, every ball straining bowlers',
batsmen's and fieldsmen's nerves and eyesight, the heat and
burden of the day a strain on everybody's endurance, roars
and screams from a multitude of 60,000 souls. Then, when
Australia were all out just before five o'clock, England's
deeds in the field were rewarded by the cheers usually re-
served for conquering heroes. Better teams than England's
may have visited Australia; none has been more productive of
entertainment and surprise.

Brown again sent in Simpson with Washbrook, which was
surely risky; for if ever an England innings has needed a
confident lead it was now; victory and perhaps a last chance of
a sight of the rubber only 179 runs away, near but so far! Alas,
Washbrook was the first to fall, clean bowled by an off-break
keeping low and turning so sharply that Washbrook's pads, as
well as bat, were useless. Johnson then defeated Bailey, who,
after his sweat and toil of the afternoon should never have
been asked to bat at this perilous period. The wicket, I
concluded, now definitely encouraged spin, or a pace pitched
farther up than the authentic fast bowlers. Everything depended on Hutton at close of play; never has a Test Match
depended more on any one batsman's courage and skill. The
responsibility was intolerably heavy. I have no appetite for

the details of the last day. Enough is known from a description of the unprecedented mishap to, if not on the part of, Hutton. Defeat by a beggarly 28 . . . I will die in the belief that this insignificant sum would have leaped England's way—from 511 balls!—if nearly every batsman had looked as bravely at a few loose balls as they looked suspiciously at the good ones. England would indeed have won and found a grip on the rubber if there had been only two hours or so left for play, in which the score 179!

There were consolations at the end. We had a second time in succession run Australia to a short head, pointing out also that if English cricket has deteriorated recently, Australian cricket too was definitely 'slipped'. The vacancy caused by Bradman's retirement is still apparent as a void. Iverson is not an O'Reilly; he is an accurate puzzling off-spinner, but I haven't yet noticed that he bowls the ball that goes 'the other way.' At Melbourne he often dispensed with a slip altogether. England's disappointment was bound to be the harder to bear because we had to admit that at Brisbane and Melbourne we were able to get to work on pitches that are favourable to the very kind of seam swing or swerve which our best bowlers today enjoy most—moreover the kind of pitch Australian batsmen like least.

If the Test Match at Melbourne was a sad disappointment, its successor at Sydney was a hollow anticlimax. It is of little use for us to complain of bad luck: England would have lost just the same even if Bailey and Wright had escaped those dangers to health and body which seem to pursue our cricketers everywhere they go in Australia. No team playing Australia can hope to get off scot free, if in two innings on a good pitch their chosen batsmen are able to score only 413 with the leading players, Hutton, Washbrook, Compton, Simpson and Parkhouse, aggregating not more than 235 for the loss of ten wickets. England threw the match away on the first afternoon after winning the toss and after having reached a hundred at the cost of Washbrook. A great cricketer changed the course of the match in one over.

Hutton was apparently thoroughly at ease, untroubled and far-seeing: Simpson showed a reliable defence at the other end: the Australian attack palpably wanted fresh ideas. But though a new ball was not yet available, Hassett asked Miller to try his arm with an old ball, and Miller seized it, ducked his head and, as though by some inspired improvisation, clean bowled Hutton. Now it is not easy to break through the defence of Hutton if you are a fast bowler using an old ball, especially if Hutton has been at the wicket two hours. But Miller did not hurl down the bumping thunderbolt which Hutton had every reason to expect at this time of day: it was a delivery of fast medium pace and, moreover, the length floated alluringly, drawing Hutton forward: then the ball swung in and broke back to the stumps after pitching. I risk these technicalities because I wish the informed reader to understand why Hutton was again dethroned in all his glory.

At Melbourne, at the pinch, he lost his wicket through an unprecedented error of judgment on his part. Miller's ball, a great one, was countered with a great batsman's science and movement: the master was mastered—simply that and nothing more. Then in the same over Miller bowled Compton for nothing: Compton, deceived by late inswing, tried to change his stroke, and his bat was as crooked as a railway signal on Sundays. None but an exceptional man, cricketer or of any other vocation, can achieve exceptional things exactly when it is urgent that effort should go beyond normal competence. Miller is the one player in this rubber who seems visited from time to time by imagination and the quick kindling flash of natural genius. But Hutton, poor Hutton: whenever before in all the history of Test Matches has one batsman, no matter how skilful and experienced, been so bowed and weighted down by the load of responsibility he has to carry today: he is achieving a sheer nobility of isolation.

F. R. Brown, by dint of nature, guts and faith in a bat as a weapon of swinging attack, demonstrated to some of his more sophisticated and technical colleagues what they, too, might have done had they shared his old-fashioned faith.

England has lost another rubber, mainly by batting tied more or less to the ground behind the crease. Last year it was Ramadhin's slow leg-spin, now it is Iverson's slow medium off-spin. Mesmerism! Still, once again there were consolations for us and for the Australian crowds who unashamedly roared for an England victory. The defeated Brown was lionised: the victorious Australian captain, Little Hassett, received a perfunctorily polite ovation. Schoolboys surrounded Brown, clamouring for his autograph, while Hassett in mufti went home alone, practically ignored, if not unrecognised. Brown, Bedser and Warr worked like Spartans for hours sustaining a crippled attack, sweating under the torrid sun, sparing no nerve or muscle, gallant with hope, gallant with frustration: Miller, who most days loves to play the cavalier courteous and magnanimous to the weak, for more than nine hours scorned egoistic delights for the cause; and though I cursed the modern economy and polity of Test cricket that leadens occasionally the feet, the winged feet, of a Miller, none the less, I could not withhold admiration at the self-control he exercised and the amount of organised principle he brought to bear on his innings of 145 not out. In fact I had scarcely thought he possessed so much sound clean stylish defensive technique. He is truly a great player, not just an improvising dilettante of genius.

There is still much to be done by Brown and his men in the two remaining games of the rubber: despite sickening setbacks and missed chances the England team has exceeded the hopes of most of us, mainly, I admit, because Australian cricket itself has declined a little from the gold standard maintained by the bank of Bradman. One or two English reputations desperately need new polish; and if we can somehow press Australia hard again at Adelaide and Melbourne, English cricket will have recovered before the tour is over a little of the prestige lost last summer by the defeats suffered against the West Indies.

SYDNEY TO ADELAIDE

A T Sydney the third Test Match presented the rubber to Australia. Injury deprived F. R. Brown of the services of two important bowlers—Wright and Bailey—before Australia's first innings began; and Brown, with Bedser and Warr, sustained England's attack for hours, achieving that ethical grandeur which is reflected in most eyes of English-speaking people whenever hard labour is rendered spectacular in the presence of comfortably-seated onlookers. But England really lost the game on the first day when, after at last Brown had won the toss, five wickets were surrendered on a good turf to the Australian bowling for only 211, acquired laboriously in five hours. It was, again, an England innings performed as though under sentence. Yet, to begin with, we had reason for cheerfulness. Hutton and Washbrook, in first together at last, played for a while as though feeling fortune's wind with them. Then Washbrook made a mistake of a kind pardonable only under a First Offender's Act. Still, there was a timely retaliation without further loss. The England innings became launched and seaworthy. A total of 350, we now thought, would not be difficult to reach and might serve the purposes of victory after the pitch had been subjected to four days of wear and tear.

Hutton was at his most assured, even as at Melbourne. Simpson accompanied him—after one or two preliminary wrong notes—as reliably and unexcitingly as a piece of honest figured bass. And, yet again, Hutton was abruptly overthrown, this time by no mistake of his own, but by a ball in a hundred, bowled by Keith Miller, which brought down Hutton in all his glory much as some interfering force of nature might bring down the sun at high noon. In the same over Miller bowled Compton, so in a few minutes England were back on the rack, pessimism not to be encouraged, maybe; but hope a virtue.

In the warmth of the fifth morning of 1951, the ground was fairly densely populated at 12 o'clock, when Hutton and Washbrook went to the wicket, their shadows like black pools in which they walked, cast by a sun beating straight down. Sydney is less majestic than Melbourne: there is space between stand and enclosure; the pretty colours of the painted seats in the ladies' pavilion lend a suggestion of social amenity not always pronounced at Test Matches in Australia. The famous 'Hill' gathered strength, but not vocabulary, which is restricted. ''It 'em', ''Ave a gow'. But during one rare period when Australia could not get an Englishman out for an hour or so, a voice from the 'Hill' shouted, with sudden inspiration, 'Put Neville Cardus on'. Lindwall bowled the first over, and Hutton drove his second ball to the off for 3, a smack in the face for any fast bowler so early as this in the New Year. Miller, at the other end, ducked his head, and his hair fell over his face like a mane. Washbrook at once struck a 3 from him to the off, so Miller let loose a 'bumper', a flying-saucer of a ball, which seemed to amuse him considerably. In little more than half an hour Hutton and Washbrook hit 31 from the fast stuff. 'At last,' we told ourselves in the English camp, 'the long-deferred stand is coming to an innings at the outset.' Our prayers last night were that Brown might win the toss, and that Hutton and Washbrook would jump to the opportunity. And here they were, palpably confident, playing cricket in a Test Match with relish.

Ian Johnson, slow offspin, came on in place of Miller; and from his sixth ball, which pitched wide of the off stump, Washbrook made a cut, not bending over the stroke, which was sliced to the slips, where Miller held a remarkable catch, going to earth quick as a ferret to a hole; he caught it one-handed as he fell over. This error of judgment on Washbrook's part was grievous and, as I think, crucial.

The downfall of Washbrook, in fact, restored to Hutton's shoulders a weight of responsibility that could be felt, if not seen, as far away as the high press box at Sydney, which is situated in the stratosphere. A cricket writer might as well go up in a balloon. I never sit in this press box without feeling that I am performing an act of levitation. Simpson, who came in next, was for a while so unhappy in himself that he caused misery in others. He groped at Johnson's spin like a man going down a steep, badly-lighted and rackety staircase. All credit to him that he contrived to stay in nearly three hours; it is not impossible to cope with cunning bowlers if you are in form, but to frustrate them when you have temporarily lost your skill—this is a proof of character, more esteemed by the angels in heaven than cleverness. England's score went beyond 100 before half-past three, with the crowd as quiet as a painted back-cloth on a brilliantly lit stage. Hutton's cricket was for the connoisseur, not for ordinary tastes. I here 'sensed' some want of faith in the Australian attack; only Ian

Johnson's inviting flight asked an awkward question now and then. The fast bowlers were out of action; Miller had even wandered from the slips to the deep offside field, where he turned occasionally to the crowd to exchange a greeting; or he looked into the blue sky at an aeroplane flying to Brisbane or London. Iverson did not spin away from the bat, and his offbreak was not yet biting on the pitch. The moment was ripe for an offensive from a great batsman. Hutton was thoroughly established; we sat back and waited.

Miller was called by Hassett from the genial company of the Sheridan Stand. I am certain Hassett expected nothing more from him than a sort of marking time until after tea, when a new ball would be available.

But in one over Miller broke the back of England's innings beyond repair. Hutton, apparently not to be dismissed by legal means, was leg-before to a ball slower than Miller's customary pace; it described an alluring curve through the air, swung in late, but not much. Hutton played beautifully forward, head down, bat ready for the defensive push to the off. The ball whipped in quicker than the length and flight had suggested, eluded the bat and—the master was mastered.

Compton played the fourth and fifth balls of this same, already historical, over; to the sixth he reached with his arms, his bat terribly crooked, as he stood on his back foot, rather stiff for him, and the ball touched the inside edge of the blade and collided sickeningly into the leg stump. What a cricketer this Miller is! A great improvisor, making up his batting, bowling and fielding as he goes along. When he extends himself in effort and purpose he does things outside the scope and reach of mere talent. To remove a Hutton after he has rooted himself to a good wicket for three hours needs a skill and craft equal to his own, with imagination added.

At tea England were 133 for three; and in Miller's second over after tea, Simpson fell; this was another lapse of a batsman's concentration. Simpson, wanting a single to reach 50, tried a leg glance and sent an easy catch straight to Loxton at square leg. Simpson expressed self-chastisement, but what was the use of that? At the afternoon's end, as I say, England were dangerously placed. Brown, not out 36, recaptured his defiance of Melbourne; indeed he recaptured his youth, fortified now with the brawn and shrewdness of middle age.

Next day he began a period of combined physical endurance and big-hearted determination which has established him as the most liked and admired English cricket captain ever to visit Australia. In the Sydney streets the other day a hawker was selling lettuces—'all,' he shouted, 'all with a 'eart as big as Freddie Brown.'

The second morning of this Sydney Test Match began in torrents of sunshine (a week later there would have been no cricket at all in Sydney for torrents of rain fell for another fornight). Brown, not out 36 overnight at once attacked: a square-drive in Miller's second over and an off-drive from Ian Johnson told us not only of fighting temper, but of batsmanship not unacquainted with first principles. Brown's innings of 79, one of the best and most commanding; let us understand how many opportunities to score freely against the Australians had been missed by other and supposedly better batsmen than Brown on the English side. It is, of course, easier to swing the bat and damn the consequence if you have everything to gain and little to lose by venture and aggression. Brown was not expected when the tour began in Australia to prove himself a more able cricketer at the age of forty than he was as a young man. None the less, his example at Melbourne and Sydney demonstrated beyond argument that the Australian bowlers, being mortal, are prone to error and change of heart.

This innings of 79 was rich with strokes as natural to cricket and as much a part of cricket as green grass and good fellowship; strong drives, upright and frank, as though saying: 'Bowl your best! and I'll bat my best—and to hell with pottering about the crease in the dark.' Don't imagine that Brown 'slogged'. A man can't score nearly a century against an accurate attack unless he observes the canons, the grammar of the game. When Brown was bowled by Lindwall, trying a drive to the on, the crowd almost groaned with sorrow. His reception, as he walked back to the pavilion's cool dark shade, was so royal that it might all have been a procession with the red carpet down and the decorations up.

Brown and Bailey scored 71 together, increasing the

England total from 187 for five to 258 for six. It was here that Bailey was hit on the right thumb by Lindwall, after two hours of noble if martyred stonewalling for 13. He tried to bat again after receiving surgical treatment, but after scoring 2 more runs he was caught at the wicket and looked pale as a ghost. He disappeared from the match, so did Wright who, in last, backed up rather late when Evans ran quickly to 'keep' the bowling, and strained his groin. So England, all out first innings for 290, went into the field just before 3 o'clock with only three bowlers—Bedser, Brown and Warr.

Their persistent energy, their steadiness and patience in the heat of Australian summer, battling in a lost cause—these things have already become part of cricket's tradition of sport that must smile fair weather or foul. The pitch, if it occasionally allowed a ball or two to turn, would not have been begrudged to a crippled attack by any good batsman.

The truth is that the Australians, for hours of inordinate length, seemed to treat England's three perspiring toilers under the sun rather unchivalrously. Such is Test cricket these times. The cause, my soul, Australia feared a crumbling wicket, if they should be asked to get a score to win, or save themselves, in a fourth innings. So even Miller, the gay Lothario, batted nearly 6 hours for 145 not out. Hassett wore down the human resistance of Bedser, Brown, Warr and the crowd by scoring 70 in 3 hours 12 minutes; Archer was 3 hours over 48. And all the time we saw Bedser and Brown, or Brown and Warr, wheeling their arms; Bedser and Brown lumbering uphill, 'bits in their mouth', like carthorses, while Warr threatened to break his back as he goaded the tired young limbs of him to unnatural spurts of temper and vitality. In the Australian innings of 426, Warr bowled 36 overs (eight balls to the over) for 142 runs and no wickets; a shamefully untrue reflection of his strenuous and fairly accurate work. Bedser bowled 43 overs for 107 runs and four wickets, including (again) Morris's, for 0. Brown bowled 44 overs for 153 runs and four wickets. He was a sort of monument of perpetual motion; his movements, as he rumbled to the bowling crease, his rotating arm, began, as the hours went by and he was 'still at it', to create the illusion of perpetual motion rendered fixed, static, unplastic. Miller's innings blazed out in imperial driving; these strokes compelled us to regret that during his long innings he had subjected himself to much unnecessary self-denial. There is something in contemporary Test cricket which clips the wings of even a bright bird such as Miller.

On the other hand, the intelligent control Miller exercised over his glamorous technique and temperament was proof of his essential calibre. He is not just a 'playboy'.

Of England's second innings, and a defeat by an innings and 13, I have little heart to write. The pitch no doubt helped Australia's spinners, Iverson particularly; he took 6 for 27 in 156 balls. Did ever Sidney Barnes receive obeisance as polite (not to say abject) as this? The English batting, again and again and yet again, was bankrupt of creative ideas. Seldom was the ball met with a resolute unmyopic blade. Once more Washbrook flattered to disappoint. In half an hour he scored 18 to Hutton's 8, and whether getting runs or countering good balls from Lindwall and Miller, he resembled a born and reliant England cricketer. But Iverson came on, and after two maiden overs to Hutton, he drew Hutton forward, and our one and only great batsman just snicked a 'top-spinner' (not an offbreak); the ball skimmed to Tallon, the wicket-keeper, who couldn't hold it, but it bounced towards Johnson at second slip, who barely touched it back to Tallon, who made a catch one-handed, upside down. The very gods have conspired against Hutton in this rubber. Why? A superb ball from Iverson clean bowled Washbrook, whose bat, playing forward, did all that a bat can do—as Doctor Johnson said, on his deathbed, of a pillow. Parkhouse showed, as at Melbourne, some relish of rapid stroke play, following more moments of dark interstices of self-doubt. He was run out because he didn't wait to be 'called'. There are times when J. M. Barrie's generally sound advice should be disregarded: 'When you make a stroke, don't stop to cheer, but run at once . . .'

Though Compton was watchful this time while he gradually accumulated 23, he did nothing to clear the England innings of encircling gloom. Iverson dictated his terms; Compton's wriggled on his hook; he didn't look a great player now.

English batsmanship in England last year could find no

answer to Ramadhin's leg-spin; now they seem at a loss against Iverson's offspin in Australia. Something is wrong with the works somewhere.

The Adelaide match was more or less given away after luncheon the closing afternoon, following a hopeful stand at the day's beginning by Sheppard and Simpson. Even the comparatively experienced Simpson failed in concentration the last over before the adjournment, and made the silliest stroke in the world to mid-wicket on the offside. Apart from Sheppard, nobody (Brown was absent hurt), seemed to make an effort to keep England's innings struggling bitterly to the end. The truth is that throughout the tour the team's assets of character and experience have depended on too few men: recently there has been in one or two instances a quite palpable, if indirect, admission of tiredness, if not of actual boredom. No doubt it is hard to have to play five hours' cricket under a hot sun for five days running (interrupted only by a lunch interval of ninety minutes and a tea interval of twenty, with refreshments brought into the field every forty-five minutes and only Sunday for a day of rest): hard indeed to suffer bondage to labour in a losing side, especially in Australia where the labourer considers himself very much worthy of his hire. I have been given cause to believe these last few weeks that players of contemporary Test cricket really do not like it and are extremely relieved when six o'clock sounds an imaginary knock-off in their ears and they all walk home to the pavilion and to the good food and society of friendly Australians and their homes. Nowadays I see many of our well-paid first-class cricketers going to golf at week-ends with an avidity they seldom express when embarking on a day in the field at their own game. Here we come to the main source of cricket's weakness at the present time as a game and as an art. It is not played for its own sake often enough: the old true amateur influence is no longer there. And how could it be, since it has departed from public life generally? Even Australians, usually opportunist stroke players, are changing to canniness and caution: even the bright free and often fluttering wings of a Keith Miller are slowly becoming clipped. In the old days, under the eye of great captains of cricket such as MacLaren, Warner, Lord Hawke, A. O. Jones, the Fosters

—under this aristocratic scrutiny and spacious, sometimes reckless, economy—the professional player had before him a constant example of independence of style. Hence the incomparable succession of professionals, brilliant and individual, such as Tyldesley, Denton, Hirst, J. T. Brown, Hayward, Braund, George Gunn, on and on to the greatest of all, Jack Hobbs. In the MCC team of today there are at least two cricketers who, much as we admire them, would have gained something of regality if they had played with the masters of the golden age, not a technical gain, but one involving a change of mental approach to Test Matches. All the current talk in England about schools to improve our cricket, with concrete pitches a panacea—this is to talk away from the heart of the matter. The greatness of the game, its immortals, all the inspiration which impelled us to go to the trouble of building and preserving Lord's, the game's literature and the endless talk amongst friends years after the event and to a life's end, all these things came to be because one day a number of men and boys and barking dogs went into a field with a bat and a ball, intent on fun and no material profit.

FINAL TEST

Now that we have expressed a nation's thankfulness for the first victory for thirteen years achieved by England against Australia at cricket, criticism is called from the kennel and put on to the scent of more or less objective truth. It was a victory well deserved and it was needed on account of sheer justice. F. R. Brown's team, though far from the best that ever sailed the seas, was at least better, technically and in spirit, than would have been suggested by five consecutive defeats. But I confess I cannot hail the victory as a sign of a turning tide, or of a renaissance in our cricket. No 'new blood' or talent contributed to the conquest; Hutton was needed to steer the ship to the harbour. I myself would have counted the rubber well lost—for I have never imagined we could win it—if a new England batsman of Hole's pedigree had revealed himself.

Yet though this England team depended sorely on Hutton, Bedser, Brown and Evans, we can realise as we glance back across the rubber, how easily the luck of the game, or a little more of good management, might have wrested the 'ashes' from the ancient enemy. The spin of the coin settled the issue at Brisbane. More heart-breaking still, in the match at Melbourne at Christmas, where England fell short of victory by only 28, Hutton inexplicably committed a crudity not in his repertory and not in his nature; he hit a ball across the spin and sent a ghastly 'skier' near the square-leg umpire. The match at Sydney was lost by a combination of mediocre cricket and physical hardship; Bailey and Wright at the halfway stage received injuries which put them out of the struggle.

At Adelaide, in truly Australian conditions—weather and wicket—England were obviously outplayed; and now none of us doubted the superiority, as an *ensemble*, of Australia over a collection of variable spare-parts, one or two of them of the finest metal. The turning-point of the fifth match occurred during the last-wicket stand of Simpson and Tattersall. Once again, England's bowlers had broken through an Australian first innings on a very easy pitch, so that the total of 217 was not higher than Bradman, Ponsford and Woodfull could muster when one of them was got rid of cheaply. But England, in response, seemed certain to miss a golden chance: nine wickets were down for 246. It was here that Simpson, on the verge of a century but not so far at all in command, demonstrated at last that he is still capable of swift movement of foot and of beautiful and punitive strokes. He played the Australian attack at leisure; he drove and pulled with an ease almost indecent. In less than an hour he added 50, with six boundary strokes which sped to an inch exactly where he intended they *should* travel. Meanwhile, Tattersall demonstrated the value of Lancashire obstinacy; he put his bat to the ball, and though apparently it was a bat of lath, and though he was surrounded by fieldsmen, they couldn't remove him for nearly an hour, by which time England was leading by 103. During this gallant stand, stylish and handsome at one end, comically vulnerable at the other, even if Tattersall had to cope with less than three overs in all, it is possible that the inability of Australia to take a wicket was beginning to affect Miller's health (or Lindwall's); for after lunch Miller summarily smashed through Tattersall's divertingly camouflaged resistance. Is it conceivable that had the rubber been at stake, England, wanting 74 to win and nine out, that this tenth wicket partnership would have happened? I am reminded of the man who went up to the Duke of Wellington one night in Wills's Club and said, 'Mr Jones, I believe?' 'If you can believe that', growled the Duke, 'you can believe anything'. I am not hinting of any want of conscious effort by Australia at the crucial period of the match. But Australian cricketers in possession of the rubber are, I think, less 'highly strung' than when on the 'kill', unsparingly and to a man. In this fifth Test Match, it was England's reputation that was at stake, not Australia's. Every lover of cultured batsmanship was happy at Simpson's revival; but O that he could have given us half an hour of it at Melbourne during Christmas!

If we look at the bowling analyses of England, we find that Bedser took 30 wickets in 195 overs for 484 runs, average 16.13. Bailey took 14 wickets for 198, average 14.14; Brown took 18 wickets average 21.61; and Wright 11 wickets average 45.45. Yet this attack, comprising one really dangerous bowler over by over, dismissed Australia five times on good pitches for pittances such as 228, 194, 181, 217, and 197. In 1946–47, Bedser's Australian figures for the Test Matches were 246 overs 3 balls, 876 runs, 16 wickets, average 54.75. And four years ago Bradman described Bedser as the best bowler of his type extant. This season one or two Australian wickets have been responsive to bowling that 'swerves' from the ground off the upright seam. There is no doubt that Bedser excelled himself at Brisbane and at Melbourne. From an abstract view of technical accomplishment, even before his work had been confirmed by wickets and 'results', I decided this was 'seam' bowling comparable to Tate's. All praise to him, and all praise to Brown, who by persistent effort, added inches to his technical stature. None the less, critical justice must be observed; and in fairness to Bedser's ill-rewarded work of 1946–47, we must remember that four years ago the

Australian XI contained Bradman and Barnes, that Morris was at his very best, and that Barnes and Morris on several occasions held the first wicket long after the new ball had lost its gloss.

From the first day's first hour of the Melbourne match of this present year, Australian cricket seemed stale and un-ambitious. Hassett once more won the toss, and at 3 o'clock on a hot humid day not a single run more than 81 had attracted the scorers' notice after two and a quarter hours' play, for the loss of Burke's wicket. The treat of a storm then seemingly galvanished Hassett into a sudden sequence of hits which ceased as soon as the clouds rolled away. It is a pity when cricketers born with rare and delightful capacities allow cir-cumstances to sway them to methods wasteful to natural talent. These, our contemporary heroes of the cricket field, many times reverse the doctrine of Falstaff; they become lions under compulsion. Morris stonewalled for two hours forty minutes, so severely that he broke a bat.

Keith Miller was immediately caught and bowled by Brown; he was out the same way to the same bowler next innings. Miller is as uncertain as a spring day in England; they can't trap him into the cage of routine efficiency. Brown removed Morris, Miller and Harvey for no runs in ten balls; and maybe after all, this was the thrust into Australia's vitals that really brought about the funeral so much desired by one and all, English and Australians. The wheel of Australia's first innings whirled from 111 for one to 123 for four; and nowadays the Australian 'tail' is capable of wagging the dog off the field. Hassett now had no choice but to retire into a shell of self-protection. He made 92 in 212 minutes before Hutton caught him right-handed at first slip, shoulder high, off Brown. Hassett bore his cross 'for the cause', and in general the proceedings were so slow that, in a match taking place weeks after the 'death' of the rubber, it seemed that the slayers were an unconscionable time disposing of the body. At close of play, in just under five hours, Australia's score stood or reclined at 206 for eight wickets, on a pitch so comfortable that to bowl on it must have been rather like bowling on a steak-and-kidney pudding. But contemporary batsmen argue that because this sort of wicket is so 'slow' they cannot compel the ball to leave the face of the bat with any appreciable speed. A man might try—as Pooh Bah observed.

On Saturday play was prevented by heavy showers, but the wicket was as easy as in the beginning when we 'resumed', as they say, on Monday. Five hours later I walked through the Fitzroy Gardens full of misgivings. At one period of the afternoon England's score was 170, with only Washbrook out; now it was 218 for six, only one run to the good. Hutton, being human, lapsed into mortal error again when, with his innings established at 79, he allowed the boy Hole to bowl him with a slow floating ball he endeavoured to drive to the off. Hutton and Washbrook, at the beginning of the England innings, 'set about' Lindwall and Miller quite flippantly. Strokes to the on from Lindwall were executed affably; Lindwall here was so tame that I was put in mind of one of those beautifully preserved glass-cased lions which we can admire at leisure in a museum. Soon, though, the sucking dove was to be heard roaring like any of your proper lions. Washbrook cut and drove 22 in next to no time: six overs produced 34. I thought there were signs of high blood-pressure in Washbrook's cricket; a sort of red sky at morning. He was abruptly caught at the wicket from a widish ball which came up not too high to the off, bowled by Miller; a redundant stroke. Hutton for a while was a model of deportment. An off drive against W. Johnston was as classical as the Elgin marbles, and more shapely. A very late glance, also off W. Johnston, was executed with the crossed legs and rapidity of Ranjitsinhji.

Iverson stole lustre from Hutton this time by pitching his off-breaks so that they turned towards the left hip of the batsman; also Iverson set a defensive field of adjacent leg 'slips'. He is not a great bowler, I am certain. His accuracy is admirable no doubt; given a dusty pitch, his spin is horrid. But apparently he has never consistently controlled a leg-break, or any ball that 'leaves' the bat. QED. One of the curiosities of this curious rubber is that Hutton found Ian Johnson as troublesome as most of the Australian bowlers; and on the occasion now under notice he tried, when his score was 37, to drive Johnson forward; in fact cover-point got himself into position to receive the stroke. But the ball veered away a

little, found the bat's 'outside edge', whence it skimmed to
Miller in the slips, and Miller—of all men—allowed the
chance to go through his fingers. Next day we would see and
witness a missed slip catch by Hutton; and these, I think, were
the only fielding mistakes committed by Miller and Hutton in
all the five Tests. Simpson, after a vague sort of beginning,
gradually rooted himself; and we saw a straight bat going to
the ball as though with eyes in the wood. The wicket was
dismally lifeless; the bowlers appeared to me, as Hutton and
Simpson strengthened their partnership, as objects of charity.
At the tea interval, England were 160 for one, and there
seemed no reason why the score should not persist for the day
without further loss.

Then after tea, we saw a great outbreak of fast bowling.
Realising the dangerous position Australia had drifted into on
the becalmed sea of a wicket, Lindwall and Miller, by almost
unbelievable energy, electrified the moribund earth. A snick
from Hutton's bat from Lindwall, singed Ian Johnson's
fingers in the slips. But it was not the sound and fury of the fast
stuff that defeated Hutton—who really does lose his wicket at
times in a manner which with Hobbs would have prompted
psychological as well as technical analysis; he was clean
bowled by a simple well-tossed ball from the youth Hole. Now
came Compton, every true lover of the game praying for him.
A lovely sweep to leg in his happiest vein lifted expectation on
happy tip-toe. For half an hour he played the bowling easily
enough, like a man 'tuning in' with some discretion. But
Lindwall, who had so far attacked Compton's legs, sent a
'snorter' just outside the off-stump, and Compton from a
spasm of a cut was caught at slip by Miller. Sheppard, a run
later, was caught at the wicket off Miller, a stroke as empirical
as at a mosquito in a dark room. Then Lindwall smashed his
way into Brown's stumps; Brown heaving his bat into the air,
chin up, legs astride. Another splintering of wood announced
the bowling by Miller of Evans—so here we were again,
another collapse of England after the passing of Hutton—170
for one, 213 for six. There were critics in the English camp
who objected to Lindwall's and Miller's attack, alleging that it
exploited too many 'bumpers'. I am sorry for the supposed
lover of the game who cannot respond to so magnificent an

effort as this of the only two fast bowlers of our time. Here we are, impoverished for great pace, denied for years the thrilling spectacle of fast bowlers 'whizzing' the air. And then, when natural genius, glory of Australian limb and sinew, wake a dead wicket into galvanic life, there are protests because now and again a ball is sent humming like a tuning-fork past a batsman's ears, as years and years ago. Ernest Jones propelled them alongside the left ear of Ranji—who propelled them to fine leg for fours; or as Cotter hurled bouncing lightning at MacLaren who murmured to himself 'Let him go on with it, I'll—well, Cotter him!' In this rubber of strange mutations of form and mood, nothing was so mysterious as this violent fusilade by Miller and Lindwall, in the light thrown next day during the England last-wicket stand; for instead of the unexpected and, you would suppose, provocative obstinacy by Tattersall, and Simpson's opportune militancy spurring the fast bowlers to another convulsion, they received it all, as Harry Fragson used to sing, 'most politely'. Simpson, who stood firm when the pace was at its most alarming was, as I say, next morning the supremely sure master of all he surveyed.

It was Bedser who led us to our first Pisgah height, there to catch a glimpse of a victory after all; we could not believe it at first, surely it was a mirage? He yet again caused the new ball to swerve viciously late, almost akin to a leg-break quick off the middle stump to the off. Morris, though, was out to a ball rather short of a length from Bedser: he swung his bat across the line of flight, aiming for the square-leg boundary, missed and was leg before. In the same over Burke had no choice but to flash his bat, and he sent a catch to Hutton in the slips. And Hassett was at once missed by Hutton in the slips off Bedser with his view of the ball rather spoiled by Evans as it travelled like a comet through the air, a streak of red. But the cat was definitely amonst the Australian pigeons at last. Bitterly did Hassett resist, his bat so straight that metrical deductions could have been drawn from it, like the great pyramid. Harvey attacked: it is his nature to look for runs. Some of his strokes were splendid, if a little flushed with suggestions of insecure, if not brief, life. The Australian score was hauled or salvaged from 6 for two to 88 for two. Another hour of Harvey

would put England out of the hunt, and our disappointment
and disillusionment would be too hard to bear now. The
scales were falling the wrong way for us—then Harvey,
attempting a forcing hit to the on from Wright, 'lost' the ball,
which kept low. He departed disconsolate—l.b.w. And only
a few moments afterwards Miller thrust his bat out precipitately at a ball artfully changed in pace by Brown, who caught
and bowled him again. Brown's triumphant grin spread from
ear to ear. Australia 89 for four, still behind; bless us if
England weren't really and truly winning! With the first threat
of defeat shading the Australian sky, young Hole came in, an
hour of the day to go, that searching closing hour no batsman
likes if his side is losing. He showed his strength of nerve, and
actually dared to drive and cut. Hassett spoke to him about it.
But next morning, with visible leaden responsibility on his
shoulders, Hassett was clean bowled after a few overs, by the
best ball in Wright's variegated and sometimes unruly repertory: a leg-break of perfect length, which floated through
the air seductively, lured Hassett forward, pitched on the
stumps and yet hit the stumps. There is no scientific counter
to this ball. In the same over Ian Johnson optimistically
leapt out of his ground, swung his bat and himself into
an effort to clear the pavilion's roof; the ball soared at
convenient altitude to mid-on, where Brown waited for it
lovingly. Australia, with six wickets gone beyond recall, led
by a bagatelle of 43. It is a testimony to the Australian
tradition of nerve and backbone that even now not a man in
the English camp was taking things for granted. Lindwall
came in to play stonewall to Hole, who, as soon as Hassett was
beaten, took charge as though the occasion were not his first
but his twenty-first Test Match. Twice in one over he hit
Wright to long-leg, a true hit, not a sweep round. A fieldsman
was placed to frustrate any other liberty that this impertinent
youth might take in the same direction, so Hole cut Wright's
next ball through the almost vacant slips, quick as a cat on the
sudden acceleration of pace. Hole is a tall, loose-limbed boy
who bends his knees not at all prettily in his 'preliminary'
stance at the wicket; but when the ball is out of the bowler's
hand he is upright and quite stylish.

When Bedser attacked with the new ball, Hole cut him

riskily through the slips for four; the next ball he drove through the covers, poised to an inch; the stroke thrilled the eye, and left the fieldsmen standing. Hole drove Bailey straight for four, one of the few straight drives in the rubber. He hit Bailey square past point for three, and when his score was 57, he chanced another 'cheeky' cut between Hutton and Washbrook in the slips. Lindwall was obstructive until the scoreboard proceeded from 142 to 192, then, an over or two before lunch, he played a ball from Bedser into his stumps. After lunch, anti-climax. Hole was bowled driving heart and soul at a yorker from Bailey; and Australia's last three wickets collapsed for five.

We expected another assault from Lindwall and Miller on Hutton and Washbrook as they began to score 95 to win. But surprisingly soon the spin bowlers were in action, and radiation left the atmosphere. Though Washbrook was out at 32, and Simpson was thrown-out cleverly, and vengefully, by Harvey, Hutton went an untroubled way to the end. It was only poetic justice that it was decreed he should pilot the ship home. No batsman in the history of Test Matches has been known to carry his lone responsibility. Nobly has he done so. Hole is potentially the best young stroke-player I have seen for years. He will go far—and so will many a ball bowled at him.

BRAVO, MR BROWN!

ENGLAND has lost the rubber again because of indecisive batting. Too many times have I seen the right foot grounded behind the crease, the bat pushed out or stabbed down in front of the left pad, or thrust suddenly out and rather across the line of the ball. And too many times has the right leg moved over to the off stump, but behind the crease or not far beyond it.

Last summer it was Ramadhin's leg-spin that mainly overwhelmed our leading batsmen, technically and intellectually:

now it is Iverson's off-spin. Less than three years ago on English turf it was Lindwall's pace.

What manner of bowling then, if it is a fair question, do our contemporary masters expect to satisfy them in Test matches: these mighty scorers and hunters before the lord in most county matches, boasting their records and sure in their hearts that Trumper and MacLaren could not have been much good: 'look at their averages?'

F. R. Brown cannot blame his attack for our present bankruptcy: on good wickets in Brisbane and Melbourne, Australia were put out in consecutive innings for 228, 194, and 181.

A crippled bowling team, dependent on three heroic spartans, Brown, Bedser and Warr, held their own on a good wicket for hours in Sydney, taming even Keith Miller and removing from the scene six batsmen including Morris, Harvey and Hassett for 252.

Jardine, with Larwood's lightning and a leg-side field, scarcely reduced the currency of Australian batsmanship more than this. It was a cruel and unworthy blow of fortune that deprived England in Sydney of Bailey and Wright at the game's crucial point, but I cannot believe that Australia would not have won if both Wright and Bailey had remained at Brown's disposal sound of limb and in form.

No cricket team can hope to escape a severe thrashing in Australia if it persists in methods which play into spin bowlers' hands. Iverson is clever with his off-break, spun in the manner of a googly. But he is not yet experienced, and anyhow he did not bowl at both ends when England pitifully collapsed for 123.

England's dire need was reinforcement from some batsman of character and experience in a hard school, who knows how to use his feet.

Brown's attack, of course, called at once for reserves after the accidents to Wright and Bailey: Tattersall certainly will steady and lend artful aid. But for the MCC to send two bowlers to Australia in the present circumstances, but no more batting fuel, is as though a new piston were sent out to a stranded engine and no more coal.

In spite of errors in the selection of the players last summer at Lord's, the present England team has astonished most of us by running Australia to a short head not once, but twice.

In Melbourne and Sydney, Brown demonstrated for all eyes to see that the Australian attack, like any attack Australian or Martian, is mortally subject to counter-attack, and that the best bowler in the world (and he doesn't at the moment of writing happen to be an Australian) tends to lose confidence if he is driven hard and sensibly.

How near this England side has come to a remarkable ascendency will be understood if we imagine how many runs more would have been to our credit if Compton had maintained form and comparative soundness of knee.

My heart and the hearts of thousands of Australians went out to Brown as he toiled on and on in the third Test, always setting his teeth and biting whenever he could. The other morning I received a letter from an Australian lover of cricket in Adelaide containing the following sentence:

'Can you explain why suddenly we Australians, usually inclined to be one-eyed, are all wanting England to win. Right at this moment, with a crowd in my home listening to the Sydney Test, I find every member of my family almost sobbing because that great scout Freddie Brown has just been bowled. How we were all hoping for him to reach his century, it is impossible to describe'.

The Australian is not given to cant or sentimentality: he has a resonant word for it. The moral to be learned from Brown's example is plain: he, at the age of 40, has twice thrown back an advancing Australian attack by some free, purposeful swings of his bat.

A younger and more accomplished batsman would find the job easier and twice as profitable: this, surely, is a reasonably safe assumption.

I shall die in the belief that England would today be boasting two victories if Edrich had been at our call in Brisbane and Melbourne: or Lowson or Watson of Yorkshire.

But while we are expressing a natural mortification, we Englishmen on the torrid, humid spot (how I envy you your cool winds in London!) must not lose sight of the fact that Australia is rich in her Miller.

In Sydney, Miller disappointed many of his friends by persistent self-denial of his hitting powers. But really the intelligent control he exercised over his brilliant technique and over his D'Artagnan temperament was proof of his greatness as a cricketer: doubtless he was intent on reinsuring Australia against the risk of having to bat a fourth innings on a dubious pitch.

His policy received the justification of subsequent events. And not many players naturally as glamorous as Miller can embrace austerity, generosity and style.

The Australians, at the time of writing, are not at all happy about their resources; they realise the gap opened by the retirement of Bradman. But the old determination is there.

Take the case of young Archer; he is technically not better than Sheppard, Simpson nor Parkhouse. All the same, he has established himself—at short notice—as one of Australia's 'opening' batsmen, in a crucial position left empty by the sudden lapse in the form of Moroney.

Australian cricketers, young or old, put their 'noses to the ball'; they seldom conspire in their undoing. No Australian I have recently met can understand the failures of Washbrook, Compton and Simpson. 'They are all in form most days. Yet they fail in the big matches'.

On paper there is not much difference in skill and experience between Hutton, Washbrook and Compton on the one hand, and Morris, Miller and Hassett on the other. The 'unknown' factor is—what?

Where the Australians unmistakably are our superiors is in bowling. Bedser has achieved wonders in this rubber; and Bailey has added inches to his stature. The others of importance have disappointed, so much that F. R. Brown has taken a large, if not a lion's share, of the attack.

When an England innings begins, Hutton and Washbrook, both of them carrying overweight of responsibility, are obliged first of all to cope with the new ball hurled at them by the two fastest of contemporary bowlers. The 'possibility', or imminence of a flying saucer of a ball, must constantly be a thought at the back of their minds.

Then, after Lindwall and Miller have been parried, on comes W. Johnston, fast-medium, accurate on the leg stump.

At the other end, Ian Johnson pitches a gnawing length, off-spin to a defensive field. If the wicket is at all dusty, or even promising some surface wear, Iverson at once spins his 'googlies'. By sweat of the brow the slow and medium stuff are also kept at bay.

But the hardworked Hutton and Washbrook (if both are still at the crease) look at the score-board: only a paltry sixty or so—and another new ball and Lindwall and Miller to be tackled again in a few overs!

It is doubtful whether Australia has for years enjoyed an attack as resourceful and varied as this; the batsman is compelled to *play without relaxation* at both ends, all the time.

Obviously, the Australian batsmen are not called on to support such a strain; there is really only Bedser to counter *technically*—unless Wright happens to be in form; and, alas! Wright's genius too often is potential, not actual.

It's the paradox of the Australian rubber of 1950–51 that it hasn't been England's weak attack that has failed us, but the highly overrated batting of those county lions, who each season at home can roar and spring like mad, but in Test matches will coo like the dove of peace itself.

Oh! that a Leyland had been included in the England team. I think he might have swung the balance. And I'm not sure Edrich wouldn't have done almost as well.

1953

AUSTRALIA'S CAPTAIN

LINDSAY HASSETT isn't at all like the picture of an Australian cricketer usually and fearfully presented to the imagination. He is not a grim-chinned man of the open spaces, horny-handed, unwieldy and even destructive to the furniture when he is confined by an interior of chairs and tables.

He is a gentle little inhabitant (off the field of play) of Melbourne, one of the most respectable cities in the world. He is not at all ferocious of aspect; not since 'Willie' Quaife has a cricketer looked so much dwarfed by the stumps. His shoulders do not stand out cliff-wise and threaten to bruise you. He is neat and dapper, resembling a jockey at times, especially in his face. His eyes twinkle; his mouth is that of a comedian.

There is about him that air of miniature caprice which causes women, young and ageing, to think of pixies at the bottom of the garden. And though his face and conversation encourage laughter, there is also conveyed in sudden grimaces an essential seriousness, even a melancholy, which Hassett himself is quick to turn to satire.

One hot night at Adelaide, during the tour of F. R. Brown's team, I met Hassett in North Terrace; he had, during the afternoon, batted for hours without a perceptible stroke. 'Are you *too* forgetting how to hit the ball?' I asked him. 'Are even *you* joining the Cricketer's Union of Universal Borers? Good Heavens, Lindsay, what's the matter with you?'

From a quite inscrutable mouth and countenance came the prompt reply: 'Wore out!'

Hassett's tendency nowadays to bat defensively and to withhold his splendid range of strokes, is due, perhaps, less to increase of years than to some imp of comedy secreted in his brain. Before the war, round about 1938, he would any day cut and drive as brilliantly as any batsman I have seen since J. T. Tyldesley; in fact, when he plundered and massacred W. J. O'Reilly at Sydney, I thought that the spirit of J. T. Tyldesley had blessedly come upon the earth again.

When Hassett first visited England in 1938 he began with 43 at Worcester, then, in consecutive innings, he scored 146, 148 (run out), 227 not out, 57 and 98, by strokes of swordlike swiftness and severity. In the Test match at Leeds, that same year, Australia in their second innings needed 105 in an awful light, and Wright bowled so skilfully that four wickets, including Bradman's, fell for 50, or thereabouts. Hassett dispersed the tense atmosphere, and England's hopes, in ruthlessly rapid time, effortlessly and as though vastly enjoying himself.

It is not altogether the responsibility brought by leadership that has gradually changed him into a cricketer mainly realistic and shrewd. His early brilliance was that of a young Australian of 25 years old. All Australians mature sooner than young men of this country; and in Melbourne the very atmosphere is sedate. But even yet, I suspect, there is in Hassett the urchin who won't grow up.

In technique it is hard to fault Hassett. His footwork is a joy to watch. He is able to add inches to his stature by mobility; he is most times near the ball and over it, whenever he chooses to play a stroke. His wrists are strong and flexible; like every great batsman, he plays late. He can drive and hook with rare power and accuracy.

In the present Australian team he is easily the most principled batsman: I mean his method is correct and based on the soundest foundations, straightness, economy, closeness to the line of attack. If he is not Hutton's equal on a 'turning pitch', the reason is not want of innate ability. There are few occasions in Australia when a batsman can find a chance to practise against spin on a damp earth, as the wickets are too frequently protected from rain in Australia.

But, in general and in substance, Hassett is the perfect foil to Hutton; it would be hard to think of two captains of cricket so likely to play tit-for-tat, both instructed in the same dour school, both excellent at the game which calls for the 'poker

204   CARDUS ON THE ASHES

face'. Neither Hutton nor Hassett will 'give anything away' or indulge in out-moded quixotry.

The Test matches of 1953 could easily become as static on the surface, but as subtly and invisibly unfolding, as a chess tournament. The rubber may well be settled by which of the two captains is the more enterprising. It will be a fascinating match in leadership and tactics.

Both Hassett and Hutton possess the pawky humour that seldom misses a bargain. Two stories will illustrate this. When I went to Australia with F. R. Brown's team, I didn't disembark at Perth but voyaged to Sydney to await their arrival and the serious business of the tour there. So when I ran into Hutton during lunch at the MCC *v.* New South Wales match, I hadn't seen him for several weeks. I naturally asked him if he was enjoying the 'trip'. Yes, he was, very much.

'But,' he added, in his own lovely Yorkshire, and soft likeable tone of voice, 'I'll tell you something.' He looked round him, and over his shoulders, as though fearful of eavesdroppers. 'Aye,' he said, 'Ah'll tell you something . . .' And he looked around again. Then he dropped his voice lower and, with a jerk of his thumb indicating place and direction, said, 'This is a queer place.'

After Australia won the rubber at Melbourne in 1951, the crowd surged over the field, calling not for Hassett but for Brown. Thousands of schoolboys shouted 'We want Freddie; we want Len.' I was escaping round the pavilion from the throng when I bumped into Hassett. 'Listen to them,' he said, adding apologetically, 'of course we've *only* won the rubber.' Suddenly he looked at me, and made a motion as though to his pocket for his pen. 'Would you,' he faltered, 'would you like my autograph?'

And when England won the fifth Test match of the same tour at Melbourne, Hassett went on to bowl the last over. England with only two wickets down wanted merely three or four runs. Hassett solemnly set his field, moving men here and there to an inch. And just before he began his run, as though seized by inspiration, he suddenly rubbed the old ball vigorously on his thigh, then doubled-up laughing at the gorgeous joke that had come to him.

So there we are: two stern captains, both 'on the watch',

both quick at the main chance but prepared not to get to blows for hours, both endowed with the humour that reveals self as clearly as it reveals others! A perfect match, surely.

Most Australian cricket captains have been shrewd and not given to romanticism. It is not easy to imagine an Australian Chapman or Arthur Gilligan, though Victor Richardson departed considerably from type and loved to make a gallant gesture.

M. A. Noble was one of the finest men I have ever met in cricket; his integrity was unswerving. But though he loved the game passionately, it was as a student, rather than as an artist. I can see him yet, between overs during a stand against Australia, walking to his position in the changing field, head down, pondering what to do to get a wicket urgently needed.

Warwick Armstrong mellowed in time, and his teams called him 'The Big Ship'. He was amiable yet unyielding. But his triumph of 1921 in England was easy; cricket here was still sadly disorganised after the 1914–1918 War, and the strength of Australia colossal. An attack of Gregory, Macdonald and Mailey scarcely needed controlling throughout the hot summer of fiery wickets.

Woodfull, like Hassett and Armstrong, came from Melbourne, and in every way he was characteristic of Melbourne. His batting made virtues of solidity and sedateness. An innings by Woodfull was as quiet, safe, uneventful and as respectable, as any Sunday in Melbourne. He was a man incapable of duplicity. He was good and honest through and through, but for all his quietness of manner, he knew his mind and would not suffer fools. He could express masterly control in the softest voice. When any Australian made a mistake clearly the consequence of slackness, a single look of reproach from Woodfull caused shame to bend the head.

Bradman, off the field, was something of an enigma. It was hard really to get to know him, or get him to realise that you really liked him. It was, so to say, hard to 'get his station', hard to find his 'wave-length'. Not all his colleagues at cricket liked him week-in and week-out. An abnormally great player who, merely because he was as good as he happened to be; attracted the attention and admiration of nearly every onlooker in the vast crowd—such a man was bound to find himself isolated from ordinary companionship. And, human nature being what it is, there were jealousies.

None the less, Bradman was respected by all who came under his command in the field. He directed them according to carefully deliberated plans. I have seldom seen a captain of cricket assert himself with more than Bradman's unobtrusive authority; he seemed able, by the merest turn of the head or motion of the hand, to communicate orders as intimately to deep long-on as to short-leg.

It must not be forgotten that Hassett was second-in-command to Bradman. Also, that if Bradman played the game with calculation, 'by the book of arithmetic', he was never unready to attack relentlessly, at the first sign of any wavering in the opposition. We shall be wise—and in this context 'we' includes Hutton—not to be deceived by Hassett's air of accommodating quiescence, his urbane quizzical manner. In any of his slowest innings he might without giving fair warning leap from his crease and hit three most violent fours from consecutive balls.

Hassett, dapper and wasteful of no energy, does not play for safety unless compelled by overwhelming odds. He will see to it that Miller and Lindwall are not overworked; but at the faintest suggestion of weakness of purpose in the England XI he will surreptitiously whisper the word of command: 'Slip her, Keith; let her go, Ray,' These 'little' generals are usually the most pugnacious!

ENGLAND'S TURN IN CORONATION YEAR?

THERE is reason to suppose that England's chance of winning the rubber in the Test matches of Coronation Year are better than any that have come our way since 1926.

In the first place it is time the tide changed (I am rather a believer in the 'law of averages'), and the pendulum is bound to swing another way soon. Again, to support our optimism, there have been portents clear enough that Australian cricket is being troubled by those mortal failings and reactions which are bred by long success and prosperity.

But while we are at liberty to make the most of favourable winds and tides, no sensible English cricketer, least of all the canny Hutton, will allow reasonable confidence in our present prespects to encourage complacency. An Australian team is invariably a more dangerous combination in England than at home—mainly because on tour it *is* a team, each player free to trust to his natural talents, with no worry whether he'll 'make the trip' at all.

Our chances in the rubber of 1953 are, I think, 'evens'; that is, if a courageous spirit informs our ranks. I have argued often in these pages, frequently in the face of much criticism, that for several years England has thrown golden opportunities away in Test matches because some 'policy', or some direct or indirect influence, has persuaded several of our leading batsmen to adopt a defensive attitude day-in and day-out, so that one or two of them have not used their natural strokes.

On more than one occasion England's strokeless batting last year, in the so-called Test matches against India, was tactically deplorable, and reprehensible from the point of view of character and sport. If these methods are repeated during the coming summer, the Australians will win; more important, the spirit of Coronation, in the year of the crowning of our young Queen, will be abused.

This is the time for boldness in the England XI—combined, of course, with a necessary discretion. Nobody but a fool would dream of throwing his bat at anything like a good-looking ball from an Australian bowler. The point is, that an Australian, like every human and perishable bowler, is likely to bowl no better and no worse than a good batsman will allow.

Given a good start to an innings, and a good wicket, no circumstances are conceivable as an excuse if a stroke player proceeds, *while well set*, to spend another hour, with no wickets falling, and score less than a dozen runs. An enormity of this kind happened at Kennington Oval last August against India.

One or two young English batsmen last summer seemed deliberately to withhold their natural strokes at a state of the game and in conditions which favoured and urgently called for quickness of feet and resolution to attack.

English cricket is as rich in young talent for batsmanship at the moment as any patriot could wish; it mustn't be handicapped by hesitancy against an Australian team by no means sure of itself deep down, though, of course, no Australian is going to 'give himself away'. We can be sure that Hassett's men will go into action with all the old show of cock-a-hoop confidence and opportunism!

There is an old saying that 'bowling wins matches'; fielding and safe catching contribute almost as much. But in recent years Bradman has demonstrated the value of aggressive batsmanship in a Test. Australia was nearly invincible while he was at his best, in spite of England's possession of one of the finest attacks ever known.

The best bowler in the world is of little use as a match-winner if your batsmen have wasted time and handed over to the enemy what is militarily known as the initiative. But what a different question assails the pit of the bowler's stomach if, half-way through his run, he sees the batsman raising his bat, the eye threatening and the feet moving!

I am still of the opinion that there is not a vast technical difference between the pick of our cricketers this year and the pick of Australia's. The rubber's honours will in the end go to the team that is the stronger in character, the more confident in outlook. Let us suppose that, in a Test match, twenty rather inaccurate balls are bowled, say, every two hours. My uneasy feeling is that the Australian batsmen will, right down the order of the innings, punish fifteen of them severely, but the English only five.

We must bear in mind, too, that attack in cricket doesn't end with the efforts of your batsmen. Much of today's negative play is caused by negative bowling. In England we have in recent years overdone the in-swinger and the 'leg-slip' field. The most dangerous weapon in the bowler's armoury is the ball that 'leaves the bat', Lindwall's masterstroke. The in-swinger is no doubt harder to score from, but seldom does it leave the batsman entirely 'without an answer'. Any bowler is wasting his time and energy if he allows a batsman liberty *not* to play two balls every over.

'For God's sake, Sydney,' said Victor Trumper on a certain famous occasion in Australia, 'when are you going to give me a moment's peace?' The question was addressed to S. F. Barnes while the prince of batsmen was half-way through one of his finest innings on a flawless pitch.

The Australian cricketers love to assume an offensive even before the first ball of the match has been bowled; for example, let us consider the field placed for Lindwall while he is getting out of his sweater. Only one man palpably in front of the wicket except the lonely bowler. No third man. A cordon of close slips and short legs.

'Take them away!', said A. A. MacLaren to Joe Darling, the Australian captain of yore, when MacLaren, having received his guard from the umpire, inspected the positions in the Sydney field at the beginning of a Test match. After raising himself on tip-toe to see to an inch where deep long-on was stationed, he turned round and discovered two crouching leg 'body-snatchers'. 'Take them away, Joe,' said A. A. MacLaren, 'they are in my way and are of no use to you.'

It is a well-known story; MacLaren drove the fast bowling of Ernest Jones straight; as a consequence, the Australian field had to 'open out'.

In 1938, at Lord's, McCormick at last found a length, and on a wicket that 'lifted' he got rid of Hutton, Barnett and Edrich for 22. Australia rampant! In walked Hammond— and what a walk! Down the pavilion steps he came, with his own high knee action, and the straight, square-shouldered calm movement over the grass to the wicket.

Eddie Paynter defended while Hammond put the Australian attack to the sword. He reached a century in two hours and twenty-five minutes; he lay back and, by strength of his right arm, he hit, he thrust the fast stuff to the ropes under the 'Father Time' grandstand. Hammond remained in possession until next day and scored 240 in six hours, and when he walked up the pavilion steps the whole of Lord's rose to him, members and all the vast crowd.

This was one of the noblest of all innings—and it is about time another innings, *half as noble*, was seen in an England innings! Too much of England's batting in recent Test matches has been frankly ignoble.

Another Paynter would also enter the England XI of 1953 like a strong supporting column. On the day at Lord's in 1938 when he was Hammond's companion during a grand stand in a crisis, he scored 99, then was l.b.w. A few minutes after he had returned to the pavilion I saw him and said, 'Bad luck, Eddie, to miss the century.' 'Hey,' said Paynter, 'T' first nine of 'em were all reight.'

With faith and humour, a competent technique can be carried a very long way. Name the two batsmen who can boast, alive or dead, the best averages in all Test matches between England and Australia. Bradman of course: 5,028 runs, 89.78 average. Next? Jack Hobbs? No. Herbert Sutcliffe? No. The answer is Eddie Paynter: 591 runs, average 84.42, thanks to 216 not out at Nottingham in 1938!

The one obvious advantage possessed by the Australians this year over the best we can at the moment gather together is Lindwall, who is easily the greatest bowler at present in the game. I have not shared the view, recently expressed but lately recanted like a hot brick, that Lindwall has for some time been 'showing his age' with a lowering arm.

The truth is that Lindwall has subtly developed into a fast-medium to very fast seam and variation bowler. He has never belonged to what George Lohmann contemptuously called the 'brute force' school of fast bowlers; he has actually used his intelligence. When he was playing in the Lancashire League, he learned much about 'green', moist wickets. So today he is likely at any moment to bowl a ball to which a batsman makes no stroke at all, only to hear the rattle of the stumps sickeningly behind him.

Lindwall has always bowled more dangerously in England than in Australia. He routed England at the Oval in 1948 for 52 on a moist wicket which was not truly a fast bowler's. And, if now and again Lindwall's arm should seem a little 'low', well then—the action favours a menacing 'skid' of the new ball, near the wicket and the batsman's zone of danger.

Trent Bridge may easily prove the least suitable of all our grounds for Lindwall's methods today. I expect he will display his most dangerous and most beautiful arts at Lord's, Leeds,

Manchester and, maybe—yet again—at the Oval. But I can well imagine that at least one or two of the Australian batsmen are as much concerned about Bedser as are some of ours about Lindwall.

I remain of the opinion that both England and Australia are rather below standard in 1953; that on the whole the technical resources of the two teams are likely to be much in the balance during the rubber, and that in the end the victory will go to imagination, character and enterprise.

I have often noticed that when cricketers themselves talk to Test match 'prospects', they seldom waste time on vague generalisations about 'form', such as the daily Press lavishes on us. Most times they begin with a very pointed question: 'What sort of wickets are going to be prepared?'

I have heard rumours about the part to be played by groundsmen in the rubber of 1953. Is it true that some strategian has proposed that everything should be done— that *fairly* can be done—to blunt the edge of the fast bowling of Lindwall and Miller?

We expect, as a matter of course, a good, reliable and fairly endurable pitch in a contemporary Test match. But a wicket without 'life' in it at all might easily prove a greater handicap to England than to Australia.

Our best chance of winning the Coronation rubber is in the right hand of Alec Bedser. A wicket that draws the teeth of his attack will be an asset to Hassett—and the pun (God forgive me!) is accidental. To say the bare-faced truth, I would rather that Hutton or any other English batsman was 'out of form' this summer than Bedser!

Australians are more accustomed than English bowlers to hard, persistent labour on wickets that don't help them. Besides, granted a thoroughly tame wicket, hundreds of runs will come inevitably from the bats of Morris, Craig, Harvey, McDonald, Miller and the rest.

Our chief hope, while our bowlers are coping with Harvey, is that pace and swing from the pitch will lure him to careless flashes or swings at the 'flight' of the ball. If the wicket is so elaborately prepared that the ball 'comes through straight' to Harvey, then he'll demolish any English attack as soon as the seam and 'shine' are gone.

The same remark applies in lesser measure to Craig. This wonderful youth has still to learn to deal with late swing, changing pace from the pitch, and sudden 'lift'.

As I say, a good durable wicket is fair and essential in any great cricket match; but the arts of the modern groundsman, if carried too far, could render Hassett's batting strength well-nigh impregnable. And the speed of Miller and of Lindwall through the air, exploited shrewdly only at intervals, might swing the balance of superiority of attack Australia's way.

The material at England's disposal seems better in batting than in bowling. Leg-spin is hard to seek—I mean really subtle and controlled leg-spin. Rhodes of Derbyshire is worth bearing in mind. For England's spearhead we shall look to Bedser and Trueman or Statham.

To unsettle the left-handed Morris and Harvey we shall need the ball that swings away from the bat. Bedser has often enough got rid of Morris quickly; but, by the time Hassett sends Harvey to the wicket, the ball may not be swinging dangerously, so now the specific challenge to Harvey should be off-spin; and here is the cue for Laker.

One of the fascinations of the rubber will be the meeting again in action of Miller and Laker. In 1948 Miller drove Laker time after time prodigiously, 'with the spin'. But in Australia, curiously enough, Tayfield's off-spinners caused Miller endless worry and trouble—and nobody would claim that Tayfield is a better off-spinner than Laker.

Tattersall may return to his best arts of flight and spin; and if Compton wins back his place in the England XI, he may help in providing a necessary variety, even a necessary eccentricity, in an attack which, good though it should prove with the new ball, doesn't promise much of subtlety for the best part of a hot day.

If the summer turns out wet—heaven forbid!—the rubber would be a gift for England, bar accident. No Australian XI not including a Trumper or a Macartney could hope to make scores preventive of defeat against Laker and Lock.

I take it that the England XI at Nottingham will be chosen from a nucleus consisting of Hutton, Sheppard, Simpson, May, Compton, Graveney, Watson, Evans, Laker, Lock,

Bedser, Tattersall, Ikin, Trueman and Bailey, with young hopefuls such as Cowdrey and Preston in the running.

All these are obvious names, and if the first Test is won by Australia, there will be natural changes, though the present Selection Committee will not, I think, be thrown by defeat into the panic which overwhelmed the Selection Committee of 1921, when all sorts and conditions of players were called to the colours—and got them!—while George Gunn, greatest player of fast bowling in the world, was not even once asked to go in first and walk up and down the pitch to Gregory and Macdonald.

The chief trouble facing the Selection Committee of Coronation Year is that there is available a more than usually talented 'pool' of ability to draw on, but not much experienced greatness. Some of our 'coming' young geniuses didn't make too impressive a sight while batting against the by no means formidable Indian bowlers last summer—as we have seen and remembered.

A ball sent through the air as fast as Miller's or Lindwall's is a hair-raising challenge to eye and nerve, if you haven't met the like of it before, and even if it is hurled or exploded at you only twice every quarter of an hour.

Let us not underrate Lindwall and Miller, strains, slipped discs, groins, backache or lumbago despite. Who wouldn't be confident, and more than confident, about England's chances in the rubber if our team included Lindwall or Miller?

At Lord's last summer Charles Palmer of Leicestershire made a century for the Gentlemen against the Players; it was one of the finest innings seen in this great match for many a long day. Only a really good player, well equipped technically, could have achieved it.

Well, no man can perform at any time more than what is 'in him'. Palmer's innings at Lord's last July was not that of a merely competent batsman; it contained quality. Here is a cricketer who shouldn't be lost sight of by the Selection Committee; he is also a useful bowler. It is easy for talent to become 'overlooked' if it is exhibited most days in the year at Leicester.

On paper it is possible to write the names of what looks like a more than tolerably good England XI to take the field at

Trent Bridge next month: Hutton, Sheppard or Simpson, May, Compton, Watson, Graveney, Bailey, Evans, Bedser, Tattersall or Lock or Laker, and Trueman.

I confess I don't like the look of the bowling. Leg spin! leg spin!—the fine craft of it is being discouraged and made obsolete by the current leg-before-wicket rule, which, as far as its effect on the art of the game is concerned, is one of the most deleterious ever devised.

If only Douglas Wright . . . but we can't begin all over again with him . . . or can we?

MILLER—AUSTRALIAN MATCH-WINNER

In every great cricketer there is as much character as skill. That is why the scoreboard and the averages can tell only half the truth about players such as Frank Woolley, Harold Gimblett and Keith Miller. Figures are positively misleading as an index to the achievements of Miller.

One day at Sydney, when F. R. Brown's England XI were playing Australia, England was apparently laying the foundation of a huge score—128 for one wicket, Hutton well set and Simpson now at ease. The time of day was ten minutes before the tea interval and the weather was hot. For nearly three hours Hutton and Simpson had sternly defended; the Australian attack was at this point waiting for the new ball, available soon after tea.

Miller had wandered from his customary place in the slips to the outfield in front of the Sheridan Stand, where all the pretty girls were presenting themselves to the sunshine. Hassett suddenly clapped his hands and called Miller in, and asked him to send down a few overs, just to mark time until the interval.

'What's the idea?' we can imagine Miller saying, 'wait for the new ball, Lindsay . . .' The other bowlers were dead-beat, so Miller took the old ball and at half-pace swung his arm, merely to oblige. In one over he dismissed Hutton and Compton, and swung the match round. Immediately after tea, he got rid of Simpson, with the new ball. So in a flash of creative cricket, Miller won a Test match. England crashed from 128 for 1 to 137 for 4, and he overthrew England's three best batsmen in 31 balls.

At Leeds in 1948 after England had batted first for 496, Australia began dubiously, and Pollard got rid of Hassett and Bradman in an over or two at the beginning of the day. The crowd and the England team were expectant. Bradman out before he or the rest of us knew what time it was!—the atmosphere was electrical with hope. Keith Miller, in next, attacked savagely from the first ball; in quick time the air was cleared for Australia. Miller scored 58, and the Australian total at the end amounted to 458.

I shall die in the belief that if Miller had not been in a characteristic vein on this bright morning at Headingley, England wouldn't have lost a crucial match in the rubber of 1948.

It is necessary for Miller to find himself in good mood to do justice to his gifts. He is prone to the ups-and-downs of the artist; he is not enslaved to technique. Strictly and austerely speaking, his technique is sometimes not above suspicion. It works less by reason than by instinct. You might as well refer to the technique of a young panther on the 'kill' or in repose! Miller is a cricketer of reflex action. I don't intend to suggest that he puts no intelligence into his play but only that at his best he is swayed rather by the logic of the heart than by the logic of the head.

He is a magnificent and typical example of Australian manhood. Tall, with good loose shoulders, handsome in a sun-stained, wind-swept way, acquiline of face, long eyelashes, brown hair that is not so much unruly as rhetorical in its falling disarray, long legs firm to the ground and astraddle as he stands in the slips, probably as he does so he is looking straight into the sun and blue sky to identify a 'plane on the way from Sydney to London—you would swear that he is the incarnation of the spirit of young masculine life in Sydney, as much the product of surf and sea as of turf and willow.

But there is the evidence of his birth-certificate that he was born in or near Melbourne, which is Australia more or less on its dignity, with rolled umbrella and top-hat. New South Wales and Sydney have assimilated Miller; today his only physical link with Melbourne and Victoria is a spoken English of soft and authoritative accent. He is a born improviser, who should always be distrustful of interfering theory. If ever he plans characteristic action, vision not calculation is the architect.

At Lord's in August, 1945, he scored 185 in two hours and

three-quarters, and on the third morning he flashed, volleyed and thundered from 61 to 185 in 45 minutes. One of his seven sixers soared to the pavilion's roof and lodged in the broad-casters' box. Only once has a ball been driven over the pavilion at Lord's, and the deed was done by another Australian, Albert Trott, playing for Middlesex in 1899; moreover, the blow was struck from a ball bowled by M. A. Noble (if I remember well) playing for the Australians.

When Miller resumed batting for the Dominions v. Eng-land on the morning of August 28 nearly eight years ago, he turned to one of the umpires, Archie Fowler, and asked if it was a fact that nobody since Trott had 'cleared the roof' of the Lord's pavilion. Fowler answered in a proud decisive affirma-tive; for, after all, Lord's is Lord's and not a proper subject or target for levity. 'Well, Archie,' replied Miller, 'I'm going to clear it myself this morning.'

And to this day Miller is of the opinion that when Trott made his great drive, the wickets must have been pitched wide from the place whence Miller swung his shoulders; aimed from a slightly different angle his hit, he maintains, would have missed the broadcasting box and overtopped the ancient roof.

I relate this story to illustrate my contention that Miller's planning is seldom blue-printed and down-to-the-earth; there is about him and his cricket the style and flavour of the picaresque. He has swagger—and it is fervently to be hoped that the solemn, humourless, kill-joy atmosphere of contemporary Test matches will never quieten his ardours.

There is danger indeed that even a Keith Miller is not immune from the terrible bacillus that has poisoned an atmos-phere that was healthy enough for Victor Trumper, Charles Macartney, Stanley McCabe, Woolley, Charles Barnett of Gloucestershire, Hammond, and—only yesterday—Denis Compton.

In the England v. Dominions match of 1945, in which Miller's glorious cricket thrilled and delighted a great crowd weary from strain and vicissitude of war, no fewer than 1,241 runs were scored in three days. Hammond hit four sixers, Miller seven, Donnelly two, Cristofani three; and the bowling on both sides was keen and excellent.

It is sad to think that cricketers of today possess the ability to play with the daring and skill of the brilliant heroes of the 'Golden Age', but hold themselves in check, denying God-sent gifts, all because Test matches have somehow come to mean and signify atrophied sport—in fact, often the negation of sport and the reasonable hazards on which true sport depends for vital existence.

Still, I am moderately contented to see Miller standing at the batting crease, his feet a little apart, tossing his hair back from over his forehead—it is a pleasure merely to watch him playing defensively with a positive straight back-swing, though I never feel that he is entirely happy if he is not attacking; and I can't enjoy him thoroughly if I suspect he is himself suffering some frustration.

I like to see him walking out to bat, looking about him so as not to miss anything, the legs moving easily but no part of the upper body moving at all. Once when he was coming through the pavilion gate at Sydney on the way to face the England attack in a Test match, a small schoolboy ran after him through the pavilion gate, defying red-faced authority. He asked the boy to hold his bat while he wrote an autograph for him.

Handsome in a sun and windswept way, and at first sight he suggests the typical Australian who 'couldn't care less'. But at the 'smell' of a half-volley or of a snick through the slips, or at the touch of a new shining red ball, the life of him darts into action. The right foot prances on the crease, and the wrists and superb forearms whip the ball to the boundary causing a crack from the fence that is like a rapid echo of the crack of the bat. At second-slip, while the bowler is walking back to his starting-place, he is relaxed and conversational, dismissing with a wave of the hand somebody's 'tip' for the 3.30, or whistling a phrase from a Beethoven piano concerto. Not until the ball is on the way does he bend. And I have seen him pounce at a catch a split-second before the chance has skimmed from the bat's edge, hold it and roll over, maybe unnecessarily, because he likes a flourish that thrills the girls as well as the schoolboys.

Frequently he is an improviser, making-up his batting and bowling as he goes along. He will turn round abruptly—

sometimes he doesn't take the trouble to measure his 'run' —and by a convulsion of the shoulders release a 'bumper' of alarming velocity and trajectory; and it is all done, I am sure, without premeditation or malice most times. Now and then, possibly, some excess of devilment goes into a Miller 'bouncer'; he is then like a man having 'shies' at a coconut stall when, after he has several times nearly knocked the Aunt Sally over, she has come swinging back again apparently at the point of no return. Naturally the thrower is driven to exasperation. In one and the same over Miller is equal to all sorts, not excluding a round-arm 'skimmer' as obsolete as a cannon-ball at Sebastopol. In this over a batsman may be asked to cope with pace and length and awkward rise from the pitch. With slower balls of tantalising curve he has twice overthrown Hutton, bringing the Master down when in full command, at Nottingham in 1948 and at Sydney in 1951. He is unpredictable and occasionally barely credible, never to be labelled under a categorical glass-case. Call him an improviser—next day he will put us temporarily in the wrong by scoring delights and living laboriously while observing the canons of batsmanship and wearing a hair shirt of self-control; this happened at Sydney in 1951 when he stayed in from noon to evening resisting the quite wicked temptation of England's crippled attack, Brown, Warr and Bedser and nobody else, on a day of merciless heat. He played a scupulous game, nearly five hours for 99. For the cause, my soul!

Call him one of the most imperious executants of the forward stroke, the left shoulder and elbow a commanding thrust not only in unison with the front foot, but all the movements of him a swift physical manifestation of a single idea. Say that whether he knows it or not he is an exponent of the doctrine of C. B. Fry: 'Play back or drive'. And in his very next innings he is capable of fooling us, capable of lunging out, right foot bogged, the body stretched to immobility, the bat stiff and sightless in front of a left foot which for the time being has obviously lost organic connection with his anatomy as a whole. I have seen him, after some such elongation, stumped from a ball he should either have driven on the run or have played back off the right foot; and as the wicketkeeper removed the bails at leisure Miller lay flat on the earth, belly down, the head and shoulders of him held up only by his right hand. Slow leg-spin is likely to double him up. Wright is always knotting the whip of his stroke-play. Miller's right-hand technique is firmer and stronger than his left hand's; he is not masterful at playing the late going away ball (if it is doing its work quickly) with the 'dead bat' of Hutton directed by a left hand and left fingers as sensitive and as much in control as those of Heifetz.

But as soon as I have written that latter sentence I am obliged to pause and remember the innings of Miller at Bradford in 1948, worth only 34 in the score-book but match-winning against Yorkshire on a bowlers' wicket. There is at least another innings to be quoted in support of Miller's batting on a nasty wicket: 99 for New South Wales against Victoria at Sydney in 1949. But whenever Miller conquers the spinning ball on a pitch of different paces, it is a case of eyesight and instinct coming to his rescue. Genius can get away with murder. From a comprehensive critical view there is no continuous line or design in a characteristic Miller innings, yet it can be ennobled by intermittent suggestions of the classical manner, moments when the man's volatility is caught in a brief, arrested attitude almost sculptural: a drive crashing to the top of a grand stand, going upward all the time, the swing of the bat easy and free, in an arc finishing over the shoulder, the back of the right wrist not far from the left cheek, the poise of him aquiline and seigniorial. Or a late-cut made by a quick bending down over the ball as it flashes past the off-stump. He seems quite still a moment after the bat has sent the ball speeding away and he looks as though into and above the stroke, a Narcissus of the cricket field, seeking in brilliance a reflection of his own art and pleased, flushed face. Or maybe it is a leg-hit which carries all his power and body round in a spiral, a magnificent expense of passion!

The classical poise of Miller's batsmanship is, as I have said, here and there endangered by some imp of energy in him that is not ready to conform and observe etiquette. This cricketer, who can stand at the batting crease with bored impatience as the field is set for him, stand there showing the condescension of one of the game's aristocracy, is not entirely blue of blood in his style; he was born under a bar-sinister. I have written of his late-cut in twopenny-coloured language. At other times he will cut late and resemble in his attitude a truant urchin out fishing when he should be in school. A bowler's fate for the day is more or less settled when Miller wakes up in the morning and finds out how he is feeling in mood.

Sir Donald has written that Miller resembles J. M. Gregory, 'whose limitations were caused mainly by his own failure to concentrate'. Very true, no doubt. But there is room, surely, in cricket today for at least one player who comes to the game most days willing to let himself go in it, without inhibitions, without even responsibility to those austere ethical canons which teach that the game is more than the player of the game. If there is the slightest likelihood that Test matches may tend to check the impulse of Miller and curb his flights into a risky void now and again, let Test matches be anathema, and done away with.

LORD'S AND LINDWALL

No rubber in the past between England and Australia has been as evenly balanced as the one now in the scales. Both teams have one or two players of Test match quality, surrounded by mediocrity.

It is never easy to foretell events if only a few 'key' men are present to control; the fumblings and ditherings of the others, the merely competent, can easily upset the apple-cart of logic any day.

At Lord's the match was thrown away in turn by England and Australia. At one point in England's first innings, the victory was in our pocket; then, on the closing afternoon, Australia's grip was so tight, apparently, that no power on earth would resist it. The frank truth is that the present Test series depends so much on the efforts of the few outstanding men that failure by any one of them will cause a drastic change in the situation.

Much as I admired the noble stand between Watson and
Bailey, the stand that saved England, I could not help asking
myself if even the courage of Bailey could for four hours
have preserved him against an Australian attack containing a Grimmett or an O'Reilly to exploit a dusty wicket,
or even against any other decent spinner as assistant to
Lindwall.

Hassett's team is the weakest in reserve bowling I have ever
known. When Lindwall is not in hot action with the new ball,
the Australian attack possess no terrors not familiar to all our
county cricketers. Indeed, if I were a batsman as good as, say,
R. T. Simpson, I would fancy my chances much more playing
the Australians minus Lindwall than against say, Surrey or
Northamptonshire.

There is not, I think, the danger in Miller's bowling that
seems to the eye still to be there, potentially if not actually; he
is certainly not the fiery attacker of 1948, when most of
England's batsmen preferred to cope with Lindwall rather
than with Miller.

W. A. Johsnton will need to improve on his bowling at
Lord's out of all recognition to stay the course of this rubber.
The other Australian bowlers are, as I say, merely a county
routine standard. England is really presented with the chance
of a lifetime.

And yet, and yet! For all the clamour with which opportunity is knocking at England's door, I doubt whether the
door will be boldly opened. I fear that England will lose the
rubber because in the Australian ranks, where as much of
mediocrity resides as in England's, there are two cricketers, if
not three, of great skill *and* imagination; whereas in the
England side, though there are three truly great cricketers,
only one of them is gifted with the vision which sees events
long before they are perceptible to the naked eye.

Denis Compton was such a seer, such a batsman, in 1947
and 1948; Miller, Lindwall and Harvey are all players of vivid
opportunism, prompted by intuition and impulse, and seldom
content to go by the book of shrewd arithmetic. Whether or
not Harvey will at Old Trafford cut and drive England's
bowling to ribbons—I write in advance of the game—as he
has remarkably failed to do up to the moment of writing, the

menace of his cavalier bat will remain over our heads, a terribly impending sword!

Miller, as we all know, is likely any afternoon to be seized by devils, though the fires of his fast bowling are on the wane. Then there is Lindwall, recently described by a very great old Test Match cricketer as the finest of all fast bowlers.

Well, I was only a small boy when I saw Richardson and Lockwood. In mature years I have seen Macdonald, Larwood, Cotter, N. A. Knox, Constantine, Gregory; and without hesitation I place Lindwall amongst the best of these, with the cautionary clause that we cannot truly compare cricketers of different periods, each the product of different conditions; at least we can't measure them technically.

For sheer pace I believe Ernest Jones, the Australian, and Kortright excelled them all, though I am reminded, as I write this sentence, that towards the end of W. G. Grace's life, when he and friends were talking cricket and the 'Old Man' was extolling George Freeman of the 1870's as one of the fastest ever, somebody said, 'But, Doctor, what about Ernest Jones?' and 'W.G.' replied, 'Heh, yes—Ernest Jones; yes, I remember him—he bowled a short one through my whiskers. Yes, yes—I should *say* he was fast; yes, I should say so.'

Kortright was so very fast that it is alleged a certain famous county batsman played forward to the first ball he ever received from him; and that he remembered nothing more until he heard the wicket-keeper behind him calling out: ''Ere you are, Bill, 'ere's your bat.' Many years ago I spoke of Kortright to J. T. Tyldesley, one of the few supremely great stroke-playing match-winning and match-saving batsmen of all time. 'Tell me, Johnny,' I asked, 'What did Kortright do with the ball?'

'He bowled fast,' answered Tyldesley. 'I know *that*,' replied I, impatiently, 'of course he bowled fast. But what did he do with the ball—did he swing it or bring it back off the pitch?' 'No,' said Johnny, 'he just bowled fast. *There was no time for anything else.*'

Lindwall is not properly to be described as a fast bowler; he commands more than speed. Another old Test match player, who challenged the other one's praise of Lindwall as the 'best of all', assures me that Lockwood was much faster than

Lindwall and, moreover, bowled a slower ball of great guile. I myself, when hardly beyond infancy, saw Lockwood hurling down balls which reared over the wicket-keeper's head after pitching. And, this old Test player tells me, Lockwood seldom bowled a deliberate 'bumper'; and his action was the smoothest imaginable.

No fast bowler's action could surpass that of E. A. Macdonald for silent curving effortless grace. He ran along the earth so lightly that often it was hard to see any footmarks on the grass after he had gone through an innings. When his arm came over, and just before the ball was released, his right wrist seemed to poise itself—I likened it to the cobra's head about to spit its venom. Macdonald, like Lindwall, bowled with variations of pace; on a soft wicket, after rain and sun, Macdonald was no mean off-spinner of medium speed.

Lindwall's action, not his general style, reminds me of Larwood, yet there is a subtle difference in the run to the wicket as well as in the actual balls delivered. Larwood ran like a young colt on the gallop. Lindwall runs easily, holding the ball a few strides in both hands in front of him, then the right hand falls behind him now in sole possession on the ball, and it hangs there with menacing looseness while Lindwall gathers a sudden and beautiful momentum before the wheel-over of the arm.

From the beginning, Lindwall's run to bowl suggests the classical sideway action, the left shoulder is all the time, every stride, veering as though to point down the wicket. He is, I think, a more dangerous bowler in England than in the clear air and on the dry wickets of Australia. He learned much, while playing in the Lancashire League, of the arts of the seam and new ball; also of the character of 'green' turf wickets.

Nobody is able to settle the question of Lindwall's supremacy as a fast bowler in point of pace. But it will be reasonable to claim on his behalf that he is probably the cleverest of all fast bowlers at using the seam; for the exploitation of seam and 'shine' is a new thing and science. In Lockwood's and Richardson's heyday, one ball only was available in the longest innings. As rare old Jack Gunn put it, 'We had to go on playin' with old ball till it coom in two.'

Lindwall swings late and keeps the ball up to the batsman most times; best of all, he threatens the stumps and urgently demands from the batsman a stroke of some sort. The purists have told us that his arm is often 'low'; true, it doesn't exactly brush the rim of the right ear. But there is artfulness in Lindwall's projectory, and in the different ways and levels from which he wheels his arm. The so-called 'low' action favours the skidding last-second swing. The whole of his splendid physique goes into every ball as naturally as breath into a living body.

Without Lindwall, Australia might suffer a crippling handicap, equal to the unthinkable disaster for England should any mishap occur to Bedser. I count Lindwall the most dangerous factor in the present rubber, especially in a challenging moment.

I am still at a loss to account for the fact that at Lord's in the second Test match Hassett didn't call on Lindwall for one last convulsion of determined hostility after tea, on that closing afternoon.

While we are trying to weigh one fast bowler with another over the ages, we should bear in mind that though Richardson, Lockwood and others did not enjoy the advantage which comes with the new ball, they were not frustrated by the over-rolled wickets of little or no pace. On the other hand, Richardson, Lockwood, Ernest Jones and the rest, had to tackle batsmen well accustomed to speed, batsmen who didn't genuflect at the first sight of a bouncing ball breast high.

It is well worth reminding ourselves, too, in this age of self-advertisement, when we are claiming records and the 'best of everything ever', as though in a national mood of vehement doubt about it all—it is well worth the while of cricketers to remember that Tom Richardson in four consecutive seasons took nearly 1,000 wickets; and in his career from 1892 to 1905 took 2,105 wickets at 18.42 runs each.

We need not measure the giants, though; none of us is big enough to do so. They stand together, Lindwall, Lockwood, Richardson, Macdonald, Knox, Brearley, shoulder to shoulder, and equally illustrious.

NEIL HARVEY—A CAVALIER

BROADLY there are two sorts or classes of batsmen. There is the batsman whose merit is measured exactly and totally by the score-board. If the score-board were not standing there, his presence at the wicket would scarcely be noticed by the crowd. Let him compile (that is the word) less than twenty runs and his visit to the wicket has been anonymous, not to say invisible. And should he amass two thousand runs in a season, average 52.17, we usually have little more than the scorer's word for it.

The other sort of batsman would hold our attention if all the scorers and the scoring boards in the world were to go on strike. He plays in a style that is beyond statistical assessment. Neil Harvey is such a batsman; he is an artist. You will no more arrive at a complete idea of his cricket by adding up the runs he makes than you will realise the quality of Mozart's music if you add up all the crotchets and quavers. Recently there has been much talk about the need to 'brighten' the game. Cricket captains at a season's beginning have spoken of this need, and of their determination to look to it, like so many political candidates in an election address. Neil Harvey has never, in all his career, needed any sort of propaganda to stir him to 'brightness'. Always he has performed, or tried to perform, strokes. His bat has been a stroke-maker all the time exactly as Yehudi Menuhin's violin has all the time been a music-maker. Naturally and inevitably enough, Harvey has on many occasions lost his wicket attempting a stroke. But I doubt if he has, once in his career, cut out his finest strokes out of fear of attempting them. And in his career of almost persistent brilliance, taking the true sportsman's chances, he has made more than 5,000 runs in Test matches, averaging round about 50 an innings—wonderful consistency on the part of a cricketer who has played less by calculation than by joyous impulse.

He, of course, is a master technician. No swashbuckling batsman could possibly achieve a Test match average of half-a-century over a longish period if he lacked knowledge of fundamentals and did not defend, at the sight of a dangerous ball, over the line. But Harvey's temperament would not be denied, even by the sight of a dangerous ball, if his team were in a strong position, of if the situation called for attack. I have heard critics complain that Harvey is too frequently 'careless'. Maybe; in fact, I know no batsman who has so frequently as Harvey got himself out to strokes which even his best friends have called 'silly'. As a fact, Harvey has seldom lost his wicket to a technically bad stroke; he has lost it, more often than not, to the wrong technically *right* stroke. In other words he has fallen because of an error of judgment—not an error of technique or style. At Old Trafford in 1956 (Laker's Test match), Harvey undoubtedly was guilty of one of the most shockingly wrong and ungrammatical strokes ever per-petrated by a well-bred batsmen. Laker, in this Australian holocaust, removed Harvey twice for noughts; and the second of them was quite straggeringly the consequence of a cross-batted, cross-eyed pull at a full-toss. Harvey drooped his head in shame; and I liked him for a revelation of honesty.

A cavalier on swift feet? His sword a lance? He has been known to put on heavy armour. At Sydney, in 1954–1955, Australia were being overwhelmed by the Tyson typhoon. On the fifth day Australia wanted only 151 to win, eight wickets in hand. Then the storm broke, the typhoon levelled the Austra-lian innings to the earth. No Australian batsman, except Harvey, was strong enough, able enough, to withstand Tyson's hurricane, backed up by the gale force of Statham, Harvey, for four hours and more, put the straightest bat to the deadly ball. But at the sight of a ball in the slightest loose he cut, glanced or hooked with a brilliance which suggested that he and his bat were making the forked blinding lightning of the storm. That dire morning for Australia, Harvey scored 92. At Leeds, in 1956, he also disciplined himself superbly for the Cause, and in four-and-a-half hours fought a stubborn rear-guard—in vain. Yet, for all his dour defence, his cricket remained good to see, beautifully poised, quietly throbbing with reserve power. It is easy for your Hutton, your Lawry, your Pullar, to stay at the crease for hours resisting temptation to hit the ball. It is not so easy for a Harvey to exercise self-control to the verge of austerity. The man born rich finds it painful to practice economy. Harvey was born with runs, strokes, lovely strokes, as a kind of inheritance. He has not so much *made* or *earned* his thousands of runs; he has spent them generously, to the enrichment of cricket.

Yet, in his very first Test match, against England in 1948 at Leeds, he was called on to bat, the first time for Australia, at a moment of incipient crisis for Australia. England, in first, had scored 496. Oh the third morning Hassett and Bradman succumbed to red-headed, magnificently Lancastrian Dick Pollard. Australia were 68 for 3 when Neil (aged nineteen) joined Keith Miller. In an hour-and-a-half he and Miller plundered 121 by glorious defiance and attack. Harvey reached a century. And it is said that after he had played a few overs at the beginning of his debut as a Test match batsman, the England bowlers having been inspired by Bradman's downfall—that in this challenging hour, he went down the wicket between overs and said to Miller: 'Don't help yourself to *ALL* the runs, Keith. Save a few for me.'

He is really a modest little man, quiet but with a twinkle in his eyes. Also he is a big man—large of nature. He could easily have taken umbrage when Richie Benaud and not Harvey was chosen as Australia's cricket captain. But Neil became Benaud's great help, the eminence (not grey!) in the modest background. He has served Australian cricket handsomely. And just as handsomely has he served it by his experienced guidance out of the public eye. He is a remarkable example of maturity and youthful shyness. He has, as they say, 'an old head'. And a young heart. His batting, though it can put the best bowlers to the sword, with fours all over the field, is not at all brutal or excessive of power. He is not, as Bradman was, an obvious 'Killer'. He charms runs out of the attack. On dancing feet he goes to meet them, and he lures them to ruin by the hypnotism of his bat's movements. These movements are willowy. Harvey's bat has never looked like a bludgeon. It is all curves and rapier-thrusts. He is not, as even the fascinating Norman O'Neill is, a batsman too dependent on the leverage of the lower grip on the bat. And if he traffics hazardly to balls swinging away on the offside—drawn to the new ball's red light as a pretty moth to the flame—well, he can't help it. He was born that way. Moreover, by playing cricket as God and nature intended that he should play, he has long since joined the ranks not only of cricket's artist-batsmen but of those who have piled up fortunes in runs and centuries.

He is still, on all wickets, Australia's greatest batsman. And he follows in, and adds lustre to, the bright tradition established by Trumper, Kippax, McCabe, Archie Jackson. I don't mention Macartney in the context of Harvey; because Macartney was a ferocious batsman. Harvey, as we have agreed, was never that—his cricket delighted and hurt not. He didn't ever assault bowler, never rubbed their noses in the dust. He lured them, allured them, to destruction. They got intoxicated with the champagne of a Harvey innings, joining in the universal chorus to him, '*For*—he's a jolly good fellow!' The Pied Piper of Australian cricket! He is not tall, but he is built like a cricketer, swift and weightless. And he is modest. His batting is, for all its glories, modest. Gentleman Harvey—no true lover of the game can think of him without pleasure and gratitude. I have not mentioned his fielding so far. As a cover point, in his younger days, he was of a piece with his batsmanship, rapid, comprehensive, graceful and electrical. It is because of cricketers of the thoroughbred order of Harvey that I have spent half-a-lifetime writing about the game, sometimes mixing it up with the higher art which has given Mozart to the world, and Schubert. Which is saying a lot of any sport, any game!

1954–55

TOUR OF AUSTRALIA

I doubt if Hutton's main problem has yet been solved—the problem arising from an embarrassment of talent, actual or potential. Seventeen players besides himself should now be at his disposal, including, I hope, the world's most versatile batsman, Denis Compton.

If every cricketer in Hutton's command were to play his best in Australia during this rubber, what a superb array of skill would be seen on the fields of Brisbane, Sydney, Adelaide and Melbourne! But with such riches at hand, how could any mortal cricket captain choose the right XI? Fortunately, or ironically, the gods usually step in to help fallible human judgment whenever wealth is lavished on us beyond our capacity to bear.

We can be pretty certain that more than one member of Hutton's contingent will, by running untrue to form, disqualify himself from the first Test Match, starting in Brisbane on November 26. Whenever an England team visit Australia, or whenever an Australian team visit England, at least one cricketer of reputation or promise fails to do justice to his gifts, and at least one cricketer still in the budding period comes to something like full bloom. Who, this time, will disappoint us? Who, this time, will go ahead and receive the recognition given only to those who emerge from mediocrity?

In both teams, English and Australian, men of reputation and youngsters on the rim of fame will be weighed in the balance. Will Lindwall maintain his position among the fast bowlers of today? Will he be ousted from it by Tyson or Statham? Will Peter May at last reproduce in Test Matches his greatness of stroke play in county cricket? Will Loader be able to swing the ball in Australian air? Will Hutton recapture his mastery as a batsman? Is he in danger of sharing

Hammond's sad fate? In the 1946–47 rubber, Hammond was far from happy, either as captain or batsman.

The present tour should settle, once and for all—or at least for some years to come—the question of whether a professional cricketer is capable of leadership during an international rubber. It is the duty of every lover of English cricket to support Hutton at this critical period of his career; to send him good wishes and to have faith in him.

Every member of the team he is leading should be prepared and glad to work himself to the bone for Hutton, for whatever some of us may think about his outlook on the game, none can doubt Hutton's grand sense of duty, his conscientiousness and integrity, his tenacity of purpose. English cricket has known no captain as ready as Hutton to devote the whole of himself to the cause, both on and off the field.

Frankly I wish he could have gone to Australia purely as a batsman and fieldsman, with no responsibility of office resting on his shoulders. It is easy to say that Hutton enjoys this kind of responsibility; every Yorkshireman has the knack of enjoying all the trials and burdens of life. 'Don't worrit yourself, lass,' says every Yorkshireman to his wife occasionally. And most times she replies: 'Get on wi' thi own worritting and leave mine alone!'

If any player in Hutton's team gives him an ounce less than his best, let his name be anathema! And let every man jack keep himself fit; let them all avoid slipped discs, fibrositis and other fashionable physical ailments hardly ever heard of in the days of W. G. Grace and George Hirst.

Once, it is true, a Middlesex professional approached P. F. Warner at the beginning of a match and said he would not be able to play. 'But why?' asked 'Plum'. The professional showed him a slightly discoloured right forefinger. 'Got 'it in the nets, sir,' he explained. And 'Plum' replied: 'Do you mean to tell me that because of a tiny bruise you don't want to play today?' Then he fixed the professional with a very solemn eye, saying: 'You should always be prepared to *bleed* for Middlesex!'

Maybe several members of the present England team will make a mistake in a contrary direction and try *too* hard. I am hoping that Tyson will be able to modify his run to the wicket without interference to rhythm and impetus. He must surely rid himself of his habit of shuffling and scratching on the turf just after he has got into, or is about to get into, his stride. The hard grounds of Australia will, in time, give him sore feet unaided by collaboration from himself.

Tyson is a cricketer of character and intelligence, and he will quickly understand that conservation of energy is the first principle a fast bowler in Australia should study and practise. To bowl wide of the wicket in Australia is wasteful, not only of time, but of breath and sinew. 'Keep the batsman playing' has been the motto of all bowlers successful in Australia.

In the game in Sydney two most notable innings were also played by a young English cricketer—two centuries by Colin Cowdrey, who first came to the wicket at a moment of incipient ruin in Hutton's ranks: four wickets down for 34. Cowdrey at once eased anxiety in the breasts of visiting English people; he at once looked as much at home as Hutton himself.

I make so bold as to say that Cowdrey's first innings definitely and once and for all announced that he is the best and most self-possessed young amateur batsman in English cricket since, say, C. F. Walters—though he is not at all like Walters in style.

I fancy that Cowdrey will surpass before long the performances of the gifted but somewhat problematical Peter May, who, each time he plays a good innings for England, leaves us still wondering what he will do next and whether he really is a pedigree batsman. In Sydney, Cowdrey was not put out of comparison even with Hutton—and Hutton on this occasion was clearly the most accomplished batsman alive.

On paper the England batting has an impressive appearance to begin with—Hutton, Compton, Cowdrey, Simpson, May, Graveney . . . yet still nobody really trusts an England innings to begin well. And as for the end!—the imagination reels at the thought of what a grisly procession might any day be witnessed as Evans, Appleyard, Bedser, Statham or Tyson come and go—one down, t'other soon after!

Yet—and still more yets—I am hopeful that, despite our failure in the First Test, Hutton will bring the 'Ashes' back to England next March.

It is hard to believe that England's batsmen will not assert themselves and their true gifts, for nobody but a fool would argue that Hutton, Compton (when fit), Simpson, Graveney, May, Cowdrey, Wilson and Edrich are not highly gifted. Australia today cannot gather together so much experience and accomplished batting as that represented by these names.

Hutton and Compton can both be called *great* players, the one providing solid technique from which an advance or a 'strategical withdrawal' can be made, according to the circumstances; the other a match-winner of imagination and genius. Australia at the moment can boast only one truly great batsman—and that is Keith Miller. Neil Narvey is a brilliant stroke-player, but if I were as good a bowler as, say, Bedser, I would usually feel confident that I could get him out. Benaud, de Courcy, Morris and Favell are all stroke-players, too—but each is often hinting at some fallibility in defence, at some 'hole in the bat.'

However, if it be true—and it *is* true—that England possesses the two greatest batsmen in the world, Hutton and Compton, it is just as true that Australia can point to the most dangerous of all living bowlers, Lindwall.

At the start of this series I was satisfied that the issue of the rubber was so even that the tiniest straw of luck might well bring down the scales one way or the other. And a tremendous lot depends on Lindwall!

The attack at Hutton's disposal is perilously dependent on speed. It is also the kind of swing or seam bowling which loses force in a dry Australian atmosphere. For this reason it will not be so well suited by the air and humidity in Melbourne, Adelaide and Sydney (in March)—where the last three Tests will be played—as by the conditions of Brisbane and Sydney (at Christmas), which applied for the first two matches.

Therefore I warn all English cricketers that even if we had won the first two Tests the prize would still not be ours. G. O. Allen's team won the first two Tests in 1936–7 in Brisbane and Sydney, but lost the next three.

In any case Hutton's shrewd captaincy would surely find fuller scope if more spin bowling were at his service. After all, a little tactical subtlety is needed to reinforce the steady persistence of the direct attack of speed. I confess that, if I were Hutton, my mind would be easier, and my task as captain of England less worrying, if my attack included the left-handed spin of Lock or the right-handed spin of Douglas Wright.

In the matches I have watched on this tour, Australian fielding has been far ahead of England's. To be blunt about it, too much of England's fielding has been slow and untidy. Something should be done about a fault which could turn the way of the battle against England and beyond redemption.

AUSTRALIAN CRICKET

THE first thing that strikes the cricket lover on his first visit to Australia is the scarcity of cricket in this land of born cricketers. The season lasts from October to March, and mostly it is hot and sunny. Yet, day after day, the great grounds of Sydney, Melbourne and Adelaide are vacant and unoccupied.

There is no day-by-day cricket in Australia, and it is possible to spend a holiday lasting several weeks in any large Australian city and not see a single hour of first-class cricket. The amount of top-grade cricket that takes place in an Australian summer could be packed into two or three weeks of an English season, weather permitting.

Cricket in Australia is played mainly on Saturday afternoons. The five states—Western Australia, South Australia, Victoria, New South Wales and Queensland—play each other twice; for the rest, the Australian cricketer and cricket lover has to be content with Saturday club games.

How, then, is it possible to become a first-class cricketer in Australia? How, with few opportunities to play the game, does Australia continue to produce from a population not larger than London's the finest all-round players in the world? The question is made the more intriguing when it is remembered that in Australia there are no long evenings of light and sunshine. Darkness descends round about seven o'clock, making net practice impossible. And every great Australian cricketer has a job in an office, bank, workshop and so on. There is no professional career open in Australia to the cricketer of talents.

Moreover, there is no organised system of cricket instruction. Much is heard in England nowadays of coaching schools and classes for young cricketers. They are excellent institutions, no doubt, as far as they go. But the greatest English players have learned the game exactly as Australians are still learning it; not by drilled instruction and deliberate theory, but by trial and error in matches, and by example set by one another in action.

A youth making his debut for a grade team in Sydney might have to go in to bat facing Lindwall, and he is immediately brought into the company of the great. A club cricketer in England might easily play every Saturday from youth to middle-age and not once face the challenge of a county cricketer's skill.

Cricketers in Australia are made the hard way; as a fact they are not made at all—they are born. They are born in an atmosphere which breeds sport as the atmosphere of Vienna once bred musicians. Constant competition governed by the ruthless law of the survival of the fittest!—here is the secret of Australia's continuously progressive evolution in sport.

As in all other walks of life, Australian sport changes in style and character from time to time. Cricket is still a national game in Australia—but only one among others. Crowds flock as ever to Test Matches. The important fact is that crowds no longer flock to the inter-state matches, as they did in the old days to see Victoria, with Ponsford, play New South Wales, with Bradman. I doubt if first-class cricket could continue to exist in Australia apart from Test Matches and the revenue brought to the cricket treasury by them.

There has also been a change in the Australian attitude to her cricket and cricketers; a striking change, during the last decade. When I visited Australia for the first time in 1936, the dominating heroes of Australian sport were Bradman, Ponsford, McCabe, O'Reilly. Nowadays it is the tennis player, not the cricketer, who is the symbol of athletic and sporting prowess and ambition in the eyes of most of the rising generation of Australians. The Davis Cup vies in interest with a Test Match in Sydney. On the roll of the nation's sporting heroes, your Sedgmans, Hoads and Quists stand for ever side by side with Trumper, Macartney, Munro the jockey and Keith Miller.

During the present rubber between England and Australia, the crowds have often seemed to be wanting England to win. Tyson, May and Cowdrey have been cheered as warmly as any Australian player. When Tyson was knocked out in the Second Test Match in Sydney by a ball from Lindwall, then returned to the field and put up as vital and bristling an exhibition of fast bowling as ever seen from Lindwall himself, the Australian crowd took Tyson to heart, and placed him once and for all in the Australians sportsman's hall of re-membrance. The name, pluck, skill and spirit of Tyson will never be forgotten in Sydney.

Other times, other manners. After the 'body-line' rumpus years ago, very few Australians wished to hail a victory by England at cricket. A new generation in Australia is finding out that a great game is none the less worth playing if it is occasionally played for fun. It is a long journey in mental outlook from Warwick Armstrong and 'Herbie' Collins to Morris and Miller.

Armstrong is dead, but Collins may still be seen watching a Test Match in Sydney. He was the most astute of all Australian cricket captains. His mind was always two overs ahead of the game. But Len Hutton's captaincy at times seems so involved, incurring so many hesitant pauses while he places and replaces the field, that he makes one think of a chess player engaged in a match against himself, half fearful of checkmating himself!

In an age of so-called democracy, leadership in cricket is following the general pattern of life and society at large. Nobody dares to dictate individually, and some of our captains remind me of the Duke of Plaza Toro in 'The Gondoliers'—they lead their regiments from behind, they find it less exciting.

It is possible now for a Test Match player to attend a race meeting rather than a Test Match—if he happens not to be playing. I doubt if D. R. Jardine would have allowed any player in his team such a liberty, and I doubt if any England player in Jardine's period would have preferred to go to the races rather than watch a crucial game in the rubber on a crucial day.

In recent years, cricketers, both in England and in Australia, have tended to take a rather mercenary and selfish view of the game, using it for their own purpose as careerists. The public has long tolerated their efforts at authorship and in the realm of pictorial advertisement. The same patient public has seen them taking far more out of the game in material rewards than they have put into it in the shape of personal risk and genius. Mediocrity has been boosted or exalted by co-operative writers on the game.

I fancy we are about to see a revival of amateur influence in English cricket. The recent advance to greatness on the part of Peter May and Colin Cowdrey is the best happening in our cricket since the days of Percy Chapman. For a little too long English cricket has been dominated by professionalism, in spirit and practice. The professional cricketer, taking him by and large, is an excellent sportsman. Still, by nature of his calling and his general way of life, he is not a leader of men; he is the sergeant-major rather than the commanding officer.

In Australia and in England alike, there is need for a revival of strong personality in leadership. A few years ago Keith Miller would have succeeded to the Australian cricket captaincy almost by divine right. Nowadays, the social habit of life is to favour the compromising and amenable attitude—and to distrust the dictates (and visions) of the individual.

THE AUSTRALIANS FALL TO TYSON

THE public's memory is short and fickle. As the forgotten Mr Dooley used to say, it's a case of 'off with the old love and on with the new—and off with that!' One year we are extolling Tate, next year Larwood, next year Bedser, and the latest hero is Tyson—all of them mortal, and therefore of perishable reputation.

Naturally, each hero is blown up beyond life size by contemporary adulation. At the moment, Tyson is dwarfing all fast bowlers in the imagination of the Australian crowds—and also, possibly, in the imagination of certain young Australian batsmen! I have seldom seen feebler attempts to cope with fast bowling than the attempts of Benaud, Davidson, Morris, and even Miller, to cope with Tyson. Indeed, some of the Australian batsmen in the present rubber have walked to the wicket with the diffidence of the condemned man who manages to get to the scaffold unsupported. Consequently England have kept the 'Ashes'.

What is happening to the Australian psychology and character? The young Australians today seem to lack toughness of type. Once, Australian batsmen were, like Yorkshire batsmen, always at their best in a tight corner. They brimmed over with optimism—cockiness if you like.

One morning in 1926, at the beginning of a Test Match between England and Australia at Lord's, I was at breakfast in a hotel in Bloomsbury. Charles Macartney, most impertinent of all Australian batsmen, happened to be staying in the same hotel. He joined me at my table. The morning was glorious—blue sky and sunshine. Macartney looked out of the window, clapped his hands and said: 'A grand day, Neville! By cripes, I feel sorry for the poor swines that bowl at me today!'

He was actually feeling sorry for them before the match had begun and before the toss had been won and lost! Such confidence is not, of course, born of conceit, but of knowledge that one is in possession of a technique. Macartney knew that he was a master batsman.

Many young Australians of the present generation simply do not understand that they are not in command of the first principles of batsmanship. In an age of 'short cuts', they have imagined they could achieve mastery by flair and glamour.

Some of these young men, in England and Australia alike, have scoffed at the great players of the past—'They'd never get runs against modern swerve and bend off the seam!' But now they are finding themselves shot out of their creases and reduced to ineffectuality by a bowler who bowls fast and straight, with little or no 'swing' or guile— just speed going the shortest distance between two points.

Against my fast bowler a batsman should remain close to the line of the ball; even a tyro batsman should prove himself equal to a firm stance *behind the ball*. Yet in Test Matches this rubber we have seen Test cricketers of contemporary vintage flashing their bats at Tyson's pace from positions where only the 'edge' will most times find contact. No great batsman should fall to slip catches or catches at the wicket from a straight fast bowler—at least, not after the said great batsman has 'looked' at the bowling for an over or two.

Tyson has bowled magnificently in the rubber of 1954–55, and it is no belittlement of his skill and stamina if I point out that he has been lucky with his opposition. In two consecutive rubbers against Australia—1928–29 and 1932–33—Larwood took 51 wickets, average 26.9. No other fast bowler has taken 51 wickets in two consecutive Australian rubbers, except Tom Richardson, who, in 1894–95 and 1897–98, took 54 wickets, average just over 30.

Let us be fair to the present, but not at the expense of the past. Larwood's opponents included Bradman, Woodfull, Ponsford, McCabe, Kippax, Fingleton and Victor Richardson. Tyson has been bowling at an Australian team who, it is admitted by everybody in Australia, are the weakest in batting for years.

The loss to the Australian XI of Hassett has already become perceptibly serious. He was thoroughly organised in the principles of defensive as well as offensive technique. Of not a single member of the contemporary Australian XI can it be claimed that he is difficult to get out unless he makes a stupid error prompted by temporary absence of mind. They are all—even Harvey and Miller—fundamentally unsound in some basic principle of technique; something is wrong with the footwork, or angle or back-lift of the bat.

It seems as though Australian cricket, once tough and masculine, has been afflicted with self-consciousness and femininity—or, to use the Australian language, 'has gone a bit "cissy"'—at least that was the impression gained after their Second and Third Test performances. But I am sure that this eclipse of masculine spirit in Australia is only for a brief period. I cannot believe that the tradition of Armstrong, Clem Hill, Darling, Trumper, Macartney, McCabe, Richardson and Bradman—all of them 'bonny fighters'—is forgotten.

Tyson and Statham in Australia have bowled superbly, make no mistake of that. They were perfectly contrasted —Tyson with his ponderous bull-at-a-gate charging energy, Statham springing to the attack with the grace of a deer.

I am not at all certain, from the highest technical standards, that Statham is not the better fast bowler of the two; he can cause the ball to swing late, now away and now into the bat. Tyson depends almost entirely on pace and straightness. We need not think the less of him for that. The great J. T. Tyldesley, when asked what C. J. Kortright 'did' with the ball, replied: 'He "does" nothing; he merely bowls fast. There is no time for anything else!'

Much too much fuss is made nowadays about 'swing' and 'bend' off the seam, 'cutters' and all the rest of the jargon. A very great old cricketer told me years ago how he had clean bowled both C. B. Fry and 'Ranji' on a perfect wicket in Brighton with balls as 'straight as a whistle'—not by subtleties of spin or swerve, but just by sheer accuracy of direction and length.

First principles! Our cricketers forget them at their peril! The first principle of batsmanship, said W. G. Grace, is 'to put your bat to the ball'. K. S. Ranjitsinhji honoured the same principle when he said: 'Watch the ball, go to it, play it.' There is nothing new under the sun. The contemporary young cricketers of Australia must learn to respect the past-masters and the ancient law.

THE YOUNG HEROES

ENGLAND'S victory in the rubber just completed must be counted one of the most decisive and surprising in all the history of these Test matches. It is difficult to explain in terms of technique exactly how it has all come to pass. Are Tyson and Statham amongst the best fast bowlers we have ever sent to Australia? Were they lucky to bowl on pitches of a more spiteful nature than is common in Australia; and if the pitches really did behave spitefully, why couldn't Lindwall, Miller, Archer and Davidson exploit them with the consistent ruthlessness of Tyson and Statham? Would any of us be prepared to hold to the opinion that Tyson and Statham make a more dangerous fast bowling combination than that of Lindwall and Miller, who only yesteryear might have been Mars and Jupiter in conjunction?

One of the most ancient sayings in cricket is that brilliant fielding wins matches; but in this rubber England's fielding, compared to Australia's, has seemed either insecure and slow in motion, when not merely peripatetic. Australia's batting suffered a grievous and not customary fallibility, true, after it had amassed the huge total of 601 for 8 wickets (declared) at Brisbane. But England's batting was also extremely precarious, and but for the efforts of two young amateurs must surely have brought ruin in its track. Australia thrice in consecutive games had victory well within reach, only to let it go by three consecutive batting collapses, each in a second innings, and each on a scale of shocking destruction and subsidence seldom equalled in Australia on dry turf.

At Sydney on the crucial morning the innings folded up with not a hint of starch in the limp fabric. At Melbourne the collapse was more catastrophic still; at Adelaide five wickets gave up the ghost in forty-five minutes for 14.

I would not belittle the fast bowling of Tyson and Statham for anything; I only wish they could have received the compliment of resolute opposition. Four years ago, during the tour in Australia of F. R. Brown's team, I sat in a Press Box at Melbourne; and Larwood sat next to me, a sedentary figure in hornrims, now reporting the game. Wickets were falling steadily, inevitably. Larwood fell into profound meditation as he saw frail batsmen follow frailer. Then he broke silence. 'Ah can't understand it,' he said, 'the way they can get 'em out nowada-ays. When Ah thinks over mi own Test career, Ah seemed to have spent all mi time bowling at Bradman.' Australia is handicapped by the presence of too many second-rate all-round cricketers, players who are not really Test match batsmen or bowlers.

But I work in a dim light of reason, as I seek for some plausible explanation of Australia's persistent breakdowns in batsmanship. Why did Morris, Harvey, Miller, Hole and Benaud repeatedly lose wickets to crude unprincipled strokes? What has happened to the old Australian power of concentration, the old Australian power to retaliate, the old Australian cocksureness? On the morning of the Test match at Lord's in 1926, I was staying in a Bloomsbury hotel, and Charles Macartney joined me at breakfast. He looked through the window, smacked his hands and said, 'Lovely day. By cripes, I feel sorry for any poor swine of a bowler who's got to bowl at me today.' He wasn't boasting; it was merely an expression of personal and anticipated enjoyment, mingled with sincere sympathy.

We can afford, and with unwonted pleasure, to leave Australian cricket to lick its own wounds. The refreshing thing about England's victory is that it was achieved by four young men. The superb wicket-keeping of Evans, the sturdy, almost ethical, service and servitude of Bailey, have been valuable but contributory influences.

England would surely have lost at Sydney but for May's century in the second innings, and Cowdrey's partnership with him after the overthrow of Hutton, Bailey and Graveney. And Cowdrey's 102 at Melbourne scored out of a total of 160, must go down in the records as one of the most magnificent acts of salvage ever accomplished by any Test match cricketer, young or old. Then, after the reliant skill of May and Cowdrey had stemmed the enemy's advance, Tyson and Statham—young Lancashire lads both, may I remind you (and not so young in the head!) blasted the way to triumph.

Cowdrey was only a month or two beyond his 22nd birthday when he wrote his name on the roll of cricket's young heroes. He began his innings in the teeth of the most devastating new-ball bowling seen at Melbourne since S. F. Barnes, in 1911, took 5 wickets for 6 in eleven overs before luncheon. Miller, on the occasion of the conception and advent of Cowdrey's masterpiece, bowled an hour and a-half, taking 3 wickets for 5. Cowdrey stood firm, did not move from the fiery spear of Miller's pace. W. J. O'Reilly described this innings of Cowdrey as 'one of the finest centuries I have seen in Test cricket'. In shattering-to-the-nerve sequence Cowdrey was called in to face five dire situations for England in his first experiences in the challenging air of an Australian v. England match in Australia—11 for 3, 147 for 3, 58 for 3, 55 for 3, and 21 for 2. I cannot recall that any young cricketer has been subjected to a more searching trial of nerve and character than these faced calmly by Cowdrey.

As I watched May and Cowdrey retrieving almost lost causes, I enjoyed a private pleasure of a kind much to be treasured these days. I was looking at, I felt sure, a revival of amateur influence and example in cricket. For too long we have watched the increase of professional control. Frankly, it has not always been to the good. The average professional cricketer is a fine sportsman and as good a fellow as the next; I have been a professional cricketer myself, so I know.

But, such is nature, that some of them have gone to work on the principle that there's nothing like leather, and that leather is best not abused. When Lord Hawke uttered his famous cry from the heart, he didn't intend to disparage the character of the professional cricketer as he knew him in the period of George Hirst, Johnny Tyldesley, J. T. Hearne, Schofield Haigh and George Lohmann; all he intended to suggest was that cricket would most likely lose much in spirit and style if it ever became heavily dependent on the services of men bound to it as a means of livelihood. The greatest batsmen were once almost always amateurs; the pace was set by the Graces, the MacLarens, the Jacksons, the Warners, the Spooners, the Frys. The 'pro' had to toe the line and play at the same pace.

The batting in Australia of May and Cowdrey during Hutton's campaign in Australia should, let us hope, prove of more value and provoke more inspiration than any victory in any rubber for years.

The balance of the mediocre ability of the two sides was no doubt swayed England's way by the astute leadership of Hutton. He was always Ian Johnson's master in gamesmanship. If he should lose the toss on a docile wicket as at Adelaide, Hutton connived that his bowlers didn't waste their energies enthusiastically; he saw to it that they laboured to the extent of not more than fifty-eight overs in five hours. Constant readjustments in field positions, made with the poised deliberation of a chess-player, wooed the clock as an ally. When everybody at Adelaide expected that Appleyard would bowl on the closing and decisive morning. Hutton at once called again on his fast attack. The pitch was not suitable for speed. Hutton was once more playing on the Australian nerve.

Following the Brisbane defeat Hutton might well have lost heart. He had blundered in judgment after winning the toss. He was out of form as a batsman. He maintained his sense of shrewdness, and in the small hours of the morning he set his teeth, wrinkled his brow; and he planned. His idea of the game is not mine; his attitude to it is contrary to mine. I see no fun at or imagination in tactics that handicap free impulses of sport. I am bored as Tyson walks slowly over his long distance to his bowling mark. I am bored whenever an attack declines the challenge of a great batsman's finest (and riskiest) strokes. I yawn whenever the England innings deliberately adopts a slower tempo for some hidden tactical motive. I am not interested in cricket if it constantly is nothing but competitive and needs perpetual reference to the score-board to justify or explain its more or less cataleptic moves and movements.

But the world judges by results. Hutton has more than retained the rubber; he has paid off old scores. In the past English cricket has had to swallow many a dish of humiliation served up by Warwick Armstrong, Collins and Bradman. The laugh is now with Hutton. No wonder there is a twinkle in his eye nowadays.

The question now at issue is whether we want our first-class cricket played this way in the future; played in a purely competitive way, with the prize more honoured than the game's brilliance and beauty as a summer spectacle. Much of the cricket recently seen in Australia was almost intolerably tedious to watch; it possessed hardly any interest except broadcasting and statistical interest. For hours a Test Match might as well have been played in a studio, or in camera, so little did the cricket appeal to the eye or to the enjoyment of individual style.

Cricket did not come by its tradition this way. Once upon a time its chief glory was that, at its best, it transcended competitive values and thrilled the imagination of the crowds *because of the way it was played.*

Nowadays, even at the start of a Test Match, an England attack may soon be seen aiming the ball outside the zone of a great batsman's best stroke. The idea is not so much designed to get him out as to *wear* him out. Not long ago, Australia's Neil Harvey, a brilliant off-side batsman, assured his friends that for months he had not received half-a-dozen balls from an England bowler that were not pitched on or outside his leg stump.

The rate of scoring in Test Matches especially in Australia, once the run-maker's paradise) has fallen abysmally. Once, a certain profession batsman was dropped from the England XI because his rate of scoring was not quick enough. Yet it was the average pace desired today, and achieved today by Hutton himself. But this discarded 'slow-coach' belonged to the period when a Test Match in England was limited to three days. The danger at present is that naturally gifted stroke-players, such as Cowdrey and May, will too frequently be subjected to the dreary routine necessary to justify the Cause and the means employed.

It is a question of what kind of cricket the public wants. A new public has come to cricket—a public mainly interested in the score-board and the results. Part of this public does not even see the actual play; they listen to broadcasts, and therefore art and style count for nothing.

Test cricket is at the cross-roads. Prize or Personality, Cricket or Competition? The hour and the demand bring forth the men. If it's results the crowd wants, Hutton has left A. C. MacLaren standing!

1956

ATTACK TO DEFEND THE ASHES

LEEDS has not so far been England's lucky ground in Test matches against Australia; in fact England has yet to beat Australia at Leeds, though ten Tests have been played there. Of them, Australia have won four—in 1909, 1921, 1938 and 1948.

If England, this year, don't play at Leeds with a more courageous spirit than our cricketers recently showed at Lord's—and I am not referring merely to wins or losses or any statistics whatever—the advantage is likely once again to go. Down Under, despite the fact that this present Australian team must be counted one of the least distinguished and menacing of any seen in this country in living memory.

But it is not so lacking in skill as many critics have led the public to suppose. We should also bear in mind that the full strength at Ian Johnson's disposal has not yet, because of accidents and ill-health, been brought into action.

By sheer determination the Australians escaped from overwhelming odds at the pinch at Nottingham, with two players pretty well ambulance cases; and at Lord's, deprived of a fast bowler in Crawford, they wrote a brilliant and exciting page or two in the history of international cricket.

Without a single victory to their credit in engagements against our counties, and proved vulnerable by Surrey, the Australians came to Lord's, still deploring the lack of Lindwall, Davidson—their most brilliant all-rounder—and Craig. And, again at the crisis, pluck and enterprise pulled the team out of a hole and clinched the victory.

When Miller was caught at the wicket in Australia's second innings, on the third day, Ian Johnson might well have given up and said, 'There go the "Ashes."' For surely if Australia had lost at Lord's, the rubber would have gone to England, simply because Australia this year are not so much stronger than England as to win twice with only three games to play—one at Kennington Oval too!

The solemn fact is that Australia thrashed England soundly at Lord's with ten men after contriving, with nine players, to wriggle out of an almost hopeless hole at Trent Bridge.

Naturally enough the old Australian confidence, not to say, cockiness, is now back in Ian Johnson's ranks, rendering half as strong again forces which on paper do not spell impregnability. The Lord's Test match was not only won thoroughly by Australia, it was as thoroughly lost by England—lost mainly because our batsmen yet again surrendered initiative to an attack containing only one Test match bowler and made on a reasonably neutral wicket.

What is psychologically wrong with English batsmen who in Test matches allow Australian bowlers to hypnotise them into immobility of mind and feet?

There must be a complete change of heart at Leeds. The Lord's Test demonstrated an old moral truth: superiority of spirit will usually win against a superiority of technique that lacks faith. It is a curious fact in English cricket nowadays that our bowlers can show grand determination; but our batsmen frequently fail in Test matches against Australia for want of determination.

Most times Leeds is a batsman's happy hunting ground in fine weather. C. Macartney, who scored a century at Leeds against England before lunch, once told me that at Leeds 'you need only to stick your tongue out at the ball and it goes for four.'

This summer, one or two wickets at Leeds have been prepared in a way which has co-operated with a bowler's spin. But I doubt if for the five-day convenience of a Test match the groundsman will refrain from using his finest arts to produce a pitch of customary Leeds reliability.

Obviously it is England's turn to go on to the offensive.

Although England hold the 'Ashes', no sane cricketer understanding Australia's mentality, would advise a negative 'What I have I'll keep' policy. And I fervently hope that at Leeds the England side will not contain too many players fresh to the atmosphere of a Test match against Australia. In such an atmosphere it is not fair to expect a cricketer to overcome inexperience and excusable nervous tension, and at the same time conquer an Australian attack very much pleased with itself.

Once, of course, Yorkshire were so strong and so highly placed in the championship table that if an England XI were to lose to Australia at Leeds, the crowd there would advise the Selection Committee to 'pick all Yorkshire side for next match'.

It was at Leeds that I overheard two spectators, one obviously from Huddersfield, the other as obviously from Batley, actually naming the England players essential to a Test match coming next week——.

'Well, 'Arry, we needn't look farther than 'Erbert Sutcliffe and Percy Holmes for opening batters, then Roy Kilner picks 'imself . . .' Very solemnly these two Yorkshiremen chose the entire Yorkshire team of that date.

I could not help overhearing their conversation, and I politely interfered:

'Excuse me,' I said, with intended irony, 'but you've left out Jack Hobbs.'

The Yorkshireman expressed astonishment, then one of them said, 'Aye, by gum, so we have!'

But the other Yorkshireman said, 'But 'ow are we goin' to get 'im in?'

On the first morning of any cricket match at Leeds the new ball can be made to swerve considerably. Sometimes, captains are relieved to lose the toss at Leeds; for of course they daren't dream of putting the other side in on turf likely, in fine weather, soon to become easy for good batting.

When Bradman scored 300 in one day against England, in 1930, he was nearly bowled first ball.

Such is cricket. No sensible player or spectator will risk prophecy yet about the result of the present rubber.

The England XI were on top of the world at Nottingham; the Australians were feeling far from happy on the eve of the Lord's Test. So the see-saw enchantingly moves, which is all to the good of the game.

In the Bradman epoch, when two batsmen stayed in all day,

flaying tired bowlers, there was little to stir anticipation, apprehension and the sense of glorious uncertainty. If only the wicket at Leeds is equally generous to batsman and bowler, we shall witness yet another great, exciting and fluctuating battle.

THE AUSTRALIANS BLAME THE PITCH

Though England's victory in the Manchester Test match settled the destination of the 'Ashes', the interest in the rubber remains keen and most important. The Australians, by winning at Kennington Oval in the game starting this week, will share not only the honours—two wins each; they will be able to bring a show of evidence to the view that in more or less equal conditions there is not much difference in skill and temperament between the two teams —a view which in my opinion is absurd.

It is fervently to be hoped that the wicket at the Oval for the Fifth Test will be firm and fast, and that the sun will shine with the splendour and continuity calculated to make every Australian cricketer engaged in the match think he is back in his own country, where wickets and turf are, of course, above suspicion.

My own heartfelt wish is that the Oval wicket will suit not only Miller, Lindwall and Archer but also our fast men. I hope indeed that the Australian conditions prevailing in 1954–1955, when Hutton's team won the rubber, are reproduced for the Fifth Test; and I earnestly wish that Tyson will be available and fit to bowl again for England.

In such conditions—Australian conditions—I am confident that Tyson and Statham could repeat the successes they achieved in 1954–1955 at Sydney, Melbourne and Adelaide.

On this present tour of our distressfully wet country, Ian Johnson's team no doubt has had an unfair share of un-Australian wickets on which to play. Rain changed the pace of the pitches in the Test Matches at Nottingham, Leeds and Old

Trafford. On dry days, at Leeds and Old Trafford, they lost the toss on pitches which apparently went bad as soon as England, including Godfrey Evans and Tony Lock, had ceased to bat on them.

Australia won at Lord's in continuously fine weather on a wicket which, in the language of our most expert commentator, was 'a fair one'. It was certainly fair to Archer, Miller and to Trueman; it was a wicket suitable to seam bowling of pace.

On this 'fair' Lord's wicket, Laker was more or less harmless and out of action at the crisis or turning point, and so was Wardle. A 'fair' wicket is one, I take it, on which Australia's quick 'new ball' bowlers may find assistance. But it is unfair if, by some metamorphosis after the match begins, the turf should take spin—especially Laker's spin—before each side has completed an innings!

I want to see conditions at the Oval as nearly as possible like Australian conditions so that Johnson and his men will have every opportunity to show that against Tyson and Statham they are not any more capable of beating England than they were at Sydney, Melbourne and Adelaide in 1954–1955.

During the present rubber the idea has got about that the Australians' only weakness is an inability to bat on a turning or crumbling pitch. The Australian batsmen, in fact, have collapsed wholesale nine times at least in the fourteen Test Matches played since and including 1953; moreover, they have collapsed as ruinously in their own country in hot, fine weather as they have collapsed here in rain or shine. What is more, they have collapsed against every sort of bowling England have been able to show them.

Now what kind of bowling would the Australians wish England to serve up to them at the Oval? They are not easy to please. And what sort of wicket would they themselves choose?—one like Nottingham in 1953, or the Old Trafford one of the same season, or the Australian wickets of Sydney, Melbourne and Adelaide of 1954–1955?

I imagine that Johnson desires nothing better for his prospects in the Final Test than sunshine, no rain, and a wicket which remains constant in texture and pace for at least three days. Perhaps providence will see to the sunshine and the rain. But, so far, no arts discovered by groundsmen can make a stretch of turf remain static of substance over several hours, with hard usage.

Where has this new idea come from that Test Matches should be played throughout, or for the better part of the time devoted to them, on pitches that remain of the same character —favourable to straight bowling, or to bowling dependent on the new ball, *but not to spin*?

The glory of cricket is that the conditions in which it is played are ever-changeful. A great cricketer is resourceful and flexible of technique. And a great cricket team should contain players able to cope with all sorts of circumstances.

Let the game at the Oval be played, as cricketers have always played the game, with every ball treated on its merits, with skill grappling with skill all the time.

I deplore the decline of standards in skill now sadly evident in Australian cricket at the present time. The revival will come, of course—perhaps, from the English point of view, too soon! But it will come only if Australians look the facts in the face and get to the root of the trouble. No good will be done by excusing.

Most important factor of all in the present eclipse of Australian batsmanship on English turf is the custom of covering wickets in Australia in first-class matches. How may any cricketer learn to bat or to bowl on a spinner's turf if he seldom gets a chance to practise on one?

But the general scarcity of spinners' wickets in Australia does not account for the fact that only yesteryear Australian batsmen were as helpless on Adelaide turf against Tyson and Statham as they have been this year against Laker on English turf. I am sorry to rub it in—but it's true!

1958

BENAUD MAY HOLD THE KEY

IT is true that in all the affairs of man the tide of events flows this way and that; action and reaction are equal and opposite. History of Tests between England and Australia shows that the pendulum swings in fair proportion—in good time. Today, it is certainly 'Australia's turn'.

Personally, though, I think Australia will need to wait a little longer. For one thing, Peter May doesn't believe in the mechanical workings of the 'law of averages'. He believes he has a splendid team; moreover, he quite vehemently believes that by willpower and determination he can control the course of events and 'create' victory. Not since Jardine has English cricket been led by a captain of May's unswerving purpose.

Here is England's first advantage over Australia. England's skipper will be psychologically tougher and tactically more astute than Australia's.

The rise in Australia's stock has been influenced by her team's triumphant record in South Africa. There, Ian Craig's men overwhelmed players who, a year earlier, had held England to a draw in a Test series. But when Ian Johnson's team came to England in 1956, remember, they had just visited and demolished the West Indies, and Johnson boasted that his resources equalled those of Bradman in 1948. We know well enough the humiliation suffered by Johnson and his ragged army.

Today, Australia's chances depend very much of the same players who, these last few years, have been battered or tormented to ruin by Tyson, Statham, Trueman, Laker and Lock in turn. Craig, Burke, Harvey, McDonald, Davidson, Archer, Benaud, Mackay, Burge . . . we know them all, and they are well and quickly recognised at sight by Statham,

Tyson, Lock and Laker. These Australians were unequal to England's present best even when supported by Miller and Lindwall. Are we to believe that a tour in South Africa has transformed general mediocrity into greatness?

True, wickets in Australia today are likely to prove more friendly to Australian batsmen than they were in 1954–55, the rubber of Tyson's and Statham's whirlwind. But the more reliable these Australian wickets are made for Craig, O'Neill, Harvey, Burke and the rest, the more they are bound to favour the greater batting skill of May, Cowdrey, Graveney, Richardson, Subba Row and company.

Admittedly, there are genuine causes for concern for the English team. It is true that wickets are protected from rain in Australian Tests nowadays, so that the spin of Lock and Laker must inevitably be diminished; and true, also, that in the absence of Wardle, May's attack will sadly miss spin from the back of the hand—the only type of spin operative on an Australian pitch until a match is near its end.

Benaud is now better able to control his leg-breaks and has the confidence so necessary for his type of bowling.

Benaud certainly needs these assets and this improvement. In the last two rubbers against England, Benaud's 18 victims cost him nearly 40 runs each. I have always believed in Benaud's exceptional all-round ability, and I am ready to admit that if Benaud really *is* now a commanding spinner from leg, he may well tighten the issue and reduce the odds which, at present, are in England's favour. English batsmen in recent years have had no acquaintance with really dangerous, good-length leg-spin.

Kline, left-handed, also spins away from the bat. Meckiff, another left-hander, may open the Australian attack with Davidson, who is yet another left-hander. Here are three bowlers who, on pitches that don't encourage much turn, will naturally threaten the leg stump or thereabouts. Scoring is likely to be slow as a consequence; the England battery of fast stuff is pretty certain to take its time getting through overs.

An intriguing point to reflect on is how far Australian wickets will resist the wear and tear of bowlers' footwork. Davidson, Kline and Meckiff, I take it, will operate from over the stumps, so their feet will make some impact on the earth outside the right-handed batsman's off stump. Of the fifth day of a Test, might not Laker therefore find a spot? Of course, the England fast attack—and here's the snag!—could easily make some rough places outside the *leg* stump which Benaud would exploit dangerously.

Frankly—despite the unhelpful pitches I predicted last month—I am expecting much from Tyson and Statham. The attack of these two in 1954–55 has not been forgotten by Harvey, McDonald, Burke, Davidson, Benaud, Favell and Archer, most of whom crumpled in the face of it; and they will form the nucleus of Australia's batting. Psychology and memories that haunt will probably collaborate with Tyson and Statham, not forgetting Loader and Trueman.

Even if Australia's young O'Neill realises expectations, and even if McDonald and Burke prove themselves sound opening batsmen, I am still confident that England will, most times, get rid of Australia for under 300, against which I am backing May's men to retaliate with a winning advantage.

As I have said, there is a tide in the affairs of man that changes. The greatest danger facing May is inscrutable fortune, which will, any day, turn against one of its darlings for no reason explicable *in* reason. Yet, as Cassius might have remarked, without quite repeating himself: 'The merit, dear Brutus, is not in our stars but in ourselves'. It will need all of Australia's present might, working at full voltage, to disturb in the slightest May's quiet, almost serene confidence.

Maybe I wouldn't put a lot of money on England's chances; but I'd put considerably less on Australia's.

1959

DOES MECKIFF THROW?

DEFEAT in Australia last winter appears to have helped stir matters in the council chamber of cricket headquarters at Lord's. For example, according to a statement by the Advisory County Cricket Committee, legislation or more severe administration of the law will now try to suppress bowling which is 'jerked' or 'thrown'.

It has been reported that consultation with umpires on this business has been going on since the winter before last; but I still wonder how much credit must go to Meckiff, the new Australian opening bowler, for this agitation for 'reform' among our cricketers.

For years it has been common belief that at least one of England's finest bowlers has taken not a few wickets by means of a 'suspect' arm action. Have any of his victims—from overseas at any rate—protested? One of our country batsmen was bowled first ball by this particular England bowler. Said his companion at the other end. 'Bad luck, Jim. Run out before you'd got your eye in!'

The question of throwing existed long before this. Ernest Jones, Australian fast bowler of the 1896–1902 period, aroused suspicion with his action not only here but at home.

Law, of course, must be observed in the form in which it is codified. But I decline to believe that, in general, a jerked or thrown delivery will over a period be as consistently dangerous or accurate as one delivered in orthodox manner by a Statham, a Truman or a Laker. We have been told time after time by observers on the spot that Meckiff's attack was all over the place, seldom on the wicket. Why wasn't he cut or hooked after he had pitched outside the danger zone? (And is it possible for a bowler to jerk or throw for any length of time without putting his shoulder or elbow out, or at least tiring the arm very soon?)

My objection to a jerk or a throw is on grounds of style —such bowling looks ugly—but I have yet to meet a batsman of reputation who would have explained the loss of his wicket to Meckiff's action. A greater player than any in May's team, after having been clean-bowled, was asked to account for his unexpected lapse. 'Well, you see', he replied, 'I clean missed the ball'. His name was Hutton.

What in the way of subtlety of flight, variation of pace and spin could a bowler achieve by a jerk comparable with the resources at the disposal of the man blessed with a rhythmic, easy swing-over? Let us reform by all means, and clean up our stables wherever there is a stink. But even if it were proved beyond argument that both Meckiff and his partner, Rorke, threw or jerked against May's team I would maintain that our batsmen should have coped with them.

Meckiff and Rorke throwing stones over ice could not excel Lindwall and Miller for pace and accuracy. Would Sir Leonard Hutton prefer to face Lindwall and Miller at their best rather than the 'suspect' Rorke and Meckiff?

I think that the game would gain by a return to pitches of pace and reasonable reliability. On such pitches bowlers are obliged to develop whatever brains nature has given them. On the so-called 'green' wickets now current, any noodle can achieve some measure of success.

No doubt, as I have said, first-class cricket in its present low technical condition *would* profit if good, fast pitches were cultivated and made general; but greater batsmen than our contemporary best have learned to play—and throughout their careers have often had to play on—wickets sometimes dangerous to fingers and thighbones. J. T. Tyldesley, Denton, Hammond, Hendren and Denis Compton, to name a few brilliant stroke-players covering a long period, all began their cricket on 'sporting', challenging turf. If I could bat with Peter May's skill I would not object to a suspect pitch—such as one or two on which England have beaten Australia and the West Indies in England in recent years—any more than I would object to a suspect bowling action.

I am all in favour of any move to keep a bowler's footmarks

off the batsman's playing area. But why has this nuisance become prevalent during the last few seasons? I never heard of it in the 'golden age' of fast bowlers; no umpire had need to caution Tom Richardson, Lockwood, Ted Macdonald, Larwood or Kenneth Farnes.

Reform perhaps might do worse than look beyond the external circumstances of actual play: a glimpse into character and outlook might be revealing. We have virtually lived into a time in which cricketers here and there have to be legislated into sportsmanship.

Broadly speaking, the laws of cricket are much the same today as ever. They have remained thus in a period which has seen the blossoming of every great player from MacLaren to May, from Hayward, Hobbs and Hendren to Bradman and Compton; from Rhodes and Richardson to Lindwall and Benaud. I believe there exist today many players with natural gifts of the highest order and that these natural gifts do not blossom because of a wrong mental approach to the game.

Many players don't seem to love first-class cricket. Some use it as just a preliminary step to a 'career' to be developed in their spare time for future purposes. We need only see a number of Test cricketers at golf . . . now they are obviously keen and enjoying themselves—seldom unfit to swing a club!

Usually something is wrong with a sportsman's mental outlook on his game as soon as he blames circumstances for his failures. (Once on a time it was not 'the done thing' for a cricketer to question an umpire's decision, whatever the provocation. In the long run, justice levels out. A great cricketer at the end of his career said that though many times he had been given out, as he thought, mistakenly, he had as often been given in when he was out.)

Reforms on paper are all very well—but the main reforms must begin with our cricketers themselves. Where there's a will there's a way. 'These are awkward skates', said Mr Winkle, when he was floundering on the ice at Dingley Dell. 'I'm afeard there's an orkard gen'lm'n in 'em, Sir', replied Sam Weller.

ILLUSTRIOUS PAGES OF HISTORY

At the approach of every rubber v. Australia a fateful question arises—whose reputation in the field of play will be enhanced and whose reputation will go under a cloud? With no disrespect to cricketers of other lands, England v. Australia remains the Test match *par excellence*. To play in these matches, to do well in them, usually means a lasting place in the most illustrious pages of cricket's history. Which cricketer in the Tests of 1961, in England, is destined for success or failure?—'R. B. Simpson, "Lord Edward" Dexter, Neil Harvey, Brian Statham, "Freddie" Trueman, Peter May, Richie Benaud, Colin Cowdrey—which of these is likely to add to fame already achieved? And which is "on the way out"?'

It is almost certain that some name not yet known internationally will command attention. But many times a young player is severely tried by the presiding genius of the game, severely sent into the mill, before innate talent is permitted to assert itself. To any fledgling failing in the Tests of 1961, I quote the scores made by Clem Hill, one of Australia's greatest left-hand batsmen, when at the age of nineteen, in our summer of 1896, he was picked to play at Lord's, in his first international match. George Lohmann bowled him first innings for 1; J. T. Hearne bowled him second innings for 5. Yet he was persevered with and allowed to play for Australia at Manchester and Kennington Oval. His batting on these occasions amounted to 9, 14, 1, 0. These failures were, surely, bitter enough to discourage the ambitions of the most optimistic and confident cricketer that ever lived—I refer, of course, to Herbert Sutcliffe.

Clem Hill was so little discouraged that when an England team visited Australia in 1896, Hill, now arrived at the mature age of twenty, began to punish and cut to ribbons England's finest bowlers. In consecutive innings he made 19, 96, 58, 81 and 188. It was this same Clem Hill who, in the Australian season of 1901–02, scored 99, 98 and 97 in successive Test innings. All young and aspiring cricketers today should bear in mind Clem Hill's quick ascent from the depths to the heights. A mere breath of ill-favour from fortune can change a cricketer's course and, suddenly, from easy prosperous seas, land him on the rocks, or blow him in a direction which never will lead to glory. One of cricket's 'mysteries' concerns the strange short sweet and bitter career in Test matches of C. L. Badcock, the young Australian who at Melbourne in 1937 dazzled a vast crowd with a century. I saw this innings and decided on the evidence of it that Badcock had some stuff of greatness in him. He was a first choice for the Australian team to play in England in 1938. His batting average for the season, all matches, was 45.82 for 1,604 runs. In four Tests he faltered pitifully—9, 5, 0, 0 (a 'pair'), 4, 5 (not out), 0 and 9, a total of 32 in 7 completed innings. How can we explain a short-circuiting of talent such as this? It is superficial to talk of 'want of Test match temperament'. Many great players have heard this old parrot-cry in their ears—Patsy Hendren, Sandham, Ernest Tyldesley, Bill Edrich, Tom Graveney, for example. There's many a slip 'twixt cup and the lip. Jim Laker, with offbreaks, bowled himself safely to posterity of rare renown—against Australia! But Tom Goddard, as excellent an offspinner as Laker, was asked once only to do his best to get Australian batsmen out with offspin, at Manchester in 1930, when he bowled 32 overs and took two wickets for 49. In the Bradman epoch offspin was regarded as 'jam' for Australian batsmen, strong on the back foot and clever at making good use, in their favour, of the l.b.w. rule then in operation.

We take our cricketers very much for granted, expecting them to behave with the consistent accuracy of a machine. They are all the playthings of luck. In cricket, as in no other game, a great master may well go back to the pavilion scoreless, run out by a miscalculation by the batsman at the other end—brought down to nullity, and he has not received a single ball! In no other game does the law of averages get to work so potently, so mysteriously. Some years ago I talked to a member of England's selection committee a week or two before the playing of a Test. He said that he was all in favour of dropping 'Blank'. 'Good heavens,' I replied, 'why?' 'He hasn't scored twenty in his last few innings,' explained the selector. 'All the more reason,' I answered, 'why you should pick him, if he is in good health.' Bradman, I admit, didn't believe in this 'law of averages'. In 1934, at Leeds, Australia bowled England out on a good wicket for 200. Australia, at the day's end, lost Brown, Woodfull and Oldfield for round about 30.

The teams that year were staying at Harrogate, and I had a 'date' with Bradman for dinner. But he left a note at the hotel's reception office saying that he was in his room and not coming down to dinner. Thinking he might be ill I went to see him. 'No,' he said, 'I'm sorry, but I'm staying up here and having an early bed tonight. Things went all wrong for us late this afternoon. I must score 200 tomorrow—AT LEAST.' I reminded him that four years ago he had scored 334 for Australia v. England on this same ground at Leeds. 'Well,' he asked, 'what if I did?' 'The law of averages is against your scoring 200 or 300 again.' 'I don't believe in any such law,' was his quiet, unboastful reply. Next day and part of the day after he amassed 304. Herbert Sutcliffe also did not believe that as a cricketer he was ever likely to suffer the influence of an evil genius. He never realised how easy it is for a batsman to lose his wicket. One Saturday, before August Bank Holiday, Yorkshire were batting against Lancashire on a heavenly turf. Sutcliffe, having made 30 or so, easily and elegantly, played a ball to cover and ran leisurely down the wicket. Eddie Paynter, who was then nearly the quickest and surest cover in the world, picked up brilliantly threw in, and missed the stumps by an inch, while Herbert was still languidly 'getting home', on the balls of his feet. Peter Eckersley, the Lancashire captain, backed-up, stopped the throw-in, and said to Sutcliffe, now safe in his crease, 'My goodness, Herbert, that was a close shave.' And Sutcliffe replied, 'Peter, I haven't the slightest idea what you are talking about.' Confidence?—the very laws of all nature, apparently, were suspended whenever Herbert was batting.

Though I believe in a law of average, I think also that born innate skill can rise above it. There is certainly one cricketer in England today who possesses gifts which are capable of asserting themselves—and against Australia—despite that so far he has not inspired headlines in the cricket reports. I refer to Brian Close, of Yorkshire. I saw him scoring 198 v. Surrey at the Oval last summer, the most masterful, brilliant and stylish innings played in my presence by any left-hander in this country since Donnelly, the New Zealand artist. Close is bulging with good cricket. A problem child? His 'psychology' could be put right by a skipper of understanding and a good strong vocabulary. It would be a good idea if the selection committee occasionally picked a cricketer to play for England for style alone. Close definitely has style. An England XI should always be worth looking at, whatever the scoreboard says. The most stylish England XI of all time was probably the one which took the field at Birmingham v. Australia in 1902. Here are the names of it—A. C. MacLaren, C. B. Fry, K. S. Ranjitsinhji, F. S. Jackson, J. T. Tyldesley, A. A. Lilley, G. H. Hirst, G. L. Jessop, L. C. Braund, W. H. Lockwood and Wilfred Rhodes. Every department of cricket was represented in this glorious company—except a 'googly' bowler—not invented or thoroughly organised in 1902. But here were brilliance of batsmanship: MacLaren, Tyldesley, 'Ranji'; here were solidity in the classic manner; C. B. Fry, F. S. Jackson and Braund. Here were all-round skill; Hirst, Jackson, Braund and Lilley. Here was Lockwood, described by 'Ranji' as the Prince of fast bowlers. Here was Rhodes, greatest of slow left-handers in 1902, with the possible exception of Colin Blythe, of Kent. Here was the most wonderful scientific hitter in all cricket's history—Gilbert Jessop. With all these remarkable exponents of cricket, England none the less lost the rubber in 1902. None the less the lustre on those names shines brightly to this day.

The West Indies, against Australia, have recently removed the rust which in the last few years has fallen on Test cricket; they have polished it so that it shines again. This summer England and Australian cricketers must not put a damper on it. A game, like any other activity in life, is pretty much what we make of it, the players and the public. Imagination from players and crowd alike is needed to bring about greatness. Fresh pages in cricket's history are waiting to be written upon. Let our pens be golden. Let us all be made to realise, every ball, every over, that cricket is not an exact science, that it is the sum total of the skill, the impulse and the mortal error of everybody taking part in it. Playthings of fortune! On whom this summer will she smile; on whom will she frown? Peter May, Richie Benaud, Neil Harvey, Colin Cowdrey, 'Lord Edward' and the rest, including, most likely, some new aspirant? The stage is ready, inviting, beautifully set. A 'tie' in a Test match's last over and when it began Australia wanted 6 runs only with three wickets to go! A Test match in which a batsman scores a century each innings and a bowler does the 'hat-trick'! The game is, as always, as great as the players (and the spectators) can make it. No cricketer worth his flannels will fail now, surely, to follow the lead of Frank Worrell and his colleagues, and go into action, even a Test match, throwing at least one hostage to fortune!

ENGLAND TO WIN

I SUPPOSE that if I try to forecast results of this summer's rubber between England and Australia I am asking for trouble and exposing myself to the sarcasm of all sensible cricketers who know well that their game is one of the most capricious of all.

Well . . . I herewith set myself up to be knocked down like an Aunt Sally by those who rejoice in the wisdom that cometh after the event. In short, I propose—prompted by a kindly but ruthless Editor—to put on those robes of prophecy, even though, as I write, the evidence of the new season is slender.

Usually, the odds in a series favour the home team—for they are acquainted with the environment: climate, conditions of pitch, field, crowd, and so on. On the other hand, the touring team gain, or should gain, from the fact that they live and play together every day over a period of months.

Australians are very gregarious; they thrive on communal contact. We may rest assured that if Richie Benaud and his comrades are obliged to surrender the Ashes it will not be for want of persistent collective effort on their part.

I am fairly confident that England will recover the Ashes —for technical reasons. Against the West Indies last winter, Australia's batsmen faltered against the off-spin of Gibbs, who is not yet in the top class of bowlers of his type. Since the end of the Bradman era Australian batsmen have, as a whole, been suspect against off-spin.

The change in the l.b.w. law no doubt contributed to this strange weakness in Australia's batting. Their technique, as a rule, is based on the back foot and its power to pivot. But the l.b.w. ruling as it stands today—permitting a batsman's dismissal to a ball turning in from outside the off stump if it hits him in a direct, imaginary line drawn between the two sets of stumps—demands confident *forward* play: not the speculative push, but the positive stroke close to the front pad.

Against Laker in 1956, Australian batsmen, one after another, revealed an almost naive incompetence to play off-spin. Their failure to master the forward stroke was at the base of their ensuing panic: to my dying day I shall remember Neil Harvey, at Old Trafford, desperately slashing a full toss straight into short-mid-on's hands.

Again, on the first day of the 1961 tour, the off-spin of Worcestershire's Martin Horton had Benaud's men in difficulties on a slow-turning wicket at Worcester, and the tourists had the unusual experience of batting twice in a drawn game against one of the weaker counties. Rain badly hit the Australians' early matches in the North, and it seemed they could ill-afford to lose the valuable batting practice on English wickets.

The strength and glory of Australian batting is revealed whenever a fast bowler pitches short. When Bradman first came to England in 1930, A. C. MacLaren, a former England captain, after a good look at Bradman, said: 'Our bowlers must draw him off his back foot'. But our bowlers, especially our quick bowlers persistently dropped the ball short and the 'Don' pulled and hooked to his heart's content. Similarly Benaud's team will have at least four best scorers— McDonald, Harvey, Simpson and O'Neill—if they are permitted to operate mainly on the back foot.

If I were England's skipper this season I would penalise all my bowlers, especially the quick ones, to the tune of a 10s. fine for every needlessly short ball. Fortunately one of the splendid features of Brian Statham's bowling is that, with all his pace, he gives the ball 'air', keeping it up the pitch and compelling strokes made off the front foot. I am hopeful that Statham is about to have one of the most successful Test Match seasons of his career.

It is of course easier to pinpoint on paper a cricket team's technical weakness than it is to root it out in practice. Much depends on a captain's insight and on his confidence in himself. Australia is fortunate to be led into action by Benaud who is quietly sure of himself and not afraid to take a tactical and imaginative risk. Peter May like Colin Cowdrey tends to fall back on defensive measures if he finds the game is going against his side. To win the rubber England must adopt attacking strategies, not only while batting but while bowling and fielding, too.

In recent years England's captaincy has been too 'protective' in the important job of changing the bowling. Fast bowlers have been taken off too soon for no other reason than that the ball is beginning to lose its shine. A bowler whatever his pace or method should be kept at his work for as long as he is taking wickets, unless he is obviously becoming physically exhausted.

A great bowler needs time to find rhythm. If a great batsman faces him, scoring freely, the bowler certainly should be free to concentrate on his 'plan' unworried by the fear that his captain will take him off.

My confidence in England's ability to win back the Ashes is encouraged by two suppositions; first, the attack at Benaud's disposal seems likely to depend too heavily on himself and Davidson, especially in dry conditions; and second, in a wet summer the strongest Australian teams usually have been technically and psychologically at a disadvantage in this country. I fancy we must need to look back as far as 1902 to find an Australian team winning a rubber in a wet English season. Then the victory was gained only by a three-run win in the fourth Test at Old Trafford.

Australia's main batting resources are McDonald, Simpson, Harvey, O'Neill and Burge—they do not look on paper the superiors in skill and temperament of May, Cowdrey, Dexter, Pullar and Subbar Row. Maybe, though, Australia will be stronger than England lower in the order with Benaud and Davidson probably at 7 and 8; and I am not at all sure that we are sound enough in batting to exclude a cricketer of Trevor Bailey's superbly reliant character and all-round technical value.

In dry weather, the batting potential of each side should work out fairly equally but there is, I repeat—and I fervently hope I am not wrong, that Australian weakness against the flighted ball which is dangerous if played from the back foot. And the weakness of technique, as I say, can be exploited not only to a spinner's advantage but by the fast bowlers, too.

Neither country promises to field a great team, and where there is on both sides a certain amount of mortal fallibility there is also the material art of which exciting cricket is made. Test cricket in this country they say is 'On Trial'. But the crowds will not be paying money to see deliberate 'bright cricket' in which batsmen get themselves out. A Bailey or a Mackay can defend if the position of the game calls for clenched teeth and a bat which is doing the work of a safe-deposit.

To sum up, I tip England to win on the strength of their bowling, if it is deployed with bold and shrewd generalship and ordered with a brave tactical appreciation.

WICKED WICKETS

IF this summer's rubber between England and Australia is won by Australia, the decisive game might turn out to have been the Lord's Test, played on a wicket calculated to unnerve the world's best batsmen.

Why, at cricket's headquarters, was such a wicket allowed to occur, especially in a season when the Lord's wicket had earned a reputation for slow pace after the first hour or so?

Was the Lord's Test match of 1961 played on the ground's 'centre'? Was the wicket chosen for the Lord's Test the one which had for some time been 'prepared'?

The wicket for the Third Test at Leeds turned out even worse of wear than the one at Lord's. When 18 wickets, the best English and Australian, fall in a single day, in *dry weather* something obviously has gone wrong. The crowds at Lord's and Leeds paid admission money hoping to see their favourite batsmen in conditions which give their talents a chance to blossom. True, at Leeds, the superb bowling of Trueman on a wicket supposedly made for spinners but which in fact suited Freddie down to the ground—or rather down to the dust —compensated the Yorkshire crowd for some disappointment. But it is high time visiting teams were given an assurance by the ruling powers that they will find wickets of some reliability and power of duration—rather more suitable to Test cricket than the pitches in a public park.

Remembering the conditions, let us take a closer look at the lessons of the first three Tests now that the rubber is all square with two to play.

For their defeat by five wickets at Lord's, England's batsmen received severe criticism by the Press and public ('Ruddy 'orful, chicken-hearted, pudding headed'). True enough, England's batsmen faltered once again, as they did in the first innings of the drawn First Test at Birmingham. But there were similar falterings among Australia's batsmen.

No critic, so far as I can recall, drew attention to the fact that on the Lord's wicket, ideal for fast bowling, Statham and Trueman had to pay 278 runs for 11 wickets, including those taken when, in Australia's second innings, four wickets fell for 19. On the Friday and Saturday, when the wicket was at its friskiest, Statham and Trueman could between them do no greater damage than six wickets for 207. Australia's 10th-wicket pair, Misson and Mackay, were able to stay there for more than an hour at a day's beginning and add 49, *with ease*. Neither Statham nor Trueman could produce the extra-crashing straight 'yorker'.

These days bowlers are so often obsessed by seam and swerve that they cannot use an old ball and bowl straight. Frankly, I am tired of reading and hearing of 'Statham's

bad luck'—or of any other bowler's 'bad luck'. On the
same Saturday on which Statham and Trueman had
been played comfortably in the middle of the bat by
Mission—Australia's No. 11—young McKenzie and Mission
dismissed Dexter, Cowdrey, Pullar and May in quick
succession.

No, Australia won at Lord's, on a wicket which might have
been 'made' for Statham and Trueman, because they played
with far more tenacity and defiance than England could
produce. At Leeds, it was a different story, and with captain
May and bowler Trueman exploiting the wicket, England
made it one-all.

On paper, England can show a stronger all-round team
than Australia—stronger at any rate in versatility of attack.
Finer batsmen than Cowdrey, May, Dexter and Barrington
are not easy to match anywhere. Statham is generally regarded by most good judges of the game as the most
dangerous of current fast bowlers. (Personally, I think that
Davidson, not as fast as Statham and not known strictly as a
fast bowler, is more dangerous than Statham, who lacks a
little of brute hostility).

What is the cause of the sudden exposure of vulnerability in
England's foremost batsmen often when they are challenged
in a Test match at the beginning of hostilities? Twice last year,
against the moderate quality of South Africa's attack, England lost their first five wickets for small scores. The England
batting, to be frank, has for years been unreliable, likely to
lose concentration. The cause? Maybe the present craze for
'entertainment' in our county cricket, connived by irrespon-
sible declarations, breeds a soft, undisciplined mentality
among English cricketers.

A crisis usually brings the best out of an Australian. The
swift, intrepid stroke-play of Peter Burge at Lord's, when
Australia's batting cream had gone for 19 runs, was as superb
as it was decisive. Burge is already a fine batsman; I am not so
sure that he is not on the verge of greatness. There is between
him and O'Neill only a difference of degree—not of kind or
class. The wicket at Leeds proved one thing which I have
never doubted: that the greatest Australian batsman is Neil
Harvey.

Given good wickets at Old Trafford and the Oval, the odds are very much against an England victory, though our batsmen should stave away defeat on each ground. But can we take for granted that really dependable wickets will be prepared on these grounds, where most weeks in a summer the turf behaves well in fine weather?

I cannot forget the dustheap on which Jim Laker took 19 Australian wickets at Old Trafford in 1956, or the spinners' 'paradise' on which Laker and Lock revelled against the West Indies in 1957. Nature, providence or the groundsman has done wonderfully patriotic work for England in Test matches played in this country in recent years!

DEXTER FOR CAPTAIN?

THERE is much talk among England's cricket followers that the England XI needs a new leader, and that Ted ('Lord Edward') Dexter, now captaining the MCC team in India and Pakistan, is supposed to be in direct succession to Peter May. But, before discussing England's captain for next year—and for the invasion of Australia in 1962–63—let me put down a few words regarding May; we don't usually cry 'Long live the King' while the throne is the prerogative of a still-ruling monarch.

England sadly lost the rubber last summer to the poorest Australian bowling side ever to visit this country. The decisive Fourth Test at Old Trafford, as everybody now knows, was thrown away on the closing morning by England, when Australia's last wicket pair were allowed to add no fewer than 98 runs. At the day's beginning Mackay, Benaud and Grout succumbed to Allen's spin for three runs, none of which were hit off Allen. Then Davidson, playing one of the most courageous innings in Test history, hit Allen for 20 (6, 4, 4, 6) in one over. Whereupon May took Allen off and—having already tried Close's off-spin—put on Statham and Trueman, who soon took the new ball. And for making this obviously sensible change May has been chastised and virtually held responsible for the losing of the match and the rubber.

A scapegoat, I suppose, has always to be found. But what are England fast bowlers expected to do when a new ball is available and the other side's No. 11, McKenzie, is at the wicket? It was no fault of May's that two experienced Test fast bowlers, at a game's turning point, could not, *with a new ball*, get rid of McKenzie.

For the sake of fair sport, let's be fair to May. Had he asked Close to try and break this great Australian last-wicket stand at Old Trafford? Certainly. Was it May's fault that Close was plundered for 33 in six overs? Suppose May had *not* tried his pace pair, and Australia had won just the same. Would not, then, his critics have said: 'Why didn't he call Statham and Trueman back?' And if, *in extremis*, he had not turned to Close, every critic and all Yorkshire would have asked: 'Didn't May know that Close is one of the country's best change bowlers?'

True, apart from the first two Tests last summer, May has been captain of an England side which has lost two consecutive rubbers against Australia. At the end of the 1961 Australian series it was reported he was undecided about his future in cricket. Well, in December he will be 32, and in the ordinary course of his interests on and off the cricket field, his days as a leading England player may well be nearing an end. But I maintain that this end, should it come soon, cannot honestly be said to have been hastened by an unpardonable lapse on his part, as captain, during England's defeat in 1961. He was let down by batting which was often irresolute and by insecure fielding.

I believe that May still has much great batsmanship to place at England's service. The question is: has he ever been a really strong psychologically influential leader? I should my-self—one of his warmest admirers—answer 'No'. He was brought up under an astute but careful skipper who believed that a game should be made 'safe' before an attack is launched. Hutton was fortunate in having at least three fast bowlers in their energetic heyday. It is easy to prove yourself a great cricket captain if your team includes enough players of match-winning resource.

The recent death of A. P. F. Chapman revived memories of a glorious fieldsman and a brave, gallant and handsome left-handed batsman. During *his* days as England captain he could turn for support (and advice) to cricketers as great as Hobbs, Jardine, Sutcliffe, Hammond, Larwood, Tate, Woolley and Hendren. Supposing that next year Dexter should have to shoulder the responsibility of the England captaincy. To whom, in his ranks, will he be able to go for really experienced, positive and determined advice? To Pullar, to Barrington, to Murray, to Allen . . . ?

And why are many people so sure that Dexter is likely to succeed where Peter May failed? Has he led Sussex with unusual tactical discernment? Has his batting thrived for Sussex while he has held the captaincy? I am all in favour of cricket captains who have what is known as 'vision', who are quick to jump to the offensive. Richie Benaud has imagination and nerve. But Benaud is basically shrewd, a close student of cricket at all hours.

Is Dexter the only candidate for the England captaincy? Is he a more far-seeing captain, *on the field*, than, say, Mike Smith of Warwickshire? (If anybody here interposes that Smith is not up to Test standards as a batsman these days, my reply is 'Rubbish'). The field is, admittedly, bare of strong personal leadership (and not only in cricket!).

Colin Cowdrey, who took over the captaincy when May was forced to return from the West Indies two years ago and led England in the winning rubber against South Africa last year, has proved a capable deputy during his few opportunities. But I have never been convinced that the Kent captain really *enjoys* leading England.

There are those who argue in favour of Colin Ingleby-Mackenzie ('It doesn't matter if he isn't up to Test standards as a player', they say, 'Look what he has done for Hampshire'). These sentiments, very admirable, are, I think, amateurish. To defeat the Australians in Test cricket, *enthusiasm* is not enough. What of Derbyshire's Donald Carr? Many feel he is as astute and 'alive' as most of his county colleagues, but as most critics and followers are bound to agree: the land is naked.

Cricket itself is not to blame if at the present time the

dominant personal leader is hard to find. We live in the period of the *average* man. Chapman, although a successful England captain, was not exactly a great thinker. But he was educated to the game—and to life—in an age of individualism. At least one or two of the professional players under his command (Hobbs or Sutcliffe or Woolley) could, given the chance, have captained an England XI with as much authority, and as good judgment, as Hutton's. And I'm inclined to think that George Duckworth, from behind the stumps, would have check-mated more than one move of Richie Benaud.

We must wait and see how Dexter fares during the next few months in India and Pakistan. But there is no touchstone for captaincy; no reliable means of saying, in advance: 'This is the born leader!' It depends very much on the men who are at his disposal. It depends, also, on the fighting quality of the other side!

Let us hope for the best in Dexter—or in anyone else who is asked to fill the post (which, let me hope, is not yet, as far as Australia is concerned, vacated once and for all by May). Some skippers are born to greatness, some achieve greatness —and others have greatness thrust upon them.

1962

RICHIE BENAUD—1962

A T the beginning of June 1961, before the first Test match between England and Australia, Norman O'Neill playing under Richie Benaud against Sussex injured a knee while fielding, and was obliged to retire. At first the damage threatened to remove for some lengthy period this brilliant young cricketer from the Australian team. The news of O'Neill's and Australia's misfortune upset me so much that I wrote at once to Benaud hoping that O'Neill would quickly be fit again. I was as much concerned about the loss, even for a while, to the game of an artist as I was about this threat to Australia's chances of victory in the rubber.

The reply of Benaud to my letter was true to his character and to the character of most Australians. He thanked me for my sympathy but finished by saying: 'I'm not worrying unduly. I think that you'll find we'll be there when the chips are down.' And so, at the decisive moment in the rubber, they indeed were there. At Old Trafford, where the rubber's issue was settled, England were winning easily on the fifth afternoon, 150 for 1 wicket, Dexter riding the storm and only 106 needed now in as many minutes. Moreover, the Australian attack seemed pretty bankrupt: Davidson weary, Mackay physically handicapped. Benaud actually called for a breathing space, and drinks were brought into action, under a hot Manchester sun. (In 1934, two Australians were afflicted by sunstroke at Manchester during a Test match.) With the afternoon apparently lost for Australia, Benaud became a vessel of plenary inspiration. He bowled round the wicket and pitched his spin on the places on the pitch worn by Trueman's footmarks at the other end. As every cricketer and history knows, the trick came off. But it is not generally realised,

even yet, how cleverly, how artfully, Benaud played it. He
clean bowled the obstructive Subba Row the last ball, or
thereabouts, before tea—with a full-toss. He knew well
enough that, an interval due, Subba Row would take no risk,
offer no stroke, to a good ball. When Dexter was racing
ahead, and defeat stared Australia in the face, Benaud said to
himself 'We can't possibly save this match but we *could* win
it!'

He has been called a 'lucky' captain of cricket. The truth is
that he, at his career's beginning, had to suffer hard blows to
his confidence. At the age of twenty-one he played in his first
Test match v. West Indies at Sydney in January 1952. He
bowled only four overs, three balls and took Valentine's
wicket for fourteen, of which number Valentine's share was
exactly none. And he scored 3 and 19. His baptism to Test
cricket in this country, in 1953, was scarcely memorable
—three matches, five innings, 15 runs, average 3; sixty-eight
overs and two wickets for 174. He, supposedly a leg-spin
bowler, failed to use the dusty wicket at Lord's when Willie
Watson and Bailey retrieved a lost cause for England by hours
of superbly dour defence. A famous player that afternoon was
emphatic that Benaud never would reach top-class as a
leg-spinner. 'He's a roller'. 'Give him time', I said. For I had
seen young Benaud, months before this forlorn afternoon for
him at Lord's—I had seen him in the nets at Sydney. Moreover, Arthur Mailey was putting faith in his potentiality as a
back-of-the-hand spinner. But Benaud again disappointed
his prophets during Hutton's and Tyson's triumphant invasion of Australia in 1954–55. He bowled 116 overs and 7
balls in the Tests for 377 runs and 10 wickets. And in nine
completed innings he scored merely 148. For Australia in the
West Indies, in 1955, he opened out his promise as a bowler,
with 18 Test wickets, average 27.

None the less he was still on the doorstep of International
achievement as recently as 1956, when he came to England
for the second time. Another failure now could easily have
seen the last of him amongst the Top People. He was nearing
his twenty-sixth birthday. An Australian Test cricketer is
usually established by this time of his life; in fact, many of
them have looked towards retirement from the International

scene by then—what ever Clarrie Grimmett may say to the contrary. Even in 1956, despite a resonant prelude to the season to the turn of an innings of 160 v. Worcestershire, Richie for a while still could not raise himself above the level of the team's subsidiary resources. He was useful week by week, but in the first of the summer's Tests, at Nottingham, which had no result, he was not particularly useful. He scored 17, and bowled (in England's second innings only) 18 overs, and took none for 41. Between this and the second and Lord's Test he played in one match, scoring 7 and 15 v. Northamptonshire; and his one wicket cost 91. Conceivably he might not have been chosen for the Lord's Test if the Australian reserves had been stronger.

On the fourth morning of this match Australia, in a second innings, had lost six wickets for 115 and were only 229 ahead. On the evening before a morning on which Richie was destined to deal England a more or less death blow (with bat not ball), I met him for the first time at a dinner given by the most generous of hosts—John Arlott. We scarcely spoke. Benaud was not yet the confident Benaud of today. But there was a 'something' about him which impressed me, a suggestion of latent and alluring personality. The impression was strong enough to urge me to write an article, to appear before the game was resumed next morning, in which I risked a forecast . . . 'Before we are much older Benaud will do something forcibly to demonstrate his natural and unmistakable gifts'. Well, on this fourth morning, in a ticklish moment for Australia, with the day fresh and Trueman after blood with 4 wickets already rendering him even more than usually voracious—(4 for 38)—Benaud arrived at the ground almost late and had to rush into action at once, pads buckled breathlessly. Immediately he attacked, risking a long-armed drive. Also he hooked Trueman for six—and Trueman was the first of thousands to applaud the stroke. Benaud trusted to his eye daringly. In two hours twenty minutes he scored 97, swinging clean round the wheel of the game in the one engagement of the rubber won by Australia. The innings, maybe, marked the turn of his career.

I have gone into these statistics of Benaud's cricket to show how little indeed, 'luck' has had to do with his development and progress. He, like any other man ever to do anything really well, had to be tested, not only in skill but in patience, philosophy and persistence. The only unmistakable good stroke from fortune to bless his onward course was at poor Ian Craig's expense, when this cricketer and captain of bright promise fell ill, and the Australian leadership passed from him to Benaud. With the swift resolution of something approaching genius, Richie grasped the chance. He directed Australia to victory in the rubber of 1958–59, in Australia. Never since then has he looked back. The entire world of cricket knows how he and Frank Worrell, by joint and imaginative agreement, saw to it that the Tests between Australia and the West Indies in 1960–61 produced some of the greatest and most thrilling and memorable cricket of our or any other time.

It is a blessing from heaven that today England and Australia are being led by two cricketers who, if a vote were taken on the point amongst all lovers of the game, the world over, would be returned the favourites as men and players— Benaud and Dexter (with, of course, Frank Worrall dead-heating!). Both Benaud and Dexter are sportsmen of enterprise. And both, I fancy, are tough of character at the pinch. Richie, as befits an Australian and Sydney-sider, understands the value of realism. This good-looking captain of Australian cricket, with his frank eyes, and pleasant smile, scarcely fits at first sight into the general picture of an Australian skipper —think of dour immovable Armstrong, the lynx-eyed Herbert Collins, the shrewd watchful Sir Donald. But Benaud is not wholly the cavalier batsmen and the speculative leg-spinner (all leg-spinners must necessarily be speculative!). He knows that the time to be there is 'when the chips are down'.

His precious contribution to the game has been, of course, not his flair as a cricket captain; not even his ability to steer an XI to victory in a rubber in England, with a bowling team fairly to be called one of the weakest ever, Benaud himself an incapacitated member of it for weeks. No; Benaud has so far enriched cricket best by his leg-spin. He is the only first-class leg-spin bowler left to cricket of 1962 (cries of 'Shame'). This beautiful and difficult art, and any kind of spin if it comes to that, has been discouraged by legislation which has aided and abetted seam bowling. Any healthy bodily fit, even brainless, young man can readily learn to swing his arm holding the ball's seam in his fingers the right way up. To master spin from the back of the hand, spin involving turn of the wrist and flick of fingers right to left—here is an art or craft calling for years of practice, and beautiful is it to watch a great leg-spinner, to follow the ball's seductive flight (or it might easily pitch half-way!) as it lures the batsmen forward, then drops on the earth; and it whips away or, the 'googly', comes back! Nothing mechanical here. Leg-spin insists on constant careful manipulation from its exponents—and constant concentration of mind.

So, you see, this 'lucky' Benaud has not only fought through preliminary set-backs of form. While opposing them he has also learned and now command's one of cricket's most skilful and enchanting arts, leg-spin with changeful flight that asks questions in the air. If England possessed today a leg-spinner of Benaud's class Dexter could go into the battle of the approaching rubber almost cocksure of confidence. Benaud, younger looking than his thirty-two years, lithe but well-built, deceptively friendly when the chips are down is, in fact, the 'key' man of the present situation between England and Australia. He will find, in Dexter, a sword worth crossing. 'Let battle commence!'

1971

IT IS UP TO LAWRY AND ILLINGWORTH

On the whole, I am glad I was born at the right time, and could sail to Australia with an England team containing Wally Hammond, Kenneth Farnes, Maurice Leyland, Hardstaff, Voce, Leslie Ames, Walter Robins, G. O. Allen, Jim Sims—to play Australia embattled with Bradman, McCabe, Brown, Jack Fingleton, O'Reilly, Fleetwood-Smith and Bert Oldfield—all characters as well as cricketers. I admit that today there are wonderful resources of science to get us to Australia in the time taken by the ancient Orient and P & O liners to arrive seaworthily through the Bay of Biscay. But oh, the fun we enjoyed on board, the opportunity presented for weeks to know our cricketers, the opportunity for rest and relaxation! Then there was the sheer beauty of being at sea, out of sight for days of land; the divine evenings, as we voyaged over the Indian ocean, and the sky changed to a sudden purple, and stars appeared as though lighted one by one by hand.

'Gubby' Allen's England team of 1936–1937 won the first two Test matches of the rubber, then lost the following three. All Tests in Australia, in those days, were played inexorably to a finish. I am still all in favour of Test matches without a time limit. There was something dramatic, as we watched, from the *first* ball; for we all knew that one team or the other we doomed to defeat, with no escape. Every ball bowled was a nail in somebody's coffin. And it is nonsense to argue that time-limitless Test matches encouraged slow scoring. The truth is that until recently, the rate of scoring in Tests between England and Australia remained much the same over decades. In the rubbers of 1897–1898, 1907–1908, and 1920–1921, the tempo of 3 runs an over of six balls was maintained by batsmen such as Trumper, MacLaren, Ranjitsinhji, Hutchings, Hobbs, Woolley, Macartney. Even in the dazzling

English summer rubber of 1930—Bradman's marvellous year —the rate of scoring did not often rise to three runs an over. Then, following Sir Leonard Hutton's conquering tour of Australia, 1954–1955, we were lucky if two and a half runs came designedly from every six balls bowled, but—and here we come to a serious *but*—the gradual decrease in rate of run-scoring over the last decade has frequently been a consequence of an outrageously dilatory delivery of overs an hour. Obviously a batsman can't score if he doesn't get the bowling. I remember watching a Test match at Lord's in company of S. F. Barnes, then nearing his ninetieth year. 'Why' he asked, in simple perplexity, 'does bowler take so much time going back to his starting place?—he's giving batsman time to rest and take a second breath. *I never did!*' And how he growled out those words—'I never did'.

Clearly the two teams at present in opposition in Australia are not over-endowed with individual presence, personal appeal. In this midst, a Denis Compton, a Keith Miller, a Freddie Trueman, a Stan McCabe—not to mention a Don Bradman or a Bill O'Reilly—would seem as though Laurence Olivier, John Gielgud, Ralph Richardson, and such, were to appear suddenly on the stage of the Muddleton Repertory Theatre. Australia and England are today captained by two first-class sergeant-majors. No Montgomery is in charge.

We can expect competence from both XI's, but I do not regret that I am not 'on the spot', to take heed of it all. There are probably only two members of the present England XI who could have found places in the England XI of, say, 1953–1954, which consisted of Hutton, Willie Watson, Peter May, Denis Compton, Tom Graveney, Trevor Bailey, T. G. Evans, Jim Laker, Tony Lock, Wardle, and Brian Statham. Knott is a brilliant wicket-keeper, but would he ever oust Godfrey? And Snow, fine fast bowler though he is beyond doubt, is not yet a Statham.

Talking of fast bowlers, I was interested that Illingworth, at the present tour's outset, put much faith in the fast bowling at his disposal. I wonder if Illingworth is aware of the fact that many times Australia has provided a sort of graveyard for fast bowlers. Consider these figures: Tom Richardson (probably the greatest of all fast bowlers) averaged 30 runs a wicket on

Australian grounds; Lockwood 60 (!); Hirst 42; Cotter 30; Gregory 31; Macdonald 65(!). In 1928–1929, Larwood's bowling in Test matches cost him 728 runs for 18 wickets, average 40.44. Moreover, Australian wickets, a decade ago, were hard and fast; nowadays, so I am informed, they tend to get slower and slower. Apparently the old Bulli soil, and Merri-creek soil, has run out. Also, I suspect, groundsmen don't work as hard, or roll as heavily, as of yore. The main trouble with cricket today springs from the material or physical conditions in which it is played, and from the mental approach to the game. There is as much inborn talent in action as ever, most of it coming to flower, strangely enough, in non-English and non-Australian players. It is difficult to believe that a fast hard wicket is a rare event in Australia; I have myself bowled on the Melbourne pitch (not the most amiable for batsmen in Australia), and it was as hard as the pavement in London's Oxford Street. Snow's 6 wickets, in the Australians innings at Brisbane recently, must be warmly applauded; it reminded me of a truly superb piece of fast bowling by Ken Farnes for England v. Australia, at Melbourne in March 1937. Australia amassed 604, with Bradman and McCabe at their most commanding and killing. Farnes, in this longitudinous innings, bowled twenty-eight overs, and took 6 wickets for 96; in the circumstances, and especially considering the batsmen opposed to him, Farnes achieved one of the most memorable of all fast bowlers' deeds of skill and endurance.

Cricket in Australia seems at the moment in eclipse. I am told that there is scarcely the same old passion for the game amongst young boys there—the great ambition, with young Australians, is towards glamour, reputation and rich financial rewards in tennis. When I lived in Sydney, there would be crowds of 20,000 at a State match. As I write this article, I read of a gathering of 8,000–9,000 for a day at a Test match in Brisbane.

It is 'up to' Lawry and Illingworth to renew the appeal of Test cricket in Australia; let each go 'all out' for victory, and not be overconcerned that one could be beaten! Speed up the overs bowled in an hour—and roll the wickets with the sweat of the brow.